# WHAT DO MORMONS REALLY BELIEVE?

## JOHN ANKERBERG
## & JOHN WELDON

**HARVEST HOUSE PUBLISHERS**
**Eugene, Oregon 97402**

*Cover by Terry Dugan Design, Bloomington, Minnesota*

**WHAT DO MORMONS REALLY BELIEVE?**
Formerly titled (and condensed from) *Behind the Mask of Mormonism*
Copyright © 2002 by John Ankerberg and John Weldon
Published by Harvest House Publishers
Eugene, Oregon 97402

Library of Congress Cataloging-in-Publication Data

Ankerberg, John, 1945–
    What Do the Mormons Really Believe? / John Ankerberg, John Weldon.
    ISBN 0-7369-0826-9
    1. Church of Jesus Christ of Latter-day Saints—Controversial literature.
    2. Mormon Church—Controversial Literature. I. Weldon, John  II. Title.
    BX8645.A68     1992
    289.3—dc20                                             91-38068
                                                         CIP

**Printed in the United States of America.**

04 05 06 07 08 09 10 / DP-VS / 10 9 8 7 6 5 4 3

*For Latter-day Saints*
*who are searching*

# Contents

## Section VI
### *What Do the Mormons Believe About Christianity?*

# The Confusion Caused by Mormonism

In *Newsweek's* September 10, 2001 cover story on the Mormon church, Kenneth L. Woodward wrote that "The church now insists that it be regarded as a Christian church, albeit one with doctrines about God, salvation, and the priesthood that differ radically from traditional Christianity…[Further] Mormon rhetoric is becoming more overtly evangelical."

The insistence of the Mormon church that it be viewed by the world as a Christian church, despite doctrines that deny basic Christianity, is the subject matter of this book. Members of the Church of Jesus Christ of Latter-day Saints—otherwise known as Mormons—strongly emphasize that they are authentic, sincere believers in the complete divine authority of the Bible, in the biblical God, in Jesus Christ, in the Holy Spirit, in the holy Trinity, in salvation by grace, in heaven and hell, and in much more that Christians also believe in.

These claims have been so widely broadcast that legitimate confusion now exists in the minds of many people, even many Christians, as to whether Mormonism should be classified as a genuine Christian religion. Do Mormons really have the same beliefs as Christians? And if so, what is all the fuss about—why do some claim Mormonism is actually an *anti-*Christian religion?

How does one proceed to determine the truth? We have written this book to help clarify what Mormons actually believe, not what they give the impression of believing. Unfortunately, this seems to place us in the position of those attempting to "tell others what they really believe," a task rarely appreciated, for obvious reasons. Part of the problem is semantic—using the same words with different meanings. When Mormons say they "believe in Jesus Christ," they are as sincere as anyone. The question is, Do they believe in the Jesus Christ of the New Testament—the true, historical Jesus—or in the Jesus approved by the LDS church? In addition, part of the problem is the vigorous program in the LDS church to promote itself as genuinely Christian (which, obviously, is succeeding in some quarters). Finally, many Mormons and Christians aren't really quite sure as to what constitutes genuine Christianity. So the confusion, while unfortunate, is understandable.

But the larger problem is that well-informed Mormons, at least, *do* know what they believe. They also know it is *not* what historic, orthodox Christianity has always believed. They have been taught that LDS doctrines are biblical; hence, they are convinced that it is traditional Christianity that is wrong in its beliefs. Mormons are the "true" Christians, having had correct doctrines and the true interpretation of the Bible restored through divine revelation by their founder and prophet, Joseph Smith.

The solution here is a relatively easy one. It is to compare and contrast the beliefs of the Bible and the authoritative beliefs of the LDS church, as well as to examine LDS claims that Joseph Smith was a true prophet of God. We have taken pains to cite sources that the LDS church considers authoritative in determining LDS beliefs and claims. However the reader should understand that there are serious doctrinal conflicts between the alleged divinely inspired teachings of both early and modern Mormonism. Worse, there is no objective manner by which to determine which should be trusted as the "true" divine revelation. As part of our analysis, we have discussed the understandable problem this presents for LDS credibility.

So how do Christians know their faith is valid, rather than the Mormons' faith? We touched briefly on the evidence for the uniqueness and truth of biblical Christianity in *Ready with an Answer, Knowing the Truth About Salvation* (Eugene, OR: Harvest House Publishers) and other books. Objective evidence of divine revelation is found in only one religion. This evidence is sufficiently robust to convince even open-minded skeptics. It includes such things as specific, fulfilled prophecies concerning the distant future, scientific prevision, and other facts that are inexplicable apart from divine omniscience and foreknowledge. It involves the miracles, teachings, and resurrection of Jesus Christ, proving His claim to be God incarnate, supplying divine authority to His words.

No critic of Christianity can logically, convincingly dispute the fact that in all history, only one Man claimed to be God incarnate, predicted His resurrection from the dead in public, and rose from the dead in proof of His claims (cf. Acts 1:3; 17:31). Whether one cares to accept it, the simple fact is that biblical Christianity is the only religion with convincing, concrete evidence to support its claims. Further, of the world's religious literature, only the Bible can logically and evidentially be considered the Word of God. Therefore, biblical truth is the only viable standard by which to judge religious truth claims, and that is why we have applied it here to the issue of LDS assertions to be the Christian church.[1]

Unfortunately, when we come to the subject of religion in general, we find that most religions do not permit the believer to exercise their God-given right of independent inquiry and critical examination, at least as far as the religion itself is concerned. To do so is to permit members to discover the truth, whereas the "real" truth has been decided beforehand by the religion in question. In fact, "God" Himself is presented as the advocate of the status quo; to question one's religion is to question God. But what kind of God would give us minds to use and then forbid their use?

To the contrary, the God of the Bible invites fair-minded, critical investigation so that the truth will be known and broadcast. "You shall love the Lord your God with...all your mind" (Matthew 22:37). "Examine everything carefully" (1 Thessalonians 5:21). The Bereans examined the Scriptures every day, to see if what Paul said was true (Acts 17:11; cf. verses 2-3). "Come now, and let us reason together, says the LORD" (Isaiah 1:18). Concerning earliest Christianity, the physician said he had "investigated everything carefully from the beginning" (Luke 1:3-4). "Let us examine and probe our ways" (Lamentations 3:40). "Test yourselves to see if you are in the faith; examine yourselves" (2 Corinthians 13:5).[2]

It only makes sense that if God gave us a mind, He intended us to use it. "The naive believes everything, but the prudent man considers his steps" (Proverbs 14:15). Regrettably, Mormons who obey this injunction may pay an unwelcome price.

Besides millions of faithful Mormons, there are also, apparently, millions of Mormons who have left the LDS church, often the result of having discovered serious doctrinal contradictions or moral and ethical breaches in church leadership, both historically and today. The only thing these Mormons know is that the LDS church is not what it claims to be. Such Mormons can only be described as being in a state of "spiritual suspension," unsure of what to believe, if anything. We hope they will understand that God is not at fault for what men do.

Sadly, if we look at LDS leadership impartially, we discover that the Mormon faithful have been kept from the truth, as we document herein. This means that church members must take special pains to test what they have been told, even if this requires real work and courage—i.e., a sacrificial love for truth. But once again, discovering the truth can be expensive. As R.K. McGregor Wright asks, "Would we be able to reject our religious beliefs if we felt God were telling us to? Are we willing to seek God and His truth if, respectively, it would cost us that? What if it would cost the alienation of one's longtime friends, family, even one's most cherished way of life?" Sooner or later one pays a price for learning and loving the truth, but the rewards, happily, are far greater—knowing God as a person and experiencing His love and fellowship now, and later, forever. And, once you have met Him, how can you leave Him?

It should additionally be noted that the arguments in defense of Mormonism have recently become more sophisticated and scholarly through FARMS and related organizations. We briefly touched upon this in our *Encyclopedia of Cults and New Religions* (1999, pp. 314-333). The arguments presented by scholarly Mormons, however, are generally found to be extraneous. No amount of research and scholarship can prove the truth of something already demonstrated as false by biblical revelation. This misuse of argument is common today even outside religious circles, and is a warning against complacency. Consider the current frustration of the scientific establishment over the nature of the evidence for naturalistic evolution: great scientific scholarship and research are put forth, to little effect. This will always be the case with something artificial to begin with, but when such beliefs are robustly defended, it may require more time and effort to sort through the issues. (Cf. our _Darwin's Leap of Faith._) Ignoring the problems is never the answer, opening one's mind and looking at the facts without prejudice is. Otherwise, the cost is merely accountability in expanding the number of falsehoods.

Nevertheless, recent scholarly LDS arguments are probably convincing to LDS members who do not take the necessary time to look at the other side fairly and examine such arguments critically. Our hope and prayer is that this book will begin to help Mormons and Christians to "examine everything carefully" and "hold fast to that which is good." In addition, the following on-line sources will prove useful for additional study and further documentation of the arguments made in this book:

Utah Lighthouse Mission—www.utlm.org

Mormon Research Ministry—www.mrm.org

Apologetics Index—www.gospelcom.net/apologeticsindex/

Recovery from Mormonism—www.exmormon.org

The Ankerberg Theological Research Institute—
www.ankerberg.com

Alpha & Omega Ministries—
http://aomin.org/Mormonism.html

# SECTION I

## WHAT IS THE MORMON CHURCH?

# Chapter 1

# The Mormon Church Today

~

In the minds of most people Mormonism has a good, clean reputation and is often thought to be a respectable Christian religion.

This is partly because in recent years the Church of Jesus Christ of Latter-day Saints (Mormon) has initiated a powerful campaign to influence millions of people with its message. Sophisticated magazine, newspaper, and television ads have reached literally tens of millions of people with the claims of Mormonism. Multiple full-page newspaper inserts proclaim, "We believe the New Testament Scriptures are true and that they testify that Jesus is indeed the Promised Messiah and Savior of the world." Headlines blare, "Mormons believe Jesus Christ is Lord and Savior" and "Mormons testify Jesus is the Christ."

These advertisements have also been placed in *Reader's Digest* and *TV Guide* and have even provided an 800 number that respondents could call and receive a free copy of the *Book of Mormon*, which is boldly advertised as "another testament of Jesus Christ."

The success of these ads is evident; back in 1989 almost 260,000 requests for a free *Book of Mormon* were received, and 86,000 of those responding wanted missionaries to make a personal visit. In addition, forty percent of the respondents said they "believed the book was the Word of God" and indicated that "they had a special feeling about it."[1] By 2001, the church had published a total of 105 million copies of the *Book of Mormon*, distributing almost six million copies in the year 2000 alone. Direct advertising is only one way by which the Mormon church seeks converts. Its methods of proselytizing are as varied as its corporate holdings. For example, the church takes advantage of the fact that every year millions of people visit Hawaii:

> Mormons own a substantial portion of Hawaii [including] the major financial institutions of this area. When you go to the [Mormon sponsored] Polynesian Culture Center they offer you a tour to [visit] their Temple....Soon after you return from your visit...you will receive a knock from a Mormon missionary asking how you enjoyed your visit and whether you would like to know more about the Church. The Mormons have many other ways of recruiting members: through door-to-door missionaries, visitor centers, the thousands of church sponsored Boy Scout troops and educational institutions, and...the Marriott Hotel chain which places Mormon literature in every room.[2]

The power of Mormonism also stems from the fact that it is perhaps the largest, most influential and missionary-minded of the various unconventional religions of the United States. In 2001, the church had over 60,000 missionaries engaged in proselytizing activities around the world, and they won over 300,000 converts. The church's current membership passed the eleven million mark worldwide in 2000.[3] By November 2000, 31 new Mormon temples had opened up, bringing the total number to 100 worldwide.[4] By September 2001, there were 106 temples in operation, with plans for 20 more. That's in addition to the more than 12,000 local churches or meetinghouses in the world.

Moreover, the church maintains financial assets valued at $25 to $30 billion, with annual revenues approaching $6 billion.[5] This makes it one of the wealthiest churches per capita in the entire world. Not unexpectedly, many of the lay leaders within the Mormon church are businessmen who help the church oversee a vast and growing worldwide financial empire.

For example, the church's real estate holdings are worth billions of dollars. In addition, the church owns or has owned five insurance companies, a newspaper, two television stations, a chain of bookstores, a shopping mall, a dozen radio stations, hundreds of thousands of acres of farmland, one of the nation's largest private television networks, and most of Salt Lake City's tallest skyscrapers.[6] The Mormon empire also runs several colleges and schools, including Brigham Young University.

Mormons tend to view financial prosperity as a sign of God's blessing (cf. Alma 1:29; 4 Nephi 1:23). Their corporate wealth confirms their belief that Mormonism is wealthy because it is pleasing to God. Tithing is a principal means of church income. According to Mormon doctrine, tithing is a law of God commanded upon the people; _Doctrine and Covenants_ (hereafter cited in the text as _D&C_) 119:3,4 calls it a "standing law...forever." A devoted former church member estimates that many Mormons "will be paying 20%–25% of their gross income to the Church."[7] Wealthy Mormon celebrities and business executives also tend to tithe generously. For example, the Osmond and Marriott families are two large contributors to the Mormon empire.*[8]

---

* Such tithing is part of the "package" of good works that will eventually earn a Mormon his supposed exaltation or godhood.[9] In fact, in Mormonism, the logical motive undergirding both tithing and missions work is the personal hope of exaltation to divinity. Any Mormon who desires godhood must tithe generously and also become a Mormon missionary.[10] In essence, two of the most effective means for expanding the Mormon empire are sustained by one of the most compelling and enticing motivators known to man—the anticipation of absolute power.

In state and national politics, Mormons have retained more than their share of influence. Richard Beal, one of the most powerful men in the Reagan administration, was a Mormon,[11] and Mormons have headed the following posts and departments: Assistant Attorney General, head of the National Security Council, Secretary of Agriculture, Treasurer of the United States, the United States Chamber of Commerce, the Department of Interior, the Federal Communications Commission, the Department of Housing and Urban Development, the Federal Research Board, the Securities and Exchange Commission, and various state government posts.[12] Mormons also head or have headed Walt Disney Productions, Sav-On Drugs, Max Factor, Standard Oil, and many other conglomerates.[13]

The Mormon church is also the single largest sponsor of Boy Scout units in the United States, and Mormon officials have admitted this is an effective manner in which to share the faith.[14] For example, former Secretary of Agriculture in the Eisenhower administration and former Mormon prophet and president, Ezra Taft Benson, comments, "Scouting is Church work. It is part of the [Mormon] Church program."[15] And,

> I have been deeply impressed with the record that has been made by the Church....In no other field do we have a better reputation than in the field of Scouting....We have...a higher proportion of Scout troops sponsored by the Church than any other church or civic organization in the world.... [And] we have the highest enrollment of boys in Scouting of any church on the earth.[16]

In fact, President Benson stated, "Religious emphasis is a part of Scouting" and, "Scouting helps prepare boys for [Mormon] Church responsibility....We want these boys to become better men and boys and honor their [Mormon] priesthood and to be faithful members of the [Mormon] Church and kingdom of God."[17]

Thus, the positive image of Mormonism is undergirded by many factors: their scouting leadership, their financial reputation, their moral emphasis, and their Christian appearance. All this is why even many Christians think that the Mormon church is a Christian organization and that individual Mormons are Christians.

In fact, the Mormon church's successful portrayal of itself as Christian explains why there may be (according to Mormons) more converts to Mormonism from Christian churches than there are official defections from Mormonism. According to research published in a Mormon magazine, "Far more persons convert to the Mormon Church from other churches or from a status of no religious affiliation than leave."[18] The report cited a 1990 study published by Mormons Howard M. Bahr and David Hunt relying on NORC General Social Survey data from 1972–1988 and the University of Wisconsin National Survey of Families and Households, 1987–1988.

This study also indicated that the conversion rates from various Christian denominations to Mormonism were proportionately similar. Jewish, Catholic, Baptist, and Christian Reformed churches had somewhat lower conversion rates, though, than several Evangelical and Fundamentalist denominations and some mainline denominations (Presbyterian, Episcopal, Christian and United Churches of Christ, among others). Studies also indicated that among leading world religions, Mormonism has the fourth highest retention rate: Islam (92 percent), Jewish (88 percent), Catholic (83.5 percent), Mormon (82 percent).[19] But such studies do not give us the whole picture.

Even though global membership of the Mormon church has climbed sevenfold since 1947, making it the fifth largest religious denomination in America, not all is well with Mormonism. For example, according to the _Los Angeles Times_, several analysts familiar with the Mormon church have stated that at least 40 percent of Mormons are inactive and that many of these are disillusioned.[20] But if even 30 percent of Mormons are inactive or disillusioned, the Mormon empire could face some serious future problems.

One purpose of this book is to reveal some of the reasons for this disillusionment. We will seek to answer the following questions: What exactly is Mormonism and what does it teach? How did the Mormon religion begin? What kind of men founded the Mormon church and are they to be considered prophets according to biblical definition and standards? Can Mormonism truly be considered a Christian religion? Are the early teachings of the inspired Mormon prophets the doctrines of the church today? Has the official history of the church been suppressed or altered? Is the average Mormon aware of the early history and teachings of the church? Has the church engaged in deliberate suppression or alteration of its own divine revelations? Does Mormonism really believe that Jesus was the product of the *physical* sexual union between God the Father and the "virgin" Mary? Are those the Mormon church labels its "enemies" really guilty of misrepresenting and distorting what Mormonism teaches? Is one branded an enemy of the church merely for raising these questions?

These are only some of the issues we will seek to answer in this volume.

# Chapter 2

# The Beginning of Mormonism

~

The official version of Mormonism's beginnings is recorded in the Mormon scripture known as the *Pearl of Great Price* (1851). By this account, the seeds of Mormonism were sown in Joseph Smith, Mormonism's founder, during a powerful divine visitation. This encounter is known as the "first vision." Allegedly, God the Father and Jesus Christ appeared to Smith as part of their plan to begin the Mormon religion and reestablish "true Christianity."

This "first vision" episode is crucial to the claims of the Mormon religion. Because of the importance of this alleged event, we will cite the *Pearl of Great Price* verbatim, after giving a brief introduction.

Joseph Smith (1805–1844) claimed that in his fifteenth year (1820), while living in Manchester, New York, a religious revival of significant proportions took place and "great multitudes united themselves to the different religious parties."[1] However, Smith alleges that the doctrinal strife among these religious parties was so great as to confuse a person entirely: with such conflicting claims, how could anyone determine which religion was correct—Presbyterians, Methodists, Baptists, or any other denomination?

Furthermore, according to Smith, the teachers of the various denominations allegedly "understood the same passage of Scripture so differently as to destroy all confidence in settling the question [of which group to join] by an appeal to the Bible."

Because of this confusion, Smith determined to seek God's counsel as to which of the various denominations was true, so that he might know which church he should join. As he explains it, James 1:5, which refers to asking God for wisdom, had a crucial impact at this juncture. In Smith's own words,

> Never did any passage of Scripture come with more power to the heart of man than this did at this time to mine. It seemed to enter with great force into every feeling of my heart. I reflected on it again and again, knowing that if any person needed wisdom from God, I did; for how to act I did not know and unless I could get more wisdom than I then had, I would never know.[2]

He concluded at this point that either he must "remain in darkness and confusion" or else he must "do as James directs, that is, ask of God."[3]

In his attempt to seek God, the teenage Joseph Smith retired to a secluded place in the woods in order to pray. He notes that it was on the morning of a "beautiful, clear day, early in the spring of 1820."[4]

After finding an appropriate spot, Smith reports that he "kneeled down and began to offer up the desires of my heart to God." But what Smith encountered terrified him:

> I had scarcely done so, when immediately I was seized upon by some power which entirely overcame me, and had such an astonishing influence over me as to bind my tongue so that I could not speak. Thick darkness gathered around me, and it seemed to me for a time as if I were doomed to sudden destruction.[5]

Smith then describes how, fearing immediate death, he called upon God for deliverance:

> But, exerting all my powers to call upon God to deliver me out of the power of this enemy which had seized upon me, and at the very moment which I was ready to sink into despair and abandon myself to destruction—not to an imaginary ruin, but to the power of some actual being from the unseen world, who had such marvelous power as I had never before felt in any being—just at this moment of great alarm, I saw a pillar of light exactly over my head, above the brightness of the sun, which descended gradually until it fell upon me.[6]

Having felt the panic of imminent destruction, Smith was amazed to find himself delivered:

> It no sooner appeared when I found myself delivered from the enemy which held me bound. When the light rested upon me I saw two personages, whose brightness and glory defy all description, standing above me in the air. One of them spake unto me, calling me by name, and said— pointing to the other—"THIS IS MY BELOVED SON, HEAR HIM."[7]

At this point, the claims of Joseph Smith are clear. Having called on God for help, he has been immediately delivered by nothing less than the astonishing appearance of God the Father and His Son Jesus Christ. At this juncture, Smith collected his senses and recalled his mission:

> My object in going to inquire of the Lord was to know which of all the sects was right, that I might know which to join. No sooner, therefore, did I get possession of myself, so as to be able to speak, than I asked the personages who stood

above me in the light, which of all the sects was right—and which I should join.[8]

Smith was answered immediately. In fact, to answer the question of "How did Mormonism begin?" we only need read the reply that the two supernatural personages supplied to Joseph Smith's question. According to Joseph Smith, God the Father and God the Son told him that

> I must join none of them, for they were all wrong, and the Personage who addressed me [God the Father] said that all their creeds were an abomination in his sight: that those professors [of Christian religion] were all corrupt; that "they draw near to me with their lips, but their hearts are far from me, they teach for doctrines the commandments of men, having a form of godliness, but they deny the power thereof."
> He [God the Father] again forbade me to join with any of them; and many other things did he say unto me, which I cannot write at this time. When I came to myself again [fully regained his senses], I found myself lying on my back, looking up into heaven. When the light had departed, I had no strength; but soon recovering it in some degree, I went home.[9]

Joseph Smith had found his answer. He was convinced that God had appeared to him to inform him that Christianity was a false religion. Thus, he recalls, "My mind [was] satisfied so far as the sectarian [Christian] world was concerned...it was not my duty to join with any of them, but to continue as I was until further directed."[10]

Smith became persuaded that, out of all the men in the world, he had been uniquely called of God. Although he admits that he "frequently fell into many foolish errors" (cf. James 1:20-22,26), he waited patiently until the next revelation.[11]

Three years later, on September 21, 1823, Smith experienced the first of several major necromantic encounters, or

contacts with the dead. At this time a spirit appeared to Smith
to tell him the location of certain "gold plates." These gold
plates contained the purported historical records of the Jewish
"Nephite" peoples concerning their early migration to the
Americas.

In his _History of the Church_, Smith records the visit by this
spirit who identified itself as "Moroni" (the son of a "Nephite"
historian named Mormon, the alleged author of the "gold
plates" from which the _Book of Mormon_ was "translated"):

> While I was thus in the act of calling upon
> God, I discovered a light appearing in my room,
> which continued to increase until the room was
> lighter than at noonday, when immediately a
> [spirit] personage appeared at my bed side,
> standing in the air....He called me by name, and
> said unto me that he was a messenger sent from
> the presence of God to me and that his name was
> Moroni; that God had a work for me to do....He
> said there was a book deposited, written upon
> gold plates, giving an account of the former inhabi-
> tants of this [American] continent, and the sources
> from whence they sprang. He also said that the
> fullness of the everlasting Gospel was contained
> in it, as delivered by the Savior [Jesus] to the
> ancient inhabitants [of America]; also that there
> were two stones in silver bows—and these stones,
> fastened to a breastplate, constituted what is
> called the Urim and Thummim—deposited with
> the plates; and the possession and use of these
> stones were what constituted [the category of]
> "seers" in ancient or former times; and that God
> had prepared them for the purpose of translating
> the book.[12]

In addition, the spirit quoted numerous passages of
prophetic scripture, either implying or stating that some of
them were about to be fulfilled. The spirit then departed,
although it soon reappeared twice to state the same message.[13]

These and other necromantic contacts were probably the result of Joseph Smith's use of magic ritual to invoke the spirit world; the specific nature of the encounters frequently fit the pattern for magical contacts, as can be seen from D. Michael Quinn, *Early Mormonism and the Magic World View* (1987) and John L. Brooke, *The Refiner's Fire: The Making of Mormon Cosmology 1844–1894* (1984).

Further supernatural encounters continued to profoundly influence the young Joseph Smith. The very next day, the seventeen-year-old lad was crossing a field when suddenly "my strength entirely failed me, and I fell helpless on the ground, and for a time was unconscious of anything."[14] The first thing Smith remembered was hearing the same spirit calling his name. Regaining his senses, he was commanded to go and locate the "gold plates" buried in a certain hill named Cumorah. After that, according to the spirit, he was to return yearly to that same spot for further instructions and teaching, and in the fourth year (in 1827) the translation of the "gold plates" would be permitted. Thus, by 1829 the translation was completed, and in 1830 the *Book of Mormon* was published. Named after its author, the alleged Nephite historian Mormon, it became one of the three scriptures unique to the Mormon faith.

In conclusion, just as the Mormon church originated in supernatural revelations, it was sustained by this means, especially by contact with various spirits, including alleged spirits of the dead such as Moroni.

In fact, from 1825 until his untimely death in 1844, Joseph Smith received several *hundred* direct revelations from the spirit world, which helped the new religious movement to grow and solidify itself.[15] Smith claimed he received revelations not only from "God," "Jesus," and "angels," but also from many of the dead. Some 135 of these revelations were printed in *Doctrine and Covenants*, the second and doctrinally most important volume of Mormon scripture.[16] For example, in this book are recorded alleged revelations from Moroni (2); the Apostles John, Peter, and James (7; 27:12; 128:20); John the Baptist (13); and others (e.g., 128).[17]

Although most of the revelations claim to be from God the Father and Jesus Christ, this is not possible for reasons that will become evident later in this book. What's more, Joseph Smith's first vision account raises serious questions. At least three earlier versions of the first vision account are known to exist.[18] Which account is to be trusted?

Mormons themselves confess that the first vision is second in importance only to Christ's "divinity": that it is the "foundation of the Church," that the church stands or falls on the authenticity of the event, and that the "truth and validity" of all Smith's subsequent work rests upon its genuineness.[19] In other words, if the "first vision account" is established as not credible—either on the basis of serious internal discrepancies or other factors—then, according to Mormonism itself, the legitimacy of the entire church collapses.

Smith's official account of this pivotal event was published in _Times and Seasons_ in 1842, twenty-two years after the episode allegedly took place. However, as we said, at least three additional earlier accounts of the first vision, all by Smith, were suppressed by Mormon authorities because they contradicted the official story.[20]

For example, the earliest account we now possess, from 1832, varies in key details from the official 1842 version. There are discrepancies in Smith's age, in the message given, and in the number of divine personages in the vision. There are also details added, such as the presence of an evil power, Smith's reason for seeking the Lord, and the existence of a revival.[21] All this lends serious doubt to the credibility of the official account.

Consider, for instance, the divine persons in the revelation. In this version only "Jesus" appears. What happened to God the Father? Jerald and Sandra Tanner reveal that the first handwritten account of Joseph Smith does not even mention the existence of the Father—who plays so crucial a role in the official version:

> It is absolutely impossible for us to believe that Joseph Smith would not have mentioned the Father

if he had actually appeared....We feel that the only reasonable explanation for the Father not being mentioned in the account which was suppressed is that Joseph Smith did *not* see God the Father, and that he made up this part of the story after the writing of the first manuscript. This, of course, throws a shadow of doubt upon the whole story.[22]

Consider another of Smith's accounts written between 1835 and 1836. In this case there is no mention of God or Christ at all—only of many spirits who "testified" of Jesus. But here again, the authority of the account—and of Mormonism's divine origin—is called into question. No longer is it God and Jesus telling Joseph Smith to begin a new church because all others are abominations; it is now only a group of nebulous "spirits." Why should anyone accept the word of a fifteen-year-old boy who claimed he talked with some unidentified spirits? Even if he did, why should anyone trust such spirits in the first place? If my fifteen-year-old boy claimed he saw a vision of God or Jesus giving him divine authority, why should Mormons believe him? So why should anyone else believe their story of Joseph Smith—especially when Smith himself kept telling different stories about his alleged divine encounter?

The dilemma posed by these various accounts of the first vision is explained by the Tanners, who conclude:

We have now examined three different handwritten manuscripts of the first vision. They were all written by Joseph Smith or his scribes, and yet every one of them is different. The first account says there was only one personage. The second account says there were many, and the third says there were two. The church, of course, accepts the version that contains two personages. If we have to accept any of the versions, we would choose the first account. It was written six or seven years closer to the event, and therefore it should give a more accurate picture of what really took place.

Also, this account, which mentions only one personage, is the only account in Joseph Smith's own
handwriting.
At any rate, when one becomes aware of the
fact that there are conflicting versions of the story,
it becomes very difficult to believe that Joseph
Smith ever had a vision in the grove.
On top of all this, there is irrefutable evidence
that an important reference to the first vision in
the _History of the Church_ has been falsified by
Mormon historians after Joseph Smith's death.[23]

How does the Mormon church respond to these charges?
They claim that the discrepancies in the accounts in fact _sup-
port_ the conclusion that the accounts are truthful! Milton V.
Blackman, Jr., professor of Church History at Brigham Young
University, presents the standard argument:

> On at least four different occasions, Joseph
> Smith either wrote or dictated to scribes accounts
> of his sacred experience in 1820. Possibly he wrote
> or dictated other histories of the First Vision....
> each of them emphasizes different aspects of the
> Prophet's experience....the existence of these dif-
> ferent accounts help support the integrity of the
> Latter-day Saint Prophet. It indicates that Joseph
> did not deliberately create a memorized version
> that he related to everyone....[consider that] the
> Four Gospels do not correspond exactly con-
> cerning the great events at the Garden's empty
> tomb.[24]

But neither this nor similar responses deal with the real
problem. Why? Because Smith never did what Mormon apologists say he did. It is one thing to recount an incident selec-
tively. It is something else entirely to recount it in several
contradictory versions. If selective reports of a single event
are given accurately, they should "add up" when totaled,
making one complete, coherent description of that single

event. Despite the contentions of critics, this *is* what we find when examining the resurrection narratives in the four Gospels—as we have shown in *Do the Resurrection Accounts Conflict? And What Proof Is There Jesus Rose from the Dead?*[25] But this central coherence is not what we find when all the facts of up to six (some claim nine)[26] different accounts of the first vision are combined. Gordon Fraser comments, "...there are at least six versions of the famed First Vision of the prophet, with his own final version, written about 1838, being the least credible."[27]

Here are some of the inconsistencies: If Jesus had really been standing before Joseph Smith, why would a multitude of spirits also have been necessary to "testify" of Him? How old was Smith? He couldn't have been two different ages in the same year. Was there a commanding evil power that Smith was delivered from—or not? In what year did the revival occur that precipitated Smith's alleged seeking of the divine wisdom? What exactly did God, Jesus, or the spirits say? Contrary answers to these questions cannot all be true at the same time. Further, Joseph Smith never discarded only minor aspects of a larger experience that he then reported in general fashion to different audiences. Absolutely decisive elements were discarded. But key incidents are almost *never* left out of a reported event, no matter when or under what circumstances they are written—especially if they are public writings intended to make an essentially crucial point: that God was reestablishing true Christianity after an immense lapse of eighteen hundred years.

For example, the four Gospel accounts of the resurrection do not leave out vital incidents. None of them leave out the fact of Christ's death, or the empty tomb itself, or the appearances of the risen Christ to the disciples.

But consider the versions of Joseph Smith's first vision. Is it conceivable that in any retelling of Smith's story he would leave out the crucial parts about 1) the Father or 2) both the Father and the Son together? For Smith to leave out critical details in recounting such a crucial event makes one suspect that whatever his initial experience may have been, it was later embellished by him or others. One is also forced to the conclusion that that initial experience could have been any-thing—from pure invention, to religious suggestion and self-deception, to spiritistic manipulation.[28]

In essence, the official account of the church cannot be accepted as reliable, and, therefore, the authority and legiti-macy of the entire Mormon church is undermined by this one conclusion alone. If even Joseph Smith was uncertain as to what he experienced, or worse yet fabricated evidence, why should anyone trust his other claims?

We are not saying Smith never had a mystical experience. We are only saying it is impossible to establish evidence of the divine origin of the Mormon church on the basis of this event. Our own personal view is that, based on his occult back-ground, Smith probably did have a vision of spirits—and that it was _their_ intent, not God's, to establish the Mormon church.

Thus, we may observe that Smith's vision was not some-thing wholly unique, as Mormon authorities emphasize. In fact, his experience fit a characteristic pattern of spiritistic con-tacts that have occurred throughout history. Indeed, many similar incidents were evident during the time Smith was making his own pronouncements as to divine visitations. Elias Smith, Asa Wild, and others were making similar claims.[29] Joseph Smith's story was thus only one of many similar episodes, and, therefore, it seems at least possible that after an initial vision of spirits, he later added the account of the Father and/or the Son appearing to him. Why? Because it would single-handedly give _his_ claims more divine authority and make them stand out from the many other revelations of spirits that clamored for the attention of the public.[30]

The evidence appears conclusive, then, that the first vision account cannot be trusted. Even if the official version were legitimate—accurately recording what Joseph Smith thought he experienced—the revelation could not possibly have been true. From a biblical viewpoint, it would logically have to be considered a spiritual deception. For example, we can know that Smith never saw the biblical Jesus, for Jesus would never appear to a practicing occultist, reject His own faithful servants as "abominations," and then proceed to begin a new, heretical church that denied and opposed everything He ever taught.

In conclusion, Mormons who trust in the first vision account need to seriously reflect on the many unanswered questions surrounding this event. Did Smith actually see anything? Did he fabricate part or all of the vision? Did he change or combine elements of several different occult visions? Did church leaders suppress damaging evidence of the event? Until they can satisfactorily answer these and other questions, perhaps they should reserve judgment on the meaning and value of Joseph Smith's personal experiences.

What can be learned from the first vision episode is that 1) it is now unwise to place trust in the official account, and that 2) as the Bible warns, one should not take "his stand on visions he has seen" (Colossians 2:18), but rather on scriptural authority alone.* But this raises another issue. What is scriptural authority to the Mormon? When Mormons add new scripture to the canon, can these claims to divine revelation be trusted either?

The first vision narrative is interesting on one more account: its display of spiritual intimidation. Confronted by destruction from one source, Smith naturally interprets his deliverance from another as divine. But how does he know that the entire event was not staged by evil forces for just this effect? Such accounts are legion in the ranks of mediumism and other forms of spiritism. Lying spirits, which the Bible identifies as demons, often claim to be God, Jesus, angels, or the human dead.[31] A similar account of evil spirits imitating divine spirits or angels is found, for example, in former medium Raphael Gasson's *The Challenging Counterfeit*: "Demons have to use some method of deception in their attempt to prove the counterfeit is of God and so they play a game of make-believe. Although they are literally evil spirits, one pretends to be the 'good' spirit while the other proclaims his 'evil'ness."[32]

Nevertheless, the early Mormons followed the leading of Joseph Smith, and they continued to rely upon dramatic supernatural revelations and visions that only claimed to be divine.

---

* The reader may pursue the issue of the various accounts in *Dialogue: A Journal of Mormon Thought*, Autumn 1966 and Spring 1971; *Brigham Young University Studies*, Spring 1969; and elsewhere.

# SECTION II

# WHAT DO THE MORMONS BELIEVE ABOUT GOD?

# Chapter 3

# Mormon Teachings on God and the Trinity

~

Jesus Himself emphasized the importance of having an accurate knowledge of the one true God. He stated, "And this is eternal life, that they may know Thee, the only true God, and Jesus Christ whom Thou hast sent" (John 17:3).

The Mormon church also emphasizes the importance of a correct understanding of God. For example, *Doctrines of the Gospel*, published by the Mormon church, emphasizes that "central to our faith as Latter-day Saints is a correct understanding of God the Father."[1] And this is the student manual used at Brigham Young University for courses Religion 231 and 232. But the Mormon church also claims that only they understand God in truth; all other conceptions are wrong. Joseph Smith testifies, "There are but a few beings in the world who understand rightly the character of God."[2] Likewise the leading Mormon theologian James Talmage claims, "[The] sectarian [Christian] view of the Godhead [contains]…numerous theories and dogmas of men, many of which are utterly incomprehensible in their inconsistency and mysticism."[3]

Nevertheless, Mormonism proceeds to claim that its confession of faith is in the one true God, the God *of the Bible.*

But when Mormons claim they believe in the *biblical* God, what they *mean* is that the Bible teaches the *Mormon* concept of God. Because of its alleged apostasy, Christianity lost the true teaching of God, and therefore the historic Christian doctrine of God is not truly biblical.

Thus, Mormons do freely concede that their concept of deity is contrary to traditional Christian faith. William O. Nelson, director of the Melchizedek Priesthood Department, agrees: "Some who write anti-Mormon pamphlets insist that the Latter-day Saint concept of Deity is contrary to what is recognized as traditional Christian doctrine. In this they are quite correct."[4] So the real issue becomes one of ascertaining the true biblical teaching on the nature of God. For the rest of this chapter we will document that the Mormon teaching on God is not biblical.

## The Key Differences

Here is a brief chart noting major differences between the Mormon concept of God and the biblical or Christian view:

| Mormon Concept of Deity *(Pagan Polytheism)* | Biblical (Christian) Concept of Deity *(Monotheism)* |
|---|---|
| 1. The Gods are many (polytheistic) | God is one (monotheistic) |
| 2. The Gods are evolving (changing, mutable) | God is immutable (unchanging) |
| 3. The Gods are material (physical) | God is immaterial (spirit) |
| 4. The Gods are sexual (physically procreating divine "spirit children") | God is asexual (having no literal descendants) |
| 5. The Gods are polygamists (taking wives and husbands) | God is celibate (unmarried) |

6. The Gods are imperfect,     God is eternally holy
   requiring salvation

   In the pages that follow, we will discuss these topics in
turn.

## Mormon Teaching No. 1—The Gods Are Many: Pagan Polytheism

How do we know that the Mormon concept of God is
pagan? Merely by examining its teachings.

The *Encyclopedia Britannica* defines paganism as "practices
and beliefs that are incompatible with monotheism." According
to the normal understanding of *pagan*, any religion teaching
that 1) there are many gods and that 2) God is finite; He
evolves and changes, and 3) that matter and spirit are eternal
is a pagan religion. Thus Mormonism is properly classified as
a religion offering pagan theology (cf. p. 150).

Monotheism—the belief in one Supreme God—stands in
contrast to paganism which rejects that central belief. The
three great monotheistic religions, Christianity, Judaism, and
Islam, all teach that there is one eternal, sovereign, immutable,
and merciful God who created the universe. By contrast—
unlike many polytheistic occult religions of the East—they do
not teach that God changes over the aeons (that God is finite),
or that there are many gods (which is polytheism), or that
matter and God are both eternal and inseparably divine.

Of course, Mormons are very uncomfortable with the
charge of polytheism or paganism, and rightly so. Historically,
these ideas have been teachings of great consequence in the
world.

It is thus not surprising that Mormons emphatically deny
they are polytheists or pagans and that they wish to consider
such charges false and "damnable." No less a church authority
than Bruce McConkie categorically insists that "the saints
[Mormons] are not polytheists."[5] Stephen Robinson, chairman
of the Department of Ancient Scripture at Brigham Young
University and author of *Are Mormons Christians?* (which he
emphatically affirms), argues that "the Latter-day Saints

[doctrine does not]...constitute genuine polytheism."[6] And he takes pains to argue that "the Latter-day Saints [should] be considered worshipers of the one true God."[7] He argues that only by "distorting and misinterpreting our doctrine" can others charge Mormonism with polytheism.[8]

But if Mormons are really polytheists, why do they think they are monotheists? Principally, it is through the uncritical acceptance of the statements of church authorities, and secondarily, it is by a process of seemingly deliberate self-deception caused by the improper use of words. When Mormons deny the charge of polytheism, they illustrate a characteristic feature of Mormon apologetics—equivocation. Equivocation involves the ambiguous use of words in order to conceal something or duplicity of meaning in a word.

The truth is that Mormons are polytheists by any standard definition of the term. For example, the *Oxford American Dictionary* defines polytheism as "belief in or worship of more than one god."[9]

Technically, Mormon theology is "henotheistic"—a form of polytheism which stresses a central deity. In Mormonism, the central deity is Elohim, whom Mormons call "God the Father." But henotheism also accepts other deities. In Mormonism the other deities accepted include Jesus, the Holy Ghost, and endless other gods who were once men and have now evolved into godhood. Even the *Encyclopedia Britannica* classifies Mormonism as polytheistic.

The fact is, when pressed, Mormons must confess that they are polytheists, not monotheists. In his discussion of polytheism in *Mormon Doctrine*, LDS doctrinal theologian Bruce McConkie freely declares that Mormons believe in "three Gods."[10]

Nevertheless, he equivocates by vainly attempting to distinguish pagan polytheism from Mormon polytheism. Further, only by stressing their primary belief in Elohim, are Mormons able to convince themselves they are really monotheists. But this is, unfortunately, self-deception.

Mormons claim they are monotheistic merely because their *principal* concern is with the one central deity, the earth god

Elohim. In other words, even though they freely confess, at least when pressed, to be *doctrinal* polytheists,[11] they think they are *practical* monotheists. But whatever Mormons may claim, they are equally concerned with at least two other gods, the earth god Jesus and the strange god they call the Holy Ghost. Consider the following discussion in the student manual used at Brigham Young University, *Doctrines of the Gospel.* Note the initial claim to worship one supreme, absolute being: "By definition, God (generally meaning the Father) is the one supreme and absolute Being...God is the only supreme governor...who is omnipotent, omnipresent, and omniscient; without beginning of days or end of life."[12]

This sounds like monotheism, but as we read further the discussion digresses from monotheism to henotheism. Thus, "Our relationship with the Father is supreme, paramount, and preeminent over all others [e.g., over Mormon relationships with other gods like the Holy Ghost]. He is the God we worship....He is the one who was once as we are now [i.e., a man]."[13]

Further, the three members of the Mormon Godhead (the Father, Son, and Holy Ghost), all of whom were once men, remain "three separate and distinct entities. Each occupies space and is and can be in but one place at one time, but each has power and influence that is everywhere present."[14]

In an attempt to quell the charge of polytheism, the manual declares, "There is a *oneness* in the Godhead as well as distinctness of personality. This oneness is emphasized in the sayings and writings of prophets and apostles *in order to guard against the erroneous idea that these three may be distinct and independent deities.*"[15]

In other words, the claim is clearly made that the Father, Son, and Spirit are *not* "distinct and independent deities." But just a few pages later, in this very same text appears: "Both the Father and Son, *being omnipotent Gods,* are designated by the name-titles, *Almighty...Almighty God...Lord Almighty...* and *Lord God Almighty....*These holy beings have all power and unlimited might."[16]

Joseph Smith himself is quoted as declaring, "In the beginning, the head of the Gods called a council of the Gods; and they came together and concocted a plan to create the world and people in it."[17] This is polytheism, not monotheism.

Consider the following excerpts from Joseph Smith's new revelation of the Creation account in the Mormon scripture known as the *Pearl of Great Price*. Does the following sound like monotheism or polytheism?

> At the beginning...the Gods organized and formed the heavens and the earth....And the Gods called the light Day....And the Gods also said: let there be an expanse in the midst of the waters.... And the Gods ordered the expanse, so that it divided the waters....And the Gods called the expanse Heaven....And the Gods pronounced the dry land Earth....And the Gods said: let us prepare the earth to bring forth grass....And the Gods organized the lights in the expanse of the heaven....And the Gods organized the two great lights, the greater light to rule the day, and the lesser light to rule the night....And the Gods set them in the expanse of the heavens....And the Gods organized the earth to bring forth the beasts after their kind....And the Gods took counsel among themselves and said: let us go down and form man in our image....So the Gods went down to organize man in their own image....And the Gods said: we will bless them....And the Gods said: Behold, we will give them every herb bearing seed....And the Gods formed man from the dust of the ground....And the Gods planted a garden, eastward in Eden....And the Gods took the man and put him in the Garden of Eden.... And the Gods said: let us make an help meet for the man.[18]

In fact, *Abraham* chapters 4 and 5 refer to the activity of the "Gods" almost fifty separate times. Anyone who thinks this is monotheism is deceiving himself.

## Different Aspects of Mormon Polytheism

Mormon polytheism encompasses two aspects. First, there is a predominant "local" polytheism as far as the earth is concerned. The earth has three distinct gods who "rule it." Thus, Mormonism's concept of the biblical Trinity is tritheistic, not monotheistic. In *Mormon Doctrine*, McConkie declares, "There are three Gods—the Father, the Son and the Holy Ghost."[19]

The principal deity is the Father, a physical god named "Elohim," said to be the primary and most "advanced" god. Mormonism teaches, "The Father is the supreme member of the Godhead."[20] The Son is the physical god "Jehovah" of the Old Testament: "Jesus Christ is Jehovah, the God of the Old Testament."[21] The Holy Ghost is another former man who has become a god, although unlike the Father and the Son, he does not have a concrete physical body, but is a man with a spiritual body of matter.

These three beings, again, all former men, are the three gods that Mormons are to concern themselves with. Again, because Mormonism claims that extra-solar gods are not the church's particular concern, this belief in tritheism is somehow held to be monotheistic. In any case, Mormons will assure absolutely everyone that they believe in only one true God.

The second aspect of Mormon polytheism is not geocentric, but universal. If there are an infinite number of earths, each with its god or gods, there are also an infinite number of gods, and whether or not Mormons are "concerned" with them they do believe in them, hence the denial of polytheism is once again spurious. Even McConkie declares the following when he refers to the three principal gods of our earth:

> To us, speaking in the proper finite sense, these three are the only Gods we worship. But in addition there is an infinite number of holy personages,

drawn from worlds without number, who have
passed on to exaltation [Godhood] and are thus
gods....This doctrine of plurality of Gods is so
comprehensive and glorious that it reaches out
and embraces every exalted personage [God].
Those who attain exaltation are gods.[22]

Brigham Young taught the same, declaring, "How many
Gods there are I do not know, but there never was a time when
there were not Gods."[23] As we will document later, Joseph
Smith claimed that he always taught polytheism, so it is odd
to find modern Mormons claiming they are monotheists if
indeed they respect Smith as God's true prophet.

To claim that one is a monotheist when it is evident from
one's own official doctrines that one is a polytheist is religious
deception. When Mormon missionaries look people straight
in the eye and confidently claim they are monotheists—and
even that they believe in the Holy Trinity—they are equivo-
cating. The truth is they are polytheists who regret the historic, biblical doctrine of the Trinity.

Again, for Mormons to claim to be monotheists solely
because one of their gods plays a more prominent role in their
affairs than other gods is like a polygamist claiming he is really
a monogamist merely because he has a favorite wife. Notice
the argument of Mormon theologian Duane S. Crowther:

Thus it becomes obvious that there are now,
and will continue to be, many [omnipotent] gods
who will rule and reign throughout eternity on an
ever increasing number of worlds which they will
create. This is not in opposition to the Biblical concept of "one God," for an earth serves as the
dwelling place for the children of only one God,
and he alone reigns over his children there as
Father and God.[24]

In other words, Mormons are monotheists because they
believe in only one god per earth! The fact that there is an

endless number of earths each with its own god(s) is somehow irrelevant. Mormons are still not polytheists! Who then denies that Mormons are polytheists? Only Mormons.

Even though Mormonism repeatedly claims to believe in what the Bible teaches, the Bible clearly rejects polytheism in the most straightforward terms. God Himself declares in Isaiah: "Before Me there was no God formed, and there will be none after Me" (43:10). He also teaches, "I am the first and I am the last, and there is no God besides Me....Is there any God besides Me?...I know of none" (44:6,8). He further emphasizes, "I am the LORD, and there is no other; besides Me there is no God....There is none except Me" (45:5,21). From Genesis to Revelation, the Bible teaches there is only one God.

### The Mormon Claim to Believing in the "Trinity"

Mormonism claims that it believes in the Trinity. Dr. Stephen E. Robinson is chairman of the Department of Ancient Scripture at Brigham Young University and director of _Pearl of Great Price_ research for the Religious Studies Center. First, he claims that Mormonism believes in the biblical God. He emphasizes, "The Latter-day Saints accept unequivocally _all the biblical teachings_ on the nature of God."[25] He further claims that Mormons believe in the biblical doctrine of the Trinity: "Latter-day Saints believe in the _biblical_ Father, Son, and Holy Ghost."[26] Even more explicitly, "If by 'the doctrine of the Trinity' one means _the New Testament teaching_ that there is a Father, a Son, and Holy Ghost, all three of whom are fully divine, then Latter-day Saints _believe in the doctrine of the Trinity_. It's as simple as that. The Latter-day Saints' first _Article of Faith_, written by Joseph Smith in 1842, states, 'We believe in the God, the Eternal Father, and in His Son, Jesus Christ, and in the Holy Ghost.' "[27]

Richard L. Evans, a member of the Council of Twelve, as interviewed in Leo Rosten's _Religions of America_, answered "yes" to the question of "Do Mormons believe in the Holy Trinity?"[28]

To the contrary, Mormons do not believe in the Trinity; they believe in *tritheism*. Again, they believe in three gods for this particular earth and accept the existence of endless other gods on endless other earths. The very fact that they caricature the biblical teaching on the Trinity indicates that they reject the concept of one triune God. We cite three examples from early and contemporary Mormonism. Joseph Smith himself ridiculed the biblical Trinity:

> Many men say there is one God; the Father, the Son and the Holy Ghost are only one God. I say that is a strange God anyhow—three in one, and one in three! It is curious organization....All are to be crammed into one God according to sectarianism [Christian faith]. It would make the biggest God in all the world. He would be a wonderfully big God—he would be a giant or a monster.[29]

This is why Joseph Smith stated that whenever he preached on the subject of God, it was *always* in reference to polytheistic belief. In his own words, he declared while preaching on Genesis 1:1: "I will preach on the plurality of Gods. I have selected this text for that express purpose. I wish to declare that I have always and in all congregations when I have preached on the subject of the Deity, it has been on the plurality of Gods."[30]

Also referring to the Christian Trinity, William Nelson, director of the Melchizedek Priesthood Department, comments, "It was hard to fathom a Deity of this nature, let alone love him."[31] And Bruce McConkie is even more skeptical:

> Who or what is God? Is he the incomprehensible, uncreated, immaterial nothingness described in the creeds of Christendom...a three-in-one nothingness, a spirit essence filling immensity, an incorporeal, uncreated being incapable of definition or mortal comprehension....an Unknown God who does not appear to men?[32]

But, these caricatures are irrelevant; the Bible clearly does teach the historic orthodox doctrine of the Trinity.

## The Biblical Teaching

Christians believe the Bible teaches that the one true God exists eternally as three Persons. The doctrine of the Trinity can be seen from five simple statements supported by the Bible.

1. There is only one true God: "For there is one God, and one mediator also between God and men" (1 Timothy 2:5; cf. Deuteronomy 4:35; 6:4; Isaiah 43:10).

2. The Father is God: "There is but one God, the Father, from whom are all things..." (1 Corinthians 8:6; cf. John 17:1-3; 2 Corinthians 1:3; Philippians 2:11; Colossians 1:3; 1 Peter 1:2).

3. Jesus Christ, the Son, is God: "...but he [Jesus] was even calling God his own Father, making himself equal with God" (John 5:18 NIV). "...while we wait for the blessed hope—the glorious appearing of our great God and Savior, Jesus Christ" (Titus 2:13 NIV; cf. John 20:28; John 1:1; Romans 9:5; 2 Peter 1:1).

4. The Holy Spirit is a Person, is eternal, and is therefore God. The Holy Spirit is a Person: "But when he, the Spirit of truth, comes, he will guide you into all truth. He will not speak on his own; he will speak only what he hears, and he will tell you what is yet to come" (John 16:13 NIV). The Holy Spirit is eternal: "How much more, then, will the blood of Christ, who through the eternal Spirit offered himself unblemished to God, cleanse our consciences..." (Hebrews 9:14 NIV). The Holy Spirit is therefore God: "Then Peter said, 'Ananias, how is it that Satan has so filled your heart that you have lied to the Holy Spirit...? You have not lied to men but to God'" (Acts 5:3,4 NIV).

5. The Father, Son, and Holy Spirit are distinct Persons: "Therefore go and make disciples of all nations, baptizing them in the name of the Father and of the Son and

of the Holy Spirit" (Matthew 28:19 NIV); "May the grace of the Lord Jesus Christ, and the love of God, and the fellowship of the Holy Spirit be with you all" (2 Corinthians 13:14 NIV).

It is clear from these verses that the Bible teaches that one true God exists eternally as Father, Son, and Holy Spirit. For almost two thousand years the Christian church has found in the Bible the doctrine of the Trinity as defined above. This can be seen by anyone who reads the Church Fathers and studies the historic Creeds.*

Our incomplete comprehension of this truth is insufficient grounds to reject what Scripture teaches. For example, scientists long believed that all energy existed either as "waves" or "particles": two contradictory forms. They could not understand how light, for example, could consist of *both* waves and particles because their natures were different. Even when scientific testing proved this to be true, some scientists found it difficult to accept this conclusion because it was "unreasonable." Nevertheless, scientists were eventually forced by the *evidence* to conclude that light was both waves and particles. Scientists may not be able to explain it logically, but they are honest enough to accept that this is what light is.

In the same manner, God has told who He is. The evidence of Scripture forces us to accept that the one true God exists eternally as Father, Son, and Holy Spirit. We cannot fully understand it or explain it logically, but we accept it because this is where the facts have led us.

Indeed, Father, Son, and Holy Spirit are so effortlessly and consistently linked in Scripture that assuming that God is not three Persons makes it impossible to understand numerous passages (e.g., Matthew 28:19; 2 Corinthians 1:21,22; 13:14; Ephesians 2:18; 3:11-16; 5:18-20; 1 Thessalonians 1:1-5).

---

* For an in-depth study of the historical development of the doctrine of the Trinity from apostolic times through the final form of the Nicean Creed adopted at the Council of Constantinople in A.D. 381, including a line-by-line comparison of the Creed with New Testament teaching, see Calvin Beisner's *God in Three Persons*. Another excellent study is E. Bickersteth's *The Trinity*.[33]

Try answering the following questions without concluding that the Bible teaches the doctrine of the Trinity:

1. Who raised Jesus from the dead? The Father (Romans 6:4; Acts 3:26; 1 Thessalonians 1:10)? The Son (John 2:19-21; 10:17,18)? The Holy Spirit (Romans 8:11)? Or God (Hebrews 13:20; Acts 13:30; 17:31)?

2. Who does the Bible say is God? The Father (Ephesians 4:6)? The Son (Titus 2:13; John 1:1; 20:28)? The Holy Spirit (Acts 5:3,4)? The one and only true God (Deuteronomy 4:35)?

3. Who created the world? The Father (John 14:2)? The Son (John 1:1-3; Colossians 1:16,17)? The Holy Spirit (Genesis 1:2; Psalm 104:30)? Or God (Genesis 1:1; Hebrews 11:3)?

4. Who saves man? Who regenerates man? The Father (1 Peter 1:3)? The Son (John 5:21; 4:14)? The Holy Spirit (John 3:6; Titus 3:5)? Or God (1 John 3:9)? Who justifies man? The Father (Jeremiah 23:6; 2 Corinthians 5:19)? The Son (Romans 5:9; 10:4; 2 Corinthians 5:19,21)? The Holy Spirit (1 Corinthians 6:11; Galatians 5:5)? Or God (Romans 4:6; 8:33)? Who sanctifies man? The Father (Jude 1)? The Son (Titus 2:14)? The Holy Spirit (1 Peter 1:2)? Or God (Exodus 31:13)? Who propitiated God's anger against man for his sins? The Father (1 John 4:14; John 3:16; 17:5; 18:11)? The Son (Matthew 26:28; John 1:19; 1 John 2:2)? The Holy Spirit (Hebrews 9:14)? Or God (2 Corinthians 5:1; Acts 20:28)?

In conclusion, it is simple to see why the Christian church has been taught the doctrine of the Trinity for two thousand years—the Bible unmistakably teaches it.*

---

*This discussion on the Christian Trinity was excerpted from the authors' _Cult Watch: What You Need to Know About Spiritual Deception_ (Eugene, OR: Harvest House Publishers, 1991).

## Mormon Teaching No. 2—The Gods Are Evolving: Each God Was Once a Finite Man

Mormonism teaches that God was not God from all eternity, but that He was once a man who evolved into Godhood. This is a doctrine that Mormonism holds is true for all who are currently gods—and there are endless numbers of them. As noted elsewhere, both historic Mormon theology and contemporary Mormonism teach that there are an infinite number of earths throughout the universe, each one presided over by its own god or gods.

How do men become gods? Mormonism believes that all current gods have attained the status of godhood through the good works they performed when they were once finite men. Joseph Smith describes the process by which men may become gods: "When you climb up a ladder, you must begin at the bottom and ascend step by step, until you arrive at the top; and so it is with the principles of the Gospel—you must begin with the first, and go on until you learn all the principles of exaltation [becoming a God]."[34] The official Mormon publication *Gospel Principles* cites this passage and then comments, "This is the way our Heavenly Father became a God."[35] It then quotes Joseph Smith's own evaluation of "The First Principle of the Gospel," which is to realize that God the Father was once a man: "It is the first principle of the gospel to know for a certainty the character of God, and to know that we may converse with him as one man converses with another, and that he was once a man like us; yea that God himself, the father of us all, dwelt on an earth, the same as Jesus Christ himself did; and I will show it from the Bible."[36]

This same source includes the observation, "God is a glorified and perfected man, a personage of flesh and bones. Inside his tangible body is an eternal spirit (see *D&C*, 130:22)."[37] Mormon authorities claim that this teaching "in no way degrades God, but certainly elevates the status of man. And sure He's a man. He's got a body of flesh and bones like you and I have."[38]

Even though the Bible teaches, "For I, the LORD, do not change" (Malachi 3:6), Mormonism thinks that God was once a man, who was Himself created by another god. As Joseph Smith taught, "The Father of Jesus Christ had a Father":

> If Jesus Christ was the son of God, and John discovered that God the Father of Jesus Christ had a Father, you may suppose that he had a Father also. Where was there ever a son without a father? And where was there ever a father without first being a son?[39]

Mormonism thus teaches that God the Father had a father who created Him and gave Him the opportunity to become God.

This is why Joseph Smith specifically rejected the Christian teaching:

> God Himself was once as we are now, and is an exalted man, and sits enthroned in yonder heavens! That is the great secret....If you were going to see him today, you would see him like a man in form....I am going to tell you how God came to be God. We have imagined and supposed that God was God from all eternity. I will refute that idea, and take away the veil, so that you may see....He was once a man like us....Here, then, is eternal life—to know the only wise and true God; and you have got to learn how to be gods yourselves.[40]

Hence, it is not surprising that Joseph Smith stated that the true translation of Genesis 1:1 taught polytheism. According to Smith, "It read first [in its original version] 'The head one of the Gods brought forth the Gods.' That is the true meaning of the words....Thus the head God brought forth the Gods in the grand council."[41] After that, "The heads of the Gods appointed one God for us [i.e., Elohim]"—and thus Elohim became the God of this world.[42]

Modern Mormons have continued to accept these early polytheistic teachings. Bruce McConkie declares that "God is a Holy Man."[43] He further teaches that "God is...an exalted, perfected, and glorified Man of Holiness (Moses 6:57) and not a spirit essence that fills the immensity of space."[44] Mormons everywhere affirm that "God is a man."[45]

The Mormon student manual *Doctrines of the Gospel* teaches that "God Himself is an exalted man, perfected, enthroned, and supreme."[46] Even Dr. Stephen Robinson, who is convinced that Mormonism is Christian, confesses, "It is indisputable that Latter-day Saints believe that God was once a human being and that human beings can become gods." The well-known couplet of Lorenzo Snow, fifth president and prophet of the LDS Church, states: "As man now is, God once was; as God now is, man may be."[47]

But Mormonism is divided on how far the process of divine evolution extends. Historically, the church has been uncertain as to whether or not the gods continue to evolve forever. Many Mormon presidents and prophets taught that the gods evolve eternally in power, knowledge, and so on—which, of course, would never quite make them truly omnipotent, omniscient, etc.[48] This is conveyed in the following early teachings:

> God himself is increasing and progressing in knowledge, power and dominion, and will do so worlds without end.[49]

> The greatest intelligence in existence can continually ascend to greater heights of perfection. We are created for the express purpose of increase ....It is the Deity within us that causes increase.... He is in every person upon the face of the earth.[50]

The writings of the second president and prophet, Brigham Young, are a rebuke to many a modern Latter-day Saint, such as Bruce McConkie, who teaches that God is omniscient, omnipotent, and omnipresent,[51] that is, that God does not forever increase in power and knowledge. In rebuking early Mormon apostle Orson Pratt, Young emphasized that such reasoning was a reflection of ignorance:

Brother Orson Pratt has, in theory, bounded the capacity of God. According to his theory, God can progress no further in knowledge and power; but the God that I serve is progressing eternally, and so are his children; they will increase to all eternity, if they are faithful. But there are some of our brethren who know just so much, and they seem to be able to learn no more. You may plead with them, scold them...and try in various ways to increase their knowledge; but it seems as if they would not learn.[52]

In fact, Young refused to believe in an omniscient deity: "Do not lariat the God that I serve and say that he cannot learn anymore; I do not believe in such a character."[53] Modern Mormons deny all this and teach that the state of omnipotence, omniscience, and so on will finally be attained, which would logically stop the process of divine "increase."

What kind of god does Mormonism believe in? Whether we take early or late Mormonism, one fact is clear: They have no genuine concept of God in the Christian meaning of the term. Even if we assume the truth of the heresies of the modern Mormon church (heresies in contrast to its earlier prophets), their god _evolved_ to godhood, hence he was not an eternal being of divine attributes.

Thus, Orson Pratt naturally wondered, with his mind "wearied and lost in the multiplicity of [divine] generations and successive worlds...how far back the genealogy extends, and how the first world was formed, and the first father was begotten?" Although concluding that the search was futile, he raised a relevant question, for why and how "do you seek for a _first_ personal Father in an endless genealogy?"[54]

Mormonism's apparent solution is to say that matter and spirit are eternal. Matter is merely a variation of spirit, a denser form of spirit, although still eternal. Apparently, in the "beginning" divine spirit/matter somehow coalesced into a man and woman who eventually evolved into godhood and became capable of sexual intercourse and the production of spirit offspring having the same divine potential. But how did matter and spirit exist eternally without a creator? If matter is eternal and in some sense divine, is this not similar to pantheism? Further, if one eternal god did begin the process, are not Mormons to be classed as idolaters for actually obeying and worshiping lesser deities created by him?

Regardless, the above concepts are not Christian teaching. The Bible asserts in the clearest terms that God is immutable— that is, that God never changes in terms of His being, essence or attributes.* For all eternity God has remained God. God was never originally a man who, incredibly, somehow became God through personal effort.

The following Scriptures all testify that God never changes: "For I, the LORD, do not change; therefore you, O sons of Jacob, are not consumed" (Malachi 3:6). "Every good thing bestowed and every perfect gift is from above, coming down from the Father of lights, with whom there is no variation, or shifting shadow" (James 1:17). "God is not a man, that He should lie, nor a son of man, that He should repent" (Numbers 23:19). "For I am God and not man, the Holy One in your midst" (Hosea 11:9). "For He is not a man as I am that I may answer Him, that we may go to court together" (Job 9:32). "From everlasting to everlasting, Thou art God" (Psalm 90:2).

In conclusion, none can deny that the Mormon god is ultimately a finite god. As Dr. McMurrin concludes in his study: "He is therefore finite rather than absolute."[55] And, "In its rejection of the classical concept of God as eternal, Mormonism is a most radical digression from traditional theism. This is perhaps its most important departure from familiar Christian orthodoxy, for it would be difficult to overestimate the importance to [Mormon] theology of the doctrine that God is a temporal being."[56]

Unfortunately, when Mormons claim their god is infinite and omnipotent, they are only engaging in further equivocation, and for obvious reasons:

---

* The incarnation of Jesus Christ is not an exclusion to this reality, for in taking on a sinless human nature, the Second Person of the Godhead did not alter His essential divine nature.

The word "finite" stirs nothing in the soul of the worshiper. But "infinite," "omnipotent," and "omniscient" are words made to order for the preacher and the popular writer. So Mormon theological writing and sermonizing are more often than not replete with the vocabulary of absolutism. But, like it or not, the Mormon theologian must sooner or later return to the finitistic conception of God upon which both his technical theology and his theological myths are founded. Here Mormonism reveals the radical nature of its heresy.[57]

### Mormon Teaching No. 3—The Gods Are Material, Not Spirit

Mormonism teaches that its gods are physical creatures, except for the Holy Ghost. In contrast to John 4:24, where Jesus Himself emphasized that God is spirit, Mormonism teaches that God is not spirit. Joseph Smith himself declared, "There is no other God in heaven but that God who has flesh and bones."[58] The Mormon scripture, *Doctrine and Covenants*, 130:22, asserts: "The Father has a body of flesh and bones as tangible as man's; the Son also; but the Holy Ghost has not a body of flesh and bones, but is a personage of spirit. Were it not so, the Holy Ghost could not dwell in us." (One wonders how Mormons explain the many biblical references teaching that both Christ and the Father also personally dwell within the believer [e.g., John 17:20-26].)

The late Mormon president and prophet, Ezra Taft Benson, reemphasizes this "basic and important" Mormon doctrine of a material god, claiming that the Christian view is false:

The Father and Son have tabernacles of flesh and bones, and the Holy Ghost is a personage of Spirit....An understanding of these basic truths is of the utmost importance....Instead of accepting God as he has declared himself to be, the Christian sects have sought by human reason and wisdom to describe God....[But] Joseph's first vision clearly revealed that the Father and Son are separate personages, having bodies as tangible as man's.[59]

The Mormon text *A Sure Foundation: Answers to Difficult Gospel Questions* also emphasizes that the Christian teaching concerning the nature of God as spirit is wrong:

> ...there is meager evidence in the Bible to support belief in a God who is a spirit essence.... Those who have received their understanding about God from errant traditional Christianity need no longer struggle with that confused and confusing doctrine. The [Mormon] Prophets' inspired declarations about the Godhead are in total agreement with the biblical evidence that Jesus and the Father have distinct, material bodies.[60]

Doctrinal theologian Bruce McConkie calls God, "A glorified resurrected Personage having a tangible body of flesh and bones."[61] The Brigham Young University student manual, *Doctrines of the Gospel*, teaches, "God is a holy, perfected personage, or being, with a body of flesh and bones (see Moses 6:57; 7:35; *D&C*, 130:22; Matthew 5:48)."[62]

In response to John 4:24, Mormons claim that God has a *spiritual* resurrected body of flesh and bones, hence that He is a true spirit. They believe that all spirit is matter although of a finer or purer form. But even Jesus taught that a true "spirit does *not have flesh and bones*" (Luke 24:39 emphasis added).

## Mormon Teachings No. 4 and No. 5—The Gods Are Sexual Polygamists: Divine Procreation and the Begetting of Spirit Children by the Gods

How are the gods created in the first place? As in many primitive and pagan religions, Mormonism teaches that the gods are sexually active. Through sexual intercourse, they beget spirit children who have the opportunity to become "exalted"—to become gods themselves through complete faithfulness to Mormon teachings.

In Mormonism, the sex act plays an important divine function that is inseparably integrated with the church's doctrines of exaltation and celestial or eternal marriage.[63] In other words, to be "exalted" in Mormonism is to become a god who is continually active sexually, begetting offspring throughout all eternity. But this is a privilege reserved *only* for those who are married in the Mormon temple.[64] If men and women are married in the temple, and through good works finally achieve exaltation (godhood), then they may continue the process of producing spirit children who will in turn also have the opportunity to become gods. President Benson states that "Temple marriage is a gospel ordinance for exaltation."[65] Bruce McConkie explains: "Marriages performed in the temples for time *and eternity*, by virtue of the sealing keys restored by Elijah, are called *celestial marriages*....By definition exaltation consists in the continuation of the family unit in eternity.... Celestial marriage is a holy and an eternal ordinance....Its importance in the plan of salvation and exaltation cannot be overestimated."[66] The Mormon emphasis upon the family originated primarily from this doctrine: the teaching that men and women married in the temple can become gods with the privilege of ruling an eternal family of spirit offspring on another world.[67]

The text *Gospel Principles*, published by the Mormon church, cites the sixth president and prophet of the Mormon church, Joseph F. Smith, as teaching the current Mormon doctrine that "all men and women are...literally the sons and daughters of Deity....Man, as a spirit, was begotten and born of heavenly parents, and reared to maturity in the eternal mansions of the Father, prior to coming upon the earth in a temporal [physical] body."[68] Further:

> Our heavenly parents...wanted us to develop every godlike quality that they have. To do this, we needed to leave our celestial home to be tested and to gain experience...to be clothed with a physical body....Since we could not progress further in heaven, our Heavenly Father called a

> Grand Council...to present us his plan for our
> progression. We learned that if we followed his
> plan, we would become like him. We would have
> a resurrected body; we would have all power in
> heaven and on earth; we would become heavenly
> parents and have spirit children just as he does
> (*D&C*, 132:19,20).[69]

Because of the belief that there are so many spirits waiting
for bodies to indwell, the Mormon church has always emphasized the importance of large families. Bodies are desperately
needed to supply the spirit children with fleshly houses. This
was, ostensibly, the early rationale for Mormon polygamy. If
one wife could produce ten bodies for the spirit children,
twenty wives could produce two hundred bodies.

This emphasis on large families is still present in the
church. The former president and prophet, Ezra Taft Benson,
happily quotes Brigham Young in *Discourses of Brigham Young*:
"There are multitudes of pure and holy spirits waiting to take
tabernacles [bodies]. Now what is our duty?—to prepare
tabernacles for them....It is the duty of every righteous man
and woman to prepare tabernacles for all the spirits they
can."[70] And President Benson himself commented, "We know
that every spirit assigned to this earth will come [to this earth],
whether through us or someone else. There are couples in the
Church who think they are getting along just fine with their
limited families but who will some day suffer the pains of
remorse when they meet the spirits that might have been part
of their posterity."[71]

In part, the apparent glory of the Mormon male is to be
sexually virile forever with his wife or many wives;[72] some
early Mormons boasted of the hundreds or thousands of
wives they would have in the resurrection.[73] In early Mormon
history and in contemporary polygamist sects, Mormons actually secured dozens and even scores of wives for eternity,
including being sealed to dead women in "baptism for the
dead" rites.[74]

Although the modern Utah church has abandoned the clear scriptural command to maintain polygamy (*D&C*, 132:4), it continues to teach that polygamy will exist in the afterlife. Nevertheless, the sexual theology of Mormonism is why the church teaches there are divine mothers in heaven:

> We are the offspring of God. He is our Eternal Father; we have also an Eternal Mother. There is no such thing as a father without a mother, nor can there be children without parents. We were born as the spirit children of Celestial Parents long before the foundations of this world were laid.[75]

> Implicit in the Christian verity that all men are the spirit children of an Eternal Father is the usually unspoken truth that they are also the offspring of an Eternal Mother. An exalted and glorified Man of Holiness (Moses 6:57) could not be a Father unless a Woman of like glory, perfection, and holiness was associated with him as a Mother....This doctrine that there is a Mother in heaven was affirmed in plainness by the First Presidency of the Church (Joseph F. Smith, John R. Winder, and Anthon H. Lund) when, in speaking of preexistence and the origin of man, they said... "all men and women are in the similitude of the universal Father and Mother, and are literally the sons and daughters of Deity."...Mortal persons who overcome all things and gain an ultimate exaltation will live eternally in the family unit and have spirit children, thus becoming Eternal Fathers and Eternal Mothers (*D&C*, 132:19-32, Talmage, *Articles of Faith*, 443).[76]

Mormon president and prophet Joseph Fielding Smith realized that this doctrine of an eternal Mother was not taught in the Bible, or even in the Mormon scriptures. Nevertheless, it was required as a logical inference and, therefore, was deemed valid on the basis of "common sense." He stated,

"The fact that there is no reference to a mother in heaven either in the Bible, the *Book of Mormon* or *Doctrine and Covenants*, is not sufficient to prove that no such thing as a Mother did exist there. If we had a Father, which we did, for all of these records speak of him, then does not good common sense tell us that we must have had a mother there also?"[77] In commenting on Genesis 1:26,27 he asks, "Is it not feasible to believe that female spirits were created in the image of a mother in Heaven?"[78]

The Mormon concept of female deities apparently caused many early Mormons to accept celestial polygamy. Brigham Young stated in 1870, "The scripture says that he, the Lord, came walking in the Temple with his train; I do not know who they were, unless his wives and children."[79]

This is why apostle Orson Pratt wrote in *The Seer* of November 1853 that God honors polygamy, since He Himself is a polygamist, along with His Son Jesus and His people, the Mormons:

> We have now clearly shown that God the Father had a plurality of wives, one or more being in eternity, by whom he begat our spirits as well as the spirit of Jesus his First Born, and another [wife] being upon the earth by whom he begat the tabernacle of Jesus [Jesus' mother Mary], as his Only Begotten in this world. We have also proved most clearly that the Son followed the example of his Father, and became the great Bridegroom to whom kings' daughters and many honorable Wives were to be married. We have also proved that both God the Father and our Lord Jesus Christ inherit their wives in eternity as well as in time....Oh, ye delicate ladies of [apostate] Christendom...if you do not want your morals corrupted, and your delicate ears shocked, and your pious modesty put to the blush by the society of polygamists and their wives, do not venture near the holy Jerusalem [Mormonism] nor come near the New Earth; for Polygamists will be honored

there, and will be among the chief rulers in that Kingdom.[80]

Pratt further stated, "If none but Gods will be permitted to multiply immortal children, it follows that each God must have one or more wives."[81] Thus, if the earth god became the divine standard for Mormon behavior, it is not surprising that polygamy was an important doctrine in the early church.

To conclude, the spirit children of male and female gods require physical bodies. After probation in a preexistent state, they require life upon an earth so that they might have the opportunity to progress to godhood just as their "parents" did. Each spirit child, produced sexually by a male and female god, inhabits a body prepared for it and grows up as a man or woman. Through diligence and good works and obedience to the Mormon church, these spirits may attain exaltation. After they die, they may become gods on new earths who then procreate with their spouses and produce more spirit children. Then these spirit children, based on their good works in the preexistent state, are in turn given an earth upon which to have the opportunity for self-perfection and evolution into godhood.

Apparently the process continues forever, with the newly-exalted spirits being their own gods over a planet or planets—just as was true for the heavenly Father and the Mother of Jesus who procreated all the former spirit children who now reside in physical bodies upon this earth. Brigham Young commented: "The Lord created you and me for the purpose of becoming Gods like Himself....We are created...to become Gods like unto our Father in heaven so that we then create 'worlds on worlds.' "[82]

Although most Mormons today deny that God and Christ are polygamists, no one can deny the logical basis for such a doctrine in early Mormon teaching. In fact, perhaps one reason why Mormon history is disgraced with sexually-related sins is because of the sexual emphasis and practices of the gods it worships (cf. the topical index at www.utlm.org; "abuse"; "polygamy").

## Mormon Teaching No. 6—The Gods Are Imperfect and Require Salvation

Because Mormonism teaches that the gods have evolved into godhood from the status of mere men, who have struggled with good and evil and perfected themselves, it cannot logically deny that all the "gods" were once imperfect and required salvation. Milton Hunter, a member of the First Council of Seventy, commented:

> God the Eternal Father was once a mortal man....He became God—an exalted being—through obedience to the same eternal Gospel truths that we are given opportunity today to obey....We must accept the fact that there was a time when Deity was much less powerful than he is today. Then how did he become glorified and exalted and attain his present status of Godhead? In the first place, aeons ago God undoubtedly took advantage of every opportunity to learn the laws of truth....From day to day he exerted his will vigorously,...he gained more knowledge....Thus he grew in experience and continued to grow until he attained the status of Godhood. In other words, he became God by absolute obedience to all the eternal laws of the Gospel.[83]

But because the gods were once finite men who earned their deity, they must have at one time been imperfect and, by implication, sinful. In fact, because the Mormon God *intended* the Fall of man on earth, and because Mormon theology teaches that experience of sin may have a beneficial influence on the process of exaltation, it is hardly surprising that Mormonism teaches that its gods were once imperfect. Orson Pratt taught:

> The gods who dwell in the Heaven from which our spirits came, are beings who have been redeemed from the grave in a world which existed

before the foundations of this earth were laid. They and the Heavenly body which they now inhabit *were once in fallen state*. Their terrestrial world was redeemed, and glorified, and made a Heaven: their terrestrial bodies, after suffering death, were redeemed, and glorified, and made Gods. And thus, as their world was exalted from a temporal to an eternal state, they were exalted also, *from fallen men to Celestial Gods* to inhabit their Heaven forever and forever. These Gods, being redeemed from the grave with their wives, are immortal and eternal, and will die no more.[84]

If, as Mormonism teaches, every god was once an imperfect and sinful man who was saved by good works which exalted him to godhood, then the logical conclusion is that God Himself requires salvation. Thus Marion G. Romney, a member of the First Presidency, taught that "God is a perfected, *saved soul* enjoying eternal life."[85]

But again, this is not what the Bible teaches. The Scripture is clear that God is an eternally righteous, holy, and perfect God. Because He was never an imperfect and sinful man, He could never require salvation (1 Samuel 15:29; Titus 1:2).

We have now examined several key contrasts between the God of Mormonism and the God of the Bible. There are also others, as the following chart indicates:

| God(s) of Mormonism | God of the Bible |
| --- | --- |
| Material | Immaterial |
| (a physical body of flesh and bones) | (spirit) |
| Mortal | Immortal |
| Changeable, evolving | Immutable |
| Physically localized | Omnipresent |
| Polygamous and/or incestuous | Monogamous (celibate) |
| Polytheistic | Monotheistic |

| | |
|---|---|
| Tritheistic (three earth gods) | Trinitarian |
| Exalted saved man | Eternal deity |
| Eternally progressing in certain attributes (early Mormonism) | Eternally immutable in all characteristics |
| Feminine counterpart (heavenly Mother) | No feminine counterpart |
| Adam, once considered God (early Mormonism) | Adam, a creation of God |
| Jesus, begotten by Elohim's physical intercourse with Mary | Jesus, begotten supernaturally by the Holy Spirit (virgin birth) |
| Polygamist Jesus (early Mormonism) | Celibate Jesus |

How can anyone maintain that the God of Mormonism is the God of the Bible? Yet, Mormons continue to insist that they believe in the biblical God. Again, in his book *Are Mormons Christians?* Dr. Stephen Robinson writes, "The Latter-day Saints accept unequivocally all the biblical teachings on the nature of God."[86] And, "Latter-day Saints believe in the biblical Father, Son, and Holy Ghost."[87]

## Worshiping a Wrong God

Mormons assert that their concept of God is clear and precise while the Christian concept is confused and unintelligible. A previous president and prophet of the church claimed, "Our doctrine of God is clear."[88] However, as the Tanners observe, "a careful examination of Mormon teachings concerning the Godhead reveals a serious state of confusion."[89]

The Mormon church cannot consistently answer the following questions: Is God holy? Who or what is God in His essential nature and attributes? Does God evolve forever? Are the standard attributes of deity applicable to God? What is the Holy Ghost? Was Jesus a polygamist? Conflicting answers have been given on all these issues.

This is one reason we encounter a state of confusion among Mormon laymen, missionaries, and scholars as to what they believe or don't believe about God—and as we shall see, about other issues as well. This is also why the average Mormon will actually deny much of Mormon theology, claiming that those who think Mormonism teaches the above beliefs are "ignorant." When no less of a leader than McConkie says that it is the Christian and not the Mormon concept of God that is "utterly incomprehensible in its inconsistency" (quoted earlier), one can only wonder whose theology he has been reading.

Not infrequently, Mormons will also accuse Christians of "blasphemy" in their view of God. But Bruce McConkie himself defined blasphemy as follows: "Blasphemy consists in either or both of the following: 1) speaking irreverently, evilly, abusively, or scurrilously against God or sacred things; or 2) speaking profanely or *falsely* about [the] Deity."[90]

McConkie defines blasphemy correctly. Unfortunately, it is Mormonism that is guilty of it. Mormonism speaks irreverently, evilly, and abusively against God when it teaches He was once a sinful man in need of salvation. Mormonism speaks falsely about God concerning His fundamental nature and essence when it teaches polygamy and a theology of finitism.

In addition, Mormons profane God, as when Joseph Fielding Smith, the tenth president and prophet of the church, committed blasphemy in calling the biblical God "a cruel monster."[91]

In conclusion, given the pagan, polytheistic nature of the Mormonism God, it would appear that the challenge of Joshua remains open to the Mormon church: "If serving the LORD seems undesirable to you, then choose for yourselves this day whom you will serve, whether the gods your forefathers served beyond the River, or the gods of the Amorites, in whose land you are living. But as for me and my household, we will serve the LORD" (Joshua 24:15 NIV).

# Chapter 4

# Mormon Beliefs About the Holy Spirit

~

The Mormon church claims that it believes in the Holy Spirit and what it terms the Holy Ghost. (Technically, the Holy Ghost [an exalted man] and the Holy Spirit [sometimes a synonymous term, but also the mind, power, or influence of God the Father] are divided into two separate concepts and/or confused with the Person of Christ; see McConkie, *Doctrinal New Testament Commentary*, 3:337-340.) Mormon authority James Talmage asserts that only Mormons possess the Holy Ghost (Spirit):

> The Holy Ghost may be regarded as the minister of the Godhead, carrying into effect the decisions of the Supreme Council [of Gods]....The power of the Holy Ghost...is the spirit of prophecy and revelation....God grants the gift of the Holy Ghost unto the obedient....The authority to so bestow the Holy Ghost belongs [only] to the higher or Melchizedek Priesthood.[1]

Thus, the officiating elder, acting in the name and by the alleged authority of Jesus Christ, says to new converts, "Receive the Holy Ghost." And, "I confirm you a member of the Church of Jesus Christ of Latter-day Saints."[2] The *Book of Mormon* claims "the [Holy] Spirit is the same, yesterday, today, and forever" (2 Nephi 2:4; cf. verse 8; 26:13). But, Mormonism presents a significantly confused portrait of the God it calls the Holy Ghost/Spirit. It is unclear whether or not he has a body, is personal or impersonal, married or single, male or female, the mind of God or a distinct deity. The modern church has clarified some of these issues, believing the Holy Ghost is without a tangible body, personal, a separate God, unmarried, and presumably male. As space does not permit the citing of specific quotations for these many issues, we merely provide documentation and conclude with Mormon authorities Jerald and Sandra Tanner that "one of the most confusing areas of Mormon theology is that area dealing with the Holy Ghost."[3] Thus, throughout Mormon history, the Holy Ghost/Spirit has been variously interpreted as:

A personal being[4]

Something like electricity[5]

A personage of spirit[6]

The "influence" of deity[7]

The third deity in the Mormon "Trinity" or Godhead[8]

*Not* the third deity in the "Trinity"[9]

The mind of the Father and Son[10]

A male (a few have suggested female) spirit[11]

Without a body[12]

May yet receive a body[13]

Impersonal[14]

Personal[15]

A spirit who "has no other effect than pure intelligence"[16]

The Lord Jesus Christ Himself[17]

A localized spirit man or the power or gift of the Holy Ghost, or an impersonal omnipresent substance, or the spirit body of Jesus Christ[18]

Biblically, however, the Holy Spirit is God, the Third Person of the Trinity. Below we present a brief outline of scriptural teaching on the Holy Spirit:

1. He is distinguished from both the Father and the Son (Isaiah 48:16; Matthew 28:19; Luke 3:21,22; John 14:16,17; Hebrews 9:8).

2. He is personal. He loves (Romans 15:30); wills (1 Corinthians 12:11); convicts of sin (John 16:8); commands and forbids (Acts 8:29; 13:2; 16:6); speaks messages (1 Timothy 4:1; Revelation 2:7); intercedes for believers (Romans 8:26); teaches, comforts, and guides into the truth (John 14:26); can be grieved (Ephesians 4:30), blasphemed (Mark 3:29), and insulted (Hebrews 10:29). The seemingly impersonal and even inanimate terminology used to describe the actions of the Holy Spirit such as "filling," "pouring out," etc. (Ephesians 5:18; Isaiah 32:15; Ezekiel 39:29), does not imply the impersonality of the Holy Spirit as some cults maintain. Rather, such terminology refers to the intimacy of the believer's personal relationship with Him.

3. He is God. The Holy Spirit has the attributes of deity: omnipresence (Psalm 139:7,8), omniscience (1 Corinthians 2:10,11), eternality (Hebrews 9:14), and omnipotence (Job 33:4). He is the Creator of the universe (Genesis 1:2; Job 33:4) and the giver of eternal life (John 3:3-8).

   He is also identified as God by the divine associations Scripture freely lends to Him: He indwells the believer (1 Corinthians 6:19 with 2 Corinthians 6:16); strives with man (Genesis 6:3 with 1 Peter 3:20); inspires the Word of God (2 Peter 1:21 with Luke 1:68-70 with Acts 1:16 and 28:25; Isaiah 6:1-13; Hebrews 10:15-17

with Jeremiah 31:31-34); sanctifies the believer (2 Thessalonians 2:13,14 with 1 Thessalonians 4:7); speaks to
Isaiah (Acts 28:25,26 with Isaiah 6:8,9); sends forth
laborers (Matthew 9:38 with Acts 13:2-4); can be tested
(Psalm 95:6-9 with Hebrews 3:7-9); and inspires divine
love (Romans 5:5 with 1 Thessalonians 3:12,13 and
2 Thessalonians 3:5).

According to Acts 5:3,4, when Ananias lied to the Holy
Spirit, he really lied to God. And according to Jesus, there is
only one eternal sin—that is the sin against the Holy Spirit
(Matthew 12:32), who is also called the Lord in 2 Corinthians
3:17 and Hebrews 10:15,16 (see 1 Thessalonians 3:11-13). Note
also the Holy Spirit's relationship to Jesus in John 14:16-18 (see
the Greek text).

Consider too the importance of the Holy Spirit in regeneration and salvation, in sanctification, in bringing glory to Jesus
Christ, and in inspiring the holy Scriptures, not to mention
many other areas (John 3:6-8; 16:13,14; 1 Peter 1:2). All this
proves the Holy Ghost/Spirit of Mormonism is not the Holy
Spirit of the Bible.

Unfortunately, Mormonism does not even know who the
Holy Spirit is. How then can Mormons logically claim to be
genuine children of God when it is the Holy Spirit who gives
true spiritual life (John 3:3-8)? "Jesus answered, 'Truly, truly, I
say to you, unless one is born of water and the Spirit, he
cannot enter into the kingdom of God. That which is born of
the flesh is flesh; and that which is born of the Spirit is spirit' "
(John 3:5,6). "The Spirit gives life; the flesh counts for nothing"
(John 6:63 NIV). And, "For all who are being led by the Spirit
of God, these are sons of God....The Spirit Himself bears witness with our spirit that we are children of God" (Romans
8:14,16).

# SECTION III

# WHAT DO THE MORMONS BELIEVE ABOUT JESUS CHRIST?

# Chapter 5

# The Mormon View of Jesus Christ

∼

From the beginning, the Mormon church has confessed its devoted allegiance to Jesus Christ. Around the world, Mormon literature emphatically claims to accept and revere the biblical Christ. For example, the publicity booklet published by the Mormon church, *What the Mormons Think of Christ*, asserts:

> Christ is our Redeemer and our Savior. Except for him there would be no salvation and no redemption, and unless men come unto him and accept him as their Savior, they cannot have eternal life in his presence.[1]

This booklet further states that "He—Jesus Christ—is the Savior of the world and the Divine Son of God."[2]

In his book *Are Mormons Christians?* written in an attempt to prove to the world that Mormons are genuine Christians, Dr. Stephen Robinson emphasizes over and over that Mormons believe in the true biblical Jesus Christ. In fact, he claims that the evidence is so persuasive that Mormons believe in Jesus Christ that critics have never even dared to raise the issue!

71

...of all the various arguments against Latter-day Saints being considered Christians, *not one— not a single one*—claims that Latter-day Saints don't acknowledge Jesus Christ as Lord....When the charge is made that "Mormons aren't Christians," the very first impression created in the minds of the average individual is that Latter-day Saints don't believe in Jesus Christ....Yet in the arguments offered to support the assertion the only issue that really matters is *never even raised*: Do the Latter-day Saints believe in Jesus Christ? Do they accept him as Lord? Do they believe that he is the way, the truth, and the life, and that no man cometh unto the father but by him? These crucial questions are never asked.[3]

Dr. Robinson has apparently not read very many Christian apologetic works. Christian treatments of Mormonism consistently maintain that Mormons do *not* acknowledge the true Jesus Christ as Lord—they cannot do this because they do not believe in the true Jesus Christ. What's more, Dr. Robinson proceeds to make another false claim: "Nor do the LDS scriptures teach anything about Christ that the rest of the Christian world would find offensive." Finally he winds up the discussion by saying, "Though all the world may say that Latter-day Saints do not know or love or worship Jesus Christ, I know that we do, and if this is not the issue in question, or if this is not enough to be counted a Christian, then the word has lost its meaning."[*4]

But Dr. Robinson is still wrong. The real issue is which "Jesus Christ" one believes in. The simple truth is that Mormons may proclaim their belief in Jesus Christ throughout the entire world, but like countless other sects and cults they

---

* In fact, far from "loving and worshiping" Him, Mormonism teaches it is an abomination to pray to Jesus unless, as a resurrected personage, He is standing immediately before one. For example, "To whom did Stephen pray? Sectarian [Christian] commentators say he prayed to Jesus and not to the Father, and they accordingly claim this instance as justification for the apostate practice of addressing prayers to the Son."[5] Further, "As an indication of how far removed most of them are from the true form of prayer is the fact many of them...are addressed directly to Christ."[6]

believe in a false, pagan Christ who has nothing whatever to do with the biblical Jesus. In fact, as the following chart shows, the Mormon Christ and the biblical Christ are so incompatible that hardly a single resemblance can be found between them.

In the pages ahead we will prove that the Mormon Jesus Christ and the biblical Jesus Christ are as far apart as day and night. Likewise the Apostle Paul had occasion to warn some of the Corinthians that they were receiving "another Christ," a false Christ that was not the true biblical Christ. "For if someone comes to you and preaches a Jesus other than the Jesus we preached...you put up with it easily enough" (1 Corinthians 11:4). This is the only issue concerning Mormonism's claims about Jesus. Does it believe in the true Jesus Christ, or not? Before we begin our discussion, we supply the following chart for contrast:

| The Mormon Jesus Christ | The Biblical Jesus Christ |
| --- | --- |
| A created being; the elder brother of Lucifer | Uncreated God |
| Common (one of many gods) and of minor importance in the _larger_ Mormon cosmology | Unique (the Second Person of the one and only Godhead) and of supreme importance throughout time, eternity, and all creation |
| Conceived by a physical sex act between God the Father (either Adam or Elohim) and Mary, thus not through a true virgin birth | Conceived by the Holy Spirit, who supernaturally "overshadowed" Mary, thus a true virgin birth |
| Once sinful and imperfect | Eternally sinless and perfect |
| Earned his own salvation (exaltation) | As God, never required salvation |
| A married polygamist? | An unmarried monogamist |

For the convenience of the reader, we divide most of this data into three basic sections:

1. Mormons reject Christ's unique deity
2. Mormons deny Christ's virgin birth
3. Mormons impugn Christ's eternal sinlessness

## Mormon Teachings About Christ

### Mormon Teaching No. 1—Mormons Deny Christ's Unique Deity

Mormonism maintains it believes and teaches the true deity of Jesus Christ. However, although it is correct that Mormons believe that Christ is *a* god, they do not in any sense accept Christ's deity according to Christian or biblical teaching. For example, Mormons teach or imply that a) Christ is a created being, b) Christ is a "common god" who is not unique in essence, but primarily in mission—in His function and priority, and c) Christ is Satan's brother. We discuss these in turn.

### a. Mormonism teaches that Jesus Christ is a created being

To understand the Mormon view of Christ, we need to remember that Mormonism teaches that every person has two births—first, birth as a spirit child in preexistence, and second, much later, birth as a human being.

According to Mormon theology, Christ was the first and foremost of subsequent billions of spirit children created through sexual intercourse between the male earth god and his celestial wife. Later, in order to produce the body for this special spirit child, the earth god again had sexual intercourse, this time with the "virgin" Mary, who then became Jesus' earthly mother.

As we will later see in our discussion of the Adam-God doctrine, early Mormon prophets taught that Christ (spirit and body) was the offspring of both the earth god *Adam* and his celestial wife—and then later of Adam and Mary. Modern

Mormons maintain that Christ was the offspring of a different exalted man (*Elohim*, not Adam) who was nevertheless still the literal, physical father of Jesus Christ. Whatever view is held, Mormonism asserts that Jesus Christ is a created being. He was created in preexistence, and through "probation, progression, and schooling" exalted himself as the premier spirit child. Theologian and commentator Bruce McConkie describes the creation of Jesus Christ in these words:

> From the time of their spirit birth, the father's preexistent offspring were endowed with agency and subjected to the provisions of the laws ordained for their government. They had power to obey or disobey and to progress in one field or another....The preexistent life was thus a long period—undoubtedly an infinitely long one—of probation, progression, and schooling....Christ, the Firstborn, was the mightiest of all the spirit children of the father (*D&C*, 93:21-23).[7]

Mormons also claim that Jesus is the "Jehovah" of the Old Testament. Thus, whenever the Bible refers to Jehovah, for Mormons, it refers to Jesus Christ in His preexistent state. (Christians, on the other hand, teach this term refers to God.) Mormon authority James Talmage explains in his *Articles of Faith*, "Among the spirit children of Elohim the firstborn was and is Jehovah or Jesus Christ to whom all others are juniors."[8]

### b. Mormonism teaches that Jesus Christ is a "common" god and of minor importance in the larger Mormon cosmology

We have now seen that Mormonism teaches that Christ was a created being. But Mormon church teaching logically implies Christ is also a common god of only relative importance. Mormons do refer to Christ as being "greater" than all other spirit children on earth. But remember, this earth is only one of an infinite number of earths, each having their own gods who have existed and evolved for aeons longer than

Christ. Further, Christ is our "senior" only by achievement and position, *not* by nature or essence.

The *essence* of Christ is no different from the essence of any spirit child of Elohim, whether of men, or Satan and his demons. Every person on earth has the same nature and essence as Jesus Christ, and He as they. Although Christ performed better than others in preexistence, He is nevertheless of one nature with all men. Thus, Mormons universally refer to Him as their "elder brother." No one can deny then that Mormonism logically teaches that Jesus Christ is not unique in essence, but only in His achievement and mission. For example, Christ is not unique in His deity, His incarnation, or His capacity as Creator.

According to Mormonism, Jesus' "divinity" is not unique, for every exalted man will attain a similar godhood. Neither is His "incarnation" unique, for *all men* are incarnated spirit beings—in preexistence the offspring of the sexual union of the gods, who then take tabernacles of flesh. Indeed, Christ was only "unique" in His *physical* birth in that rather than having a merely human father like the rest of us, His mother had physical sex with God. (See point 2 on pages 78-83.)

Christ is also not unique as Creator of this earth, because Mormonism teaches that Adam, Joseph Smith, and others *helped* Him to create it. Christ "was aided...by 'many of the noble and great' spirit children of the Father...Adam... Noah...Joseph Smith..." etc.[9]

Thus, the Mormon Jesus Christ is, in almost all respects, rather like the rest of us—at least as far as Mormons conceive of men. He just worked harder to exalt Himself in preexistence— He had more ambition, devotion, and perhaps intelligence. But in basic nature He was no different from any of us. Mormon leader Milton R. Hunter, a member of the First Council of Seventy, asserted, "Jesus is man's spiritual brother. We dwelt with Him in the spirit world as members of that large society of eternal intelligences, which included our Heavenly Parents."[10] Mormon authority James Talmage explains: "Human beings generally were similarly existent in spirit state prior to their embodiment in the flesh....There is no impropriety, therefore, in speaking of Jesus Christ as the Elder Brother of the rest of humankind."[11]

### c. Mormonism teaches that Christ is Satan's brother

Indeed, Mormon theology holds that Jesus Christ is even the spirit brother of Satan himself. Since Satan (and his demons) were also preexistent spirit creations of Elohim and his celestial wife, Satan is therefore Christ's brother as well. In fact, the devil and all demons are the spirit brothers of everyone on earth! In other words, Christ, the devil, and all of us are literally brothers! Jess L. Christensen, director of the LDS Institute of Religion at Utah State University in Logan, Utah, writes in _A Sure Foundation_, "Both the scriptures and the prophets affirm that Jesus Christ and Lucifer are indeed offspring of our heavenly Father and, therefore, spirit brothers.... Jesus was Lucifer's older brother."[12] Thus, one Mormon writer concludes, "As for the devil and his fellow spirits, they are brothers to man and also to Jesus and sons and daughters to God in the same sense that we are."[13] In essence then, according to Mormon theology, the difference between Christ and the devil is not really one of kind, but only one of degree.

Who can maintain that this is Christian or biblical teaching? In light of the above doctrines—and many more—we must be careful _not_ to accept Mormon claims concerning their belief in Christ's uniqueness or His deity. They may claim to exalt Him, for, as McConkie says, "He shall reign to all eternity as King of Kings and Lord of Lords, and God of Gods."[14] But what is often not understood is that literally millions of other people will likewise reign, for as Brigham Young emphasized, all men are "the king of kings and lord of lords in embryo."[15]

### Mormon Teaching No. 2—Mormons Deny Christ's Virgin Birth Through the Holy Spirit: Mormonism's Spirit Adultery and Incest—The Father and Mary's Sexual Union

In his controversial Adam-God discourse of April 9, 1852, Brigham Young taught by alleged divine inspiration that the body of Jesus Christ was the product of sexual intercourse between God (Adam) and Mary, who then subsequently married Joseph. But since God (Adam) was also the literal, physical Father of Mary (Mary being his literal spirit offspring through celestial intercourse), this amounts to an incestuous and adulterous relationship, for at the same time she was betrothed in marriage to Joseph.

In essence, Mormonism teaches that Mary had sex with both her literal Father in heaven (God Himself) and her literal spirit brother, Joseph! Unfortunately, one apparent effect of this teaching, at least in the minds of some, was to give divine sanction to "spiritual" adultery and even incest—and thus to render the incidents of incestuous polygamy and adultery in Mormon history more acceptable.

In any case, because of this teaching, Mormonism denies that Jesus Christ is the product of the Holy Ghost and maintains He is the offspring of the Father only. Why? Because according to Mormon theology the Holy Ghost does not have a physical body. As such, He could not have literally, physically, had sexual intercourse with Mary in order to produce the body of Jesus. On the other hand, Mormon theology teaches that the Father does have a physical body "of flesh and bones." He could easily have had physical sex with Mary to produce the body of Jesus. This is why Brigham Young taught that if Christ had been conceived by the Holy Ghost it would have to have been through physical, sexual intercourse. And, if this were true, it would be "very dangerous" to give women the Holy Ghost lest He impregnate them and Mormon elders be held accountable for fornication! Also, it would of necessity require that Jesus be the literal son of the Holy Ghost rather than the literal son of the Father, which was not acceptable to Brigham Young and also to modern Mormons. Thus, the role of the Holy Spirit in the virgin birth of Jesus Christ, so clearly stated in Matthew 1:18 and Luke 1:35, is rejected by Mormons. Below we produce a lengthy portion of Brigham Young's "inspired" pronouncements which he himself defined as "the word of the Lord" (see p. 221):

I will tell you how it is. Our Father in heaven begat all the spirits that ever were, or ever will be, upon this earth; and they were born spirits in the eternal world. Then the Lord by his power and wisdom organized the mortal tabernacle of man. We were made first spiritual, and afterwards temporal.

Now hear it, O inhabitants of the earth, Jew and Gentile, Saint and Sinner! When our Father Adam came into the Garden of Eden, he came into it with a _celestial body_, and brought Eve, _one of his wives_, with him. He helped to make and organize this world. He is MICHAEL, _the Archangel_, THE ANCIENT OF DAYS! about whom holy men have written and spoken—he _is our_ Father _and our God, and the only God with whom we have to do._ Every man upon the earth, professing Christians or non-professing, must hear it, and will know it sooner or later....When the Virgin Mary conceived the child Jesus, the Father had begotten him in his own likeness. He was not begotten by the Holy Ghost. And who is the Father? He is the first of the human family [i.e., Adam]; and when he took a tabernacle [body], it was begotten by _his Father_ in heaven, after the same manner as the tabernacles of Cain, Abel, and the rest of the sons and daughters of Adam and Eve.

Jesus, our elder brother, _was begotten in the flesh by the same character that was in the Garden of Eden_ [i.e., Adam], and who is our Father in heaven. Now, that all who may hear these doctrines [will] pause before they make light of them, or treat them with indifference, _for they will prove their salvation or damnation._

Now remember from this time forth, and forever that _Jesus Christ was not begotten by the Holy Ghost._...If the son was begotten by the Holy Ghost, it would be very dangerous to baptize and

confirm females and give the Holy Ghost to them,
lest he should beget children to be palmed upon
the Elders by the people, bringing the Elders into
great difficulties.[16]

No wonder this bizarre and even blasphemous doctrine
has caused the Mormon church so much trouble. And no
wonder Mormons don't know what to do with this statement
by Brigham Young!

Thus, Mormons today accept the "virgin" birth of Jesus
Christ to have been accomplished through physical sexual
intercourse between God (now Elohim) and Mary, but they
deny that God was Adam. Nevertheless, because "sexu-
ality...is actually an attribute of God...[and] God is a procre-
ating personage of flesh and bone, Latter-day prophets have
made it clear that despite what it says in Matthew 1:20, the
Holy Ghost was not the father of Jesus."[17] (This, incidentally,
contradicts Alma 7:10 in the *Book of Mormon*.)

In his *Doctrines of Salvation*, the tenth Mormon president
and prophet, Joseph Fielding Smith, taught, "Christ was
begotten of God. He was not born without the aid of Man and
*that Man was God!*"[18] Theologian McConkie declares, "Christ
was begotten by an Immortal Father *in the same way* that
mortal men are begotten by mortal fathers."[19]

The former president and prophet of the Mormon church,
Ezra Taft Benson, also believes that God the Father had physical sex with Mary:

The paternity of Jesus Christ is one of the "mys-
teries of godliness" comprehended only by the
spiritually minded....An ancient [Mormon]
prophet had a vision. He saw Mary and described
her as "a virgin, most beautiful and fair above all
other virgins." He then saw her "carried away in
the Spirit...for the space of a time." When she
returned, she was "bearing a child in her arms...
even the Son of the Eternal Father" (1 Nephi
11:15,19-21)....Jesus Christ is the Son of God in the
most literal sense. The body in which he performed

his mission in the flesh was sired by that same Holy
Being we worship as God, our Eternal Father. Jesus
was not the son of Joseph, nor was he begotten by
the Holy Ghost. He is the son of the Eternal Father.[20]

The logical implication of Mormon theology seems evident. Mary was apparently married to both God Himself and
Joseph! Brigham Young stated: "The man Joseph, the husband
of Mary, did not, that we know of, have more than one wife,
but Mary the wife of Joseph had another husband [i.e.,
God]."[21]

Mormons believe that Mary had to be the "legitimate" wife
of God, of course, otherwise even God would have been guilty
of adultery! Apparently, while Mormons will accept God
having sex with many different wives, they will not have Him
engaging in illicit sex! In _The Seer_ of October 1853, Mormon
apostle Orson Pratt was more than frank—freely confessing
that God Himself is not bound by the moral laws He gave to
men (on adultery, for instance):

> The Father and Mother of Jesus, according to
> the flesh, must have been associated together in
> the capacity of Husband and Wife; hence the
> Virgin Mary must have been, for the time being,
> the lawful wife of God the Father....It would have
> been unlawful for any man to have interfered with
> Mary, who was already a spouse to Joseph; for
> such a heinous crime would have subjected both
> the guilty parties to death, according to the law of
> Moses. But God having created all men and
> women, had the most perfect right to do with his
> own creation, according to his holy will and plea-
> sure: He had a lawful right to overshadow the
> virgin Mary in the capacity of a husband, and
> beget a Son, although she was a spouse to another;
> for the law which he gave to govern men and
> women was not intended to govern himself, or to
> prescribe rules for his own conduct. It was also

lawful in him, after having thus dealt with Mary,
to give her to Joseph as her espoused husband....
Inasmuch as God was the first husband to her, it
may be that he only gave her to be the wife of
Joseph while in this mortal state, and that he
intended after the resurrection to again take her
as one of his own wives to raise up immortal
spirits in eternity.[22]

Thus, God had sex with Mary, "instead of letting any other
man do it"—and therein lies the alleged "uniqueness of
Jesus"! As Brigham Young wrote:

When the time came that his first born, the Sav-
iour, should come into the world and take a tabernacle [body], the Father came Himself and
favoured that spirit with a tabernacle instead of
letting any other man do it....And that is all the
organic difference between Jesus Christ and you
and me....If you see and understand these things,
it will be by the Spirit of God; you will receive
them by no other spirit.[23]

Not everyone would agree with that last statement. The
lying spirits the Bible identifies as demons characteristically
teach such doctrines to men who listen to them (1 Timothy
4:1).

Such teachings are hardly biblical; they are similar to occult
and pagan teachings, not Christian ones. Dr. Anthony
Hoekema appropriately concludes:

What these men are saying is that, according
to Mormon theology, the body of Jesus Christ was
a product of the physical union of God the father
and the virgin Mary. One shudders to think of the
revolting implications of this view, which brings
into what is supposed to be "Christian" theology
one of the most unsavory features of ancient
pagan mythology![24]

The Bible clearly denies Mormon teaching when it affirms Christ's true virgin (Gk. *parthenos*) birth:

> Now the birth of Jesus Christ was as follows. When his mother Mary had been betrothed to Joseph, before they came together she was found to be with child by the Holy Spirit (Matthew 1:18).
>
> "And behold, you will conceive in your womb, and bear a son, and you shall name him Jesus."...And Mary said to the angel, "How can this be, since I am a virgin? [*parthenos*]" And the angel answered and said to her, "The Holy Spirit will come upon you, and the power of the Most High will overshadow you; and for that reason the holy offspring shall be called the Son of God" (Luke 1:31,34,35).

## Mormon Teaching No. 3—Mormons Impugn the Eternal Sinlessness of Christ

While Mormons staunchly claim they affirm that Christ is sinless, this is unfortunately more equivocation.[25] Mormons accept the sinlessness of Christ while on this earth, but they do not logically maintain He was sinless for all eternity past.

Mormon theology holds that men can become gods only after an extended period of prelife probation, during which they are free to choose between good and evil. All Mormon spirits of the past have learned to choose good by their experience of evil. James Talmage declared in his *Articles of Faith* (pp. 53-54) that "a knowledge of good and evil is essential to the advancement that God has made possible for His children to achieve; and this knowledge can be best gained by actual experience with the contrast to good and its opposite plainly discernible." The sixth president and prophet of the Mormon church, Joseph F. Smith, wrote, "It was part of the divine plan that man...would be shut out of the presence of God and be subject to all the vicissitudes of mortality, the temptations and trials of the flesh, thus gaining experience and being placed in a position of trial, temptation, and being purified by passing through the trials and tribulations of the flesh" (cited in Joseph Fielding Smith, *Answers to Gospel Questions*, vol. 4, pp. 81-82). Thus, if Mormon theology teaches that Christ (a good Mormon) earned His own salvation and godhood through moral trial and error, then Mormons can hardly maintain that He was forever sinless. In fact, Mormonism teaches that Christ earned His own salvation and godhood.

As we explained earlier, Jesus was only one of innumerable spirit offspring of the earth god and his celestial wife, and therefore no different in nature from any other spirit. He, too, had to undertake schooling and progression in the spirit world for aeons upon aeons and then attain His own salvation. He had to be tested with good and evil, initially at least, falling into evil like every other spirit son. Further, just like every good Mormon, Jesus also had to *earn* the right to become God.

The following statements indicate that Mormonism views Jesus Christ as a created being who earned His own salvation, eternal life, and godhood. Bruce McConkie confesses that "Christ...is a saved being."[26] The official student manual, *Doctrines of the Gospel*, teaches that "the plan of salvation which he [Elohim] designed was to save his children, Christ included; and that neither Christ nor Lucifer could of themselves save anyone."[27] (According to Mormon theology, in prehistory both Lucifer and Christ presented plans of salvation to Elohim; Elohim chose Christ's plan, which provoked Lucifer's rebellion.)

The same manual also quotes the tenth president and prophet Joseph Fielding Smith on the subject:

> The Savior did not have a fullness [of deity] at first, but after he received his body and the resurrection all power was given unto him both in heaven and in earth. Although he was a God, even the Son of God, with power and authority to create this earth and other earths, yet there were some things lacking which he did not receive until

after his resurrection. In other words, he had not received the fullness until he got a resurrected body.[28]

Thus, even though according to the late president and prophet Ezra Taft Benson "Jesus was a God in the pre-mortal existence," He was still imperfect and lacking certain necessary things.[29]

Bruce McConkie taught, "These laws [of salvation], instituted by the father, constitute the gospel of God, which gospel is the plan by which all of his spirit children, Christ included, may gain eternal life."[30]

McConkie also stated that "Jesus Christ is the Son of God....He came to earth to work out his own salvation."[31] And that "by obedience and devotion to the truth he attained that pinnacle of intelligence which ranked him as a God."[32] The Mormon publicity booklet *What the Mormons Think of Christ* asserts that "Christ, the Word, the First Born, had of course, attained unto the status of Godhood while yet in pre-existence."[33]

Remember, this was an indeterminate period of time that involved aeons. If Christ learned to choose good over evil by experience and *attained* perfection by "probation, progression and schooling," it is difficult indeed to logically conceive of Christ as being perfectly sinless throughout the entire period of His probation and preexistence.

## Some Additional Concerns

### Why Do Mormons Refer to Christ As Eternal?

When Mormons refer to Christ as "eternal" many Christians assume this to be an affirmation of Christ's deity. But this is only another illustration of Mormon equivocation. Mormonism does not accept that Jesus is eternal as the Second Person of the Godhead, which is Christian teaching. The only sense in which "Jesus" is eternal is according to their vague, mercurial doctrine of spirit intelligence. Mormonism believes that *all life* existed eternally as some type of seemingly un-differentiated mass of incorporeal intelligence. Human life apparently passes through at least four stages:

1. As vague, undefined, uncreated, eternally-existing "intel-ligences";

2. As "spirit children" in the pre-mortal spirit world, having been mysteriously remolded by means of the physical, sexual intercourse of God and one of his wives (we then enter a lengthy period of probation, schooling, and progression which determines the nature and quality of our life on earth—being born into a Mormon family is a reward for attained excellence in preexistence);

3. As earthly beings, where we inhabit physical bodies and, if we are good Mormons, have the opportunity to earn exaltation (attain godhood); and

4. As resurrected beings in postmortem states of various degrees of glory determined by our achievement on earth (the celestial, terrestrial, or telestial kingdoms).

Christ must have "existed" then in some nebulous form before His spirit birth, probation, and schooling, and His sub-sequent fleshly life on earth. The Mormon scripture *Doctrine and Covenants* teaches that "man was also in the beginning with God. Intelligence, or the light of truth, was not created or made, neither indeed can be" (*D&C*, 93:29). Thus, just as "the [material] elements are eternal" (*D&C*, 93:33), so "Spirit ele-ment (that is, 'the intelligence of spirits') always existed.... 'The intelligence of spirits had no beginning.'"[34]

The spirit children or offspring of the gods are apparently the result of fashioning or "remolding" of "spirit intelligence" (in whatever form) through sexual union. Apparently, sexual intercourse between the gods somehow has the power to refashion this mercurial spirit "intelligence" into spirit chil-dren. Doctrinal theologian McConkie explains:

> Spirit entities as such, in their organized form
> as the offspring of Deity, have not existed as long

as God has, for he is their Father, and he begat them as spirits. Thus, there are two principles: 1) That "man was also in the beginning with God," meaning that the spirits of men were created, begotten, and organized, that they came into being as spirits at the time of their spirit birth; and 2) That "intelligence, or the light of truth, was not created or made, neither indeed can be" (_D&C_, 93:29), meaning that spirit element, "the intelligence of spirits, 'the substance from which they were created as entities, has always existed and is as eternal as God himself.' "[35]

It would seem evident then that one reason Mormons think they can become literal gods is that they existed as eternal "spirit element" prior to their birth as spirit children and that this spirit element "substance" partakes in some sense of the very nature of deity. Nevertheless, this teaching denies and rejects the nature of Jesus Christ as the eternal Second Person of the Godhead. Biblically, Christ was never some nebulous, unformed spirit element who came into existence as a preexistent spirit by the sexual intercourse of pagan gods. In nature and essence, He has always existed as the eternal Second Person of the Trinity: "Jesus Christ is the same yesterday and today and forever" (Hebrews 13:8 NIV).

## Was Christ a Polygamist?

Some early Mormons taught that both God and Christ were polygamists. Thus, even on earth, Christ would have violated the will of God concerning at least one sin— polygamy. In Deuteronomy 17:17 and Leviticus 18:18 God warned against plural marriage, both for kingly rulers and others. The New Testament also upholds marriage to only one woman (1 Timothy 3:2,12; Titus 1:6). Jesus Himself upheld the standard of marriage to only one woman based on the pattern of Adam and Eve, which was obviously God's choice, for He brought to Adam only one wife, not several (Matthew 19:4,5; Mark 10:2-8). Nevertheless, Jedediah M. Grant, second

counselor to Brigham Young, stated in 1853 that "a belief in
the doctrine of a plurality of wives caused the persecution of
Jesus and his followers. We might almost think they are 'Mormons.'"[36] Grant implies Jesus was persecuted and crucified
because "He had so many wives," including Elizabeth (he
possibly refers to the wife of Zecharias), Mary, "and a host of
others."[37] If Jesus was married to another man's wife, of
course, that was adultery.

That some Mormons taught that Jesus was married to
another man's wife should not surprise us. After all, Joseph
Smith, Brigham Young, and many other Mormon leaders were
married to other men's wives while they themselves were
married to their own numerous wives. In a statement about
Jesus, apostle Orson Hyde observed:

> I discovered that some of the Eastern papers
> represent me as a great blasphemer, because I said,
> in my lecture on Marriage, at our last Conference,
> that Jesus Christ was married at Cana of Galilee,
> that Mary, Martha, and others were his wives, and
> that he begat children. All that I have to say in
> reply to that charge is this—they worship a Savior
> that is too pure and holy to fulfill the commands
> of his Father....If Jesus begat children, he only
> "did that which he had seen his Father do."[38]

Orson Pratt stated, "The founder of the Christian religion,
was a Polygamist....The Messiah chose to...by marrying
many honorable wives himself, show to all future generations
that he approbated the plurality of Wives under the Christian
dispensation."[39]

While Mormons today generally teach that Christ was not
a polygamist, a significant number do, especially among the
many polygamist Mormon cults.[40]

## The Differences Are Real

In conclusion, then, the Mormon Jesus Christ is a vague,
eternal "spirit element" organized into a spirit child by sexual

intercourse of the earth god and his celestial wife. He is the common brother of Lucifer, one of many spirit children who earned his salvation, immortality, and godhood. And perhaps, as some Mormons say, He was a polygamist as well.

Yet Mormon missionaries will come to the prospective convert's door with this crude polytheism and say in full sincerity they are committed Christians who believe in the biblical Jesus Christ! True Mormons do not believe in Christ; they do not even know Christ. Indeed, they officially reject and attack as heresy the idea that a man or woman should seek a personal relationship with Christ.[41] The Mormon church is thus _not_ the church of Jesus Christ—it is the church of Joseph Smith.

Yet even Mormons will admit, "If a professing minister of salvation is not a witness for Christ, he is not a prophet." We find that assessment hard to disagree with. But in conclusion, note once again the contrast between the biblical Christ and the Mormon Christ.

| Biblical Christ | Mormon Christ |
| --- | --- |
| Deity | Not true deity (earned godhood) |
| Sinless | Sinful |
| Virgin born | Not virgin born |
| Eternal | Created |
| Unmarried | Polygamist? |

So, not only is the Mormon view of God not Christian, but the Mormon view of Christ is also not Christian. Mormons may claim that they believe in the biblical God and Trinity, but, in fact, they have invented a new God, a new Jesus Christ, and a new Holy Ghost/Spirit that have little to do with the God of orthodox Christian faith.

# Chapter 6

# What Mormons Say About Jesus' Work on the Cross

~

Mormonism repeatedly claims that it believes in the biblical atonement of Jesus Christ. One frequently finds statements in Mormon literature to the effect that "Christ died for our sins." When talking with Mormons, they will affirm over and over that they believe Christ has died for their sins. But Mormons mean something different by these statements from what Christians mean.

First, let us give you some examples of what Mormonism claims about the atonement. Theologian Bruce McConkie claims that "salvation comes because of the atonement."[1] James Talmage argues that Jesus "bore the weight of the sins of the whole world, not only of Adam but of his posterity."[2]

The *Doctrines of the Gospel: Student Manual* emphasizes:

> No doctrine in the gospel is more important than the atonement of Jesus Christ....The Savior...suffer[ed] for the sins of all the children of God....The infinite atonement affects worlds without number and will save all of God's children except sons of perdition.[3]

One former president and prophet of the Mormon church, Ezra Taft Benson, taught, "In Gethsemane* and on Calvary, he worked out the infinite and eternal atonement....It was in Gethsemane that Jesus took on himself the sins of the world...That holy, unselfish act of voluntarily taking on himself the sins of all other men is called the Atonement."[4]

The *Book of Mormon* also claims that Christ died for our sins. It has Jesus saying, "I...have been slain for the sins of the world" (3 Nephi 11:14). And it teaches that "the sufferings and death of Christ atone for their [men's] sins, through faith and repentance" (Alma 22:14).

But while these statements sound Christian, Mormons mean something different by them. Mormons really do *not* believe that Christ has effectively died for their sins and paid the actual penalty of divine justice necessary for their forgiveness. As we show in the pages that follow, Christ's death made forgiveness of sins possible, but it was conditioned upon obedience to law.

Further, Mormons believe that forgiveness of sins is *not* immediately received upon exhibiting true faith, demonstrating repentance, undergoing baptism, and so on. Rather, the true forgiveness of sins requires a lengthy probationary period. Worse yet, serious sins will cause the *loss* of salvation. In this sense, even *Mormon* salvation does not necessarily constitute forgiveness of "serious sins."[5]

In Mormonism, the death of Christ accomplished two principal things, neither of them directly equivalent to actually forgiving a person's sins.[6]

First, Mormons claim that Christ's atonement produced a release from physical death. Christ defeated physical death so that all men will one day be raised from the dead. Second, Christ's atonement defeated spiritual death in that men now have the opportunity to earn the right to come back into the presence of God through obedience to law. We may thus document at least three principal Mormon teachings concerning the atonement: 1) the atonement delivers from physical death

---

* Mormons believe that most or all of Christ's atonement was wrought at Gethsemane, not on the cross. See *Achieving a Celestial Marriage Student Manual*, p. 6.

by way of resurrection from the dead; 2) the atonement delivers from spiritual death in that it makes forgiveness of sins possible by law keeping; and 3) the Christian view of the atonement is therefore a delusion. Let's examine these Mormon teachings more closely.

1. The atonement delivers from physical death.

The *Book of Mormon* asserts that Christ's death paid the penalty for Adam's fall: "The Messiah cometh in fullness of time, that he may redeem the children of men from the fall" (2 Nephi 2:26). Mormonism teaches that the Fall not only brought physical death but also some degree of spiritual death, often defined as removal from God's presence, and death to the "things of righteousness."[*7]

Christ's atonement conquered physical death in freely providing a resurrection for all men and it conquered "spiritual" death *insofar as* men keep the law.

Thus, the only *actual* accomplishment of the atonement was that it made possible the resurrection of all men. As Mormon theologian Duane Crowther comments, "The Lord died in order to bring about the resurrection of the dead."[9] Again, this was all it *actually* accomplished. Any other benefits derived from the atonement must be earned by good works and obeying Mormon requirements.[10]

Likewise, when Mormonism claims that Christ's death brought immortality, that does not mean that it brought true salvation. As we will see in chapter 7 (see pp. 107-108), one can be resurrected to immortality and still be "damned." Thus, along with Jehovah's Witnesses and other cults, Mormonism teaches that the atonement merely provides the opportunity to

---

* Mormonism has had a difficult time defining what it means by "spiritual death." As McMurrin points out: "It is the state of being cast out of the presence of the Lord, i.e., banishment from the garden, but beyond this, 'spiritual death' has been difficult for the Mormon theologians to define and they have usually passed over it somewhat casually....It is typical of the Mormon theologians...to concentrate primarily on the factor of physical death rather than spiritual death....[Adam's] condition of exclusion from the divine presence does not in any way constitute sin; he is not by nature sinful, nor does a necessary compulsion to actual sin condition his freedom.... Nothing is more evident than the determination to avoid any suggestion that Adam's guilt can in any way be imputed to mankind."[8]

earn salvation through personal merit. Just as a college degree does not actually secure a salary, but only makes earning one possible, so Christ's death does not actually secure salvation, but only makes earning it possible by good works. In fact, even if all the faith in the world were placed in Christ's death on the cross, this still would not forgive a single sin—not apart from law keeping.

In Mormonism, then, the actual *saving value* of the atonement is virtually nonexistent. As Dr. McMurrin observes:

> Mormon theology has with considerable ingenuity constructed its doctrine of salvation around the fall and the atonement, but with radically unorthodox meanings....The meaning of the grace of God given through the atonement of Christ is that man by his freedom can now merit salvation....But that Christ has taken the sins of the world upon himself does not mean, in Mormon theology, that he has by his sinless sacrifice brought the free gift of salvation to mortals steeped in original and actual sin and therefore unworthy of the grace bestowed upon them. In the Mormon doctrine, Christ redeems men from the physical and spiritual death imposed upon them by the transgression of Adam...But he does not in any way absolve them of the consequences of their own actual evil or save them with high glory in the absence of genuine merit.[11]

In fact, while denying the blood atonement of Christ, the *early* Mormon church, quite logically, accepted the blood atonement of men! Mormonism actually taught that the forgiveness of certain sins required a man's death. Should certain sins be committed (for example, lying, adultery, stealing), the guilty person was to have his own blood shed in order to atone for them because the death of Christ could not forgive such sins. Brigham Young himself emphasized, "I could refer you to plenty of instances where men have been righteously slain, in order to atone for their sins."[12] In other words, a person could "justifiably" be slain to atone for his or her sins!

In one sense we may question whether or not much change has taken place in the modern church's view of the atonement compared with its early prophets' teaching. The early church taught that the blood atonement of men was necessary because the atonement of Christ was *partial*—"men can commit sins which it can never remit."[13] Today, the atonement is *still* partial: it only brings resurrection from the dead, and it doesn't offer even the *possibility* of forgiving *all* sins. At least one sin cannot always be forgiven—murder (and perhaps also apostasy).[14] For example, a previous president and prophet of the church stated that "all sins [can be forgiven by good works] but those excepted by the Lord—basically, the sins against the Holy Ghost, and murder" (cf. Alma 39:5,6).[15]

2. The atonement delivers from spiritual death in that it makes forgiveness of sins possible by law keeping (the atonement per se does not forgive sins: personal righteousness does).

Some Mormon claims to the contrary, the death of Christ did *not* forgive anyone's sins; again, it only made possible the forgiveness of sins by law keeping. The Mormon scriptures teach this. For example, *Doctrine and Covenants* 76:50,52 declares, "This is the testimony of the gospel of Christ concerning them who shall come forth in the resurrection of the just....That *by keeping the commandments they might be washed and cleansed from all their sins.*"[16]

Likewise, the 1961 *Mormon Missionary Handbook* instructs Mormon missionaries to carefully teach new converts that Christ's death has *not* removed their sins—that only obedience can do this. Under the section titled "Fourth Discussion: The Gift of God Is Eternal Life," point 7, it supplies the proper dialogue with new converts:

> *Elder:* Why is it so important for you to live the commandments then, Brother Brown?
> *Brown:* If I keep the commandments the Lord removes my sins.

*Elder:* I testify that is true. He has already paid for your sins, Brother Brown. BUT WHEN ARE THOSE SINS REMOVED FROM YOU?

*Brown:* When I keep the commandments, including repentance and baptism.

[Correct] He removes our sins if we keep his commandments.[17]

Under the "Fifth Discussion: Law of Eternal Progression," point 2 reads, "Through the atonement and by obedience my sins will be removed."[18] Under the "Sixth Discussion: Be Ye Therefore Perfect," points 6-11 teach:

6. I must conform to the first principles and ordinances of the gospel to receive a remission of my sins.

7. I will live under the Ten Commandments.

8. I will continue to live the Word of Wisdom.

9. God has given us the law of tithing to teach us unselfishness.

10. I will live the law of tithing.

11. By obedience and through the grace of Christ I will be saved from spiritual death.[19]

The thirteenth president and prophet of the Mormon church, Spencer W. Kimball, emphasizes, "This progress toward eternal life is a matter of achieving perfection. *Living all the commandments guarantees total forgiveness of sins* and assures one of exaltation....Perfection therefore is an achievable goal."[20]

President and prophet Ezra Taft Benson taught that the atonement of Christ's death is effective for "redeeming all of us from physical death, and redeeming those of us from spiritual death *who will obey the laws and ordinances of the gospel.*"[21]

The *Doctrines of the Gospel: Student Manual* claims that Jesus only came to save those who would obey Him because mercy is extended only to those who keep God's commandments.

Thus, "if we do not keep God's commandments, we must suffer for our own sins."[22]

This is why the Mormon text *A Sure Foundation* concludes, "We believe that it is Christ's atonement that saves us but that we must endure to the end in doing good works *if his atonement is to take effect on our behalf*....It is by the atonement of Christ that we are saved, but *it is necessary that we keep the commandments* and obey the ordinances God has given us."[23]

In his *Articles of Faith*, James Talmage writes of the justness of having sins be forgiven by good works:

> As...these sins are the result of individual acts *it is just that forgiveness for them should be conditioned on individual compliance with prescribed requirements*—"obedience to the laws and ordinances of the gospel."[24]

In essence, although without Christ's atonement salvation would not be possible, salvation *itself* is the reward for individual merit. This was why point 3 of the Articles of Faith of Joseph Smith stated, "We believe that through the atonement of Christ, all mankind may be saved, by obedience to the laws and ordinances of the gospel." Dr. McMurrin correctly observes,

> Here is a clear statement that, although the atonement is necessary, salvation is earned. Though the atonement brings immortality and resurrection to all men, salvation is a matter of degree, and the degree attained is a consequence of merit. Every man must answer for his own sins and salvation can come through obedience to law. Here is the opposite pole from Luther's justification by faith only.[25]

All of this is why Mormon discussions of the atonement are noticeable for their *lack* of affirming actual forgiveness of sins through Christ's death alone. This is why Mormons don't know the true Gospel—they have never heard it. The claim of one former twenty-year Mormon (who taught doctrine in the church) was that he never once heard that Christ *actually* died on the cross for *his* sin. This is not unique for Mormonism; it is characteristic.[26] Thus, forgiveness of sins comes indirectly through Christ's death, which cancels the effects of the Fall, but directly only by good works, which themselves cancel sin. Hence, "The spiritual death of the Fall is replaced by the spiritual life of the atonement, in that all who believe and obey gospel law gain spiritual or eternal life."[27] Obviously then, the atonement alone *does not* forgive sins, no matter what Mormons may claim—only law keeping does. All this is why Christ's atonement is "really just a starting point," and that true salvation and actual forgiveness of sins must be earned.[28] The Mormon publication *Gospel Principles* reiterates, "The Savior atoned for us by suffering in Gethsemane and by giving his life on the cross," and "Christ did his part to atone for our sins. Each of us must repent and obey to make Christ's atonement effective in our lives."[29]

But consider this. This same text shows how difficult it actually is for Mormons to find forgiveness. It teaches that forgiveness of sins is conditioned upon repentance.[30] But what is "repentance" in Mormonism? "The privilege of repenting is made possible through the atonement of Jesus Christ."[31] This text then tells us that repentance means we must 1) recognize our sins, 2) feel sorrow for our sins, 3) forsake our sins, 4) confess our sins, 5) make restitution, 6) forgive others, and 7) keep the commandments of God.[32]

And what does it mean to keep the commandments of God? Keeping the commandments involves 1) paying tithes, 2) keeping the Sabbath day, 3) obeying the *Word of Wisdom* (such as not drinking coffee), 4) sustaining the authorities of the church, 5) loving the Lord, 6) loving humanity, 7) consistently saying family prayers, etc.[33]

Repentance involves all this and *then* spending "the balance of your lives trying to live the commandments of the Lord so he can eventually pardon you and cleanse you."[34] In other words, a Mormon's sins are not forgiven at all until *all of this is accomplished*. Thus, "As a result of repentance, the atonement of Jesus Christ becomes effective in our lives, and our sins are forgiven."[35] If this is true, how can *any* Mormon know his sins are ever forgiven? (see pp. 139ff).

Because the atonement has not forgiven sins, no Mormon can know he or she is saved *until* all the requirements for salvation are met. But these requirements involve spiritual progression even beyond the grave. As in reincarnation, it may literally take aeons before one attains to the status of a god. If one's "sins may be forgiven beyond the grave,"[36] and if it allegedly took the earth god Elohim a *very* long time to gain salvation, certainly, as embryonic deities, Mormons cannot expect salvation in this brief life alone.[37]

All this denies the biblical teaching that Christ's death paid the full penalty for our sins, resulting in complete forgiveness at the moment of faith (see 1 Corinthians 15:3; Hebrews 9:12; 10:10-14). "He forgave us all our sins" (Colossians 2:13).

But if the atonement of Christ has already remitted the penalty of sin, how can keeping the commandments do so? Conversely, if it is taught that keeping the law forgives sin, how can Mormonism logically teach that the atonement accomplishes this? All this is why Mormons have to regard the Christian view as erroneous.

3. The Christian view of the atonement is classified as a great error and a pernicious delusion.

Consider the words of early Mormon theologian C.W. Penrose, which are, in various ways, frequently echoed by modern church authorities:

> The Latter-day Saints are often accused by the people in the Christian world of being very much deluded. Our religion is counted a delusion and snare. I was thinking, however, during the meeting this afternoon about the great number of Christian preachers who today are standing up in various parts of the world informing the people who listen to them that simple belief on the Lord Jesus, who died on Calvary, is all that is necessary

to save them and exalt them in the presence of God the Father. And it seems to me that if there is one delusion more pernicious than another it is that very doctrine, which seems to be a fundamental principle of all the various Christian sects....[We find]...preached the great error that mere belief in the work which Jesus Christ wrought out is sufficient for the salvation of the people. The inhabitants of the earth are informed that it is not by any works of righteousness which they may perform that they can gain any favor whatever in the sight of God, but it is the righteousness of Christ alone which is acceptable to the Father and which they can gain the benefit of if they simply believe in him.

[However], the plan of the true Gospel...does not consist in mere belief in the righteousness of another....It is men who are *not* sent who preach the nonsense we hear in the world. It is the men who are *not* sent who deceive mankind with their strong delusions, and then turn round and call the Latter-day Saints deluded. If they were sent of God they would not preach such nonsense, they would not deceive mankind and thus become the cause of so much sin and evil in the world.[38]

Mormonism, then, does not believe in the biblical atonement of Jesus Christ. It teaches that, at best, Christ's death only supplies the opportunity whereby individuals may work to forgive their own sins and eventually perfect themselves and become exalted as gods. When Mormons claim that Christ died to save all men or that Christ died for their sins, one must understand that such phrases do not have biblical or Christian meanings. But when Mormonism claims that Christ's death does not forgive the believer's sins, they deny what the Bible clearly teaches:

For I delivered to you as of first importance what I also received, that Christ died for our sins according to the Scriptures (1 Corinthians 15:3).

The next day he saw Jesus coming to him, and said, "Behold, the Lamb of God who takes away the sin of the world!" (John 1:29).

Who gave Himself for our sins, that He might deliver us out of this present evil age, according to the will of our God and Father (Galatians 1:4).

In Him we have redemption through His blood, the forgiveness of our trespasses, according to the riches of His grace (Ephesians 1:7).

In whom we have redemption, the forgiveness of sins (Colossians 1:14).

And He Himself is the propitiation [atoning sacrifice] for our sins; and not for ours only, but also for those of the whole world....In this is love, not that we loved God, but that He loved us and sent His Son to be the propitiation for our sins (1 John 2:2; 4:10).

...But he entered the Most Holy Place once for all by his own blood, having obtained eternal redemption (Hebrews 9:12 NIV).

Because by one sacrifice he has made perfect forever those who are being made holy (Hebrews 10:14 NIV).

We agree with the Mormon church when it emphasizes that "no doctrine in the gospel is more important than the atonement of Jesus Christ."[39] What is regrettable is that in Mormonism "the atonement of Christ becomes merely a handy tool to be used by the individual in his or her own do-it-yourself salvation kit."*[40]

----

* Robinson uses these words to convey an alleged *distortion* of Mormon belief—which is why we have quoted them.

# SECTION IV

# WHAT DO THE MORMONS BELIEVE ABOUT SALVATION?

# Chapter 7

# What the Mormon Church Teaches About Salvation

~

What does Mormonism believe about salvation as a whole? First, Mormonism claims that it alone offers true salvation to the world. No other church on the face of the earth can tell a man or woman how to be saved other than the Mormon church. This teaching flows from its claim to be the only true church on earth; therefore, "There is no salvation outside the Church of Jesus Christ of Latter-day Saints."[1]

Second, Mormon salvation is dependent upon the Fall of man.

According to the Mormon church, God planned that the Fall and sin would play an essential role in human salvation. God intended for there to be sin so that 1) mankind would be *capable* of having children who 2) could then grow in spiritual experience and discernment of right and wrong. In other words, the Fall *enabled* Adam and Eve to conceive children who would then have the opportunity to become gods by learning to choose good rather than evil.

Without the Fall there would have been no progeny of Adam and Eve, no physical bodies for the preexisting spirit children, no mankind for the earth god to rule, no increase of his kingdom from his children, and no experiential growing into godhood for any Mormon.

The Fall is thus a disguised blessing of nearly unparalleled proportions to Mormon people. Mormons are grateful to Adam for bringing about the Fall—which works to permit the true salvation (exaltation) of Mormons. Thus, Adam's role in salvation—his disobedience and Fall—is almost as important as that of Christ's (see Ankerberg and Weldon, *Behind the Mask of Mormonism*, pp. 211-218).

Third, the Mormon church distinguishes two kinds of redemption: *general* and *individual*. Although the term *salvation* is used to describe the general category of redemption, this type of "salvation" or general redemption is only a partial redemption, not true or complete salvation. This general redemption is wrought by the atonement of Christ. It covers the effects of the Fall (physical and spiritual death) and produces resurrection from the dead. It also determines, on the basis of personal merit, where (among several options) any given individual will finally spend eternity. In essence, *general* redemption constitutes resurrection to immortality in a lesser kingdom of servant status without the possibility of godhood and eternal progression. On the other hand, *individual* redemption, or full salvation, constitutes resurrection to godhood in the highest celestial kingdom, or a lesser servant status within that kingdom.

In this chapter we will discuss the Mormon teaching on salvation as a whole. We will look at its basic division into the general and individual categories. And in the next chapter, we will examine what Mormonism claims concerning salvation by grace.

## General Redemption:
## Partial Salvation (Resurrection)

In Mormonism, general redemption is resurrection from the dead. Bruce McConkie teaches concerning the resurrection or general redemption, "In and of itself the resurrection is a form of salvation meaning that men are thereby saved from death, hell, the devil, and endless torment (2 Ne. 9:17-27)....In this sense, the mere fact of resurrection is called salvation by grace alone. Works are not involved."[2]

But, even in this so-called "general" redemption of grace, that is, mere resurrection, men are still judged according to their works and consigned on that basis to different states in the afterlife. (In the *general* category of redemption this would be either the lower terrestrial or telestial kingdom, which we'll discuss more in a moment.)

Those with less-than-appropriate works are consigned to these lower kingdoms, and have no chance for full salvation or deification. Despite Mormon claims that they are saved from death, hell, the devil, and endless torment, they are saved only from annihilation. In general, when Mormons speak of eternal torment or punishment, they refer to the punishment of forever remaining single and never becoming a god.[3]

But again, it must be stressed that while works are not required in order to *be* resurrected, they *do* determine whether one is consigned to the celestial, terrestrial, or telestial kingdoms and one's placement within those kingdoms.

Further, to properly understand Mormon salvation, we must learn Mormonism's unique use of the terms pertaining to salvation. These may sound Christian, but they are given new meanings. Thus, in Mormon theology *immortality* is not the same condition as described by the term *eternal life. Immortality* means resurrection alone, and it can even involve "damnation." To be damned in Mormonism is, generally, not to be granted entrance into the celestial kingdom. Thus, Mormonism equates redemption by grace with a condition of damnation: "Immortality [general salvation] comes by grace alone, but those who gain it may find themselves damned in eternity" (Alma 11:37-45).[4] On the other hand, *eternal life* means inheriting godhood, or at least inheriting the celestial kingdom. "Eternal life, the kind of life enjoyed by eternal beings [gods] in the celestial kingdom, comes by grace plus obedience."[5]

Consider the following definitions and discussion of general salvation by Mormon theologian McConkie:

> Unconditional or general salvation, that which comes by grace alone without obedience to gospel law, consists in the mere fact of being resurrected.

> In this sense, salvation is synonymous with immortality; it is the inseparable connection of body and spirit so that the resurrected personage lives forever.[6]

He then proceeds to discuss the implications of general salvation:

> This kind of salvation eventually will come to all mankind, accepting only the sons of perdition [primarily apostate Mormons]....But this is not the salvation of righteousness, the salvation which the saints [Mormons] seek. Those who gain only this general or unconditional salvation will still be judged according to their works and receive their places in a terrestrial or a telestial kingdom. They will, therefore, be damned; their eternal progression will be cut short; they will not feel the full measure of their creation, but in eternity will be ministering servants to more worthy persons [better Mormons].[7]

Refer to the following chart, The Mormon Concept of Salvation, in order to see the hierarchy of these kingdoms:

## The Mormon Concept of Salvation

| | |
|---|---|
| True salvation: Immortality by personal merit made possible by the atonement. | **Celestial Kingdom** (individual redemption; three levels)<br><br>1. Exaltation for Perfect Mormons [godhood and eternal increase (spirit children)]<br>2. lesser servant status<br>3. same |
| Damnation: Immortality (resurrection) or "salvation by grace" (degrees of glory determined by personal merit). | **Terrestrial Kingdom** (general redemption; righteous non-Mormons) |
| | **Telestial Kingdom** (the wicked; their purgatorial expungement of sins was accomplished before their resurrection in the Mormon Spirit prison) |
| Salvation denied. | **Sons of Perdition** (e.g., apostate Mormons) |

In essence, general salvation means salvation to one of two kingdoms:

1. The terrestrial kingdom, where righteous non-Mormons go;
2. The telestial kingdom, where the wicked go.

But do those in the telestial kingdom progress into the terrestrial one? Generally, no. Theologian Crowther states,

> This is not to say there will be no progress by those who inherit the lesser glories, only that there are limits set beyond which they cannot pass. The passages cited above strongly imply that there is no progression from one kingdom of glory to another kingdom of a higher degree, though the church has never taken a formal doctrinal stand on this point.[8]

Only a few have taught that those in the telestial kingdom can and will progress into the terrestrial kingdom. But Mormons do seem to agree that those in the terrestrial kingdom apparently cannot progress into the celestial kingdom. Further, only in the highest part of the celestial kingdom do marriage and procreation continue for eternity. In the other kingdoms everyone is single and so never inherit the joys of deification and eternal marriage, or eternal progression.

There is also said to be room for "eternal" advancement within each kingdom. In the citation below we can see that the concepts of purgatory and salvation after death are part of Mormonism's general salvation. The tenth president and prophet, Joseph Fielding Smith, stated:

> Those who reject the [Mormon] gospel, but who live honorable lives, shall also be heirs of salvation, but not in the celestial kingdom. The Lord has prepared a place for them in the terrestrial kingdom. Those who live lives of wickedness may also be heirs of salvation, that is, they too shall be redeemed from death and from hell _eventually_.

> These, however, must suffer in hell the torments of the damned *until* they pay the price of their sinning, *for the blood of Christ will not cleanse them.* This vast host will find their place in the telestial kingdom.[9]

Finally, there is another class of people who are termed "sons of perdition." These are not the "damned" of the two lower kingdoms, and their fate, at least according to Mormon theology, is not easily determined. Some Mormons hold there is an eternal hell while most others deny it, a disagreement that reflects the contradictions in their scriptures, prophets, and historical theology.

Devout Mormons have no desire to achieve any of the lower kingdoms or even to live in the lower portions of the celestial kingdom. Their desire is to live in the highest portion of the celestial kingdom where they will be gods and have sexual increase. George Q. Cannon, a member of the First Presidency, commented in a conference report, "I never heard a prayer offered, especially in the family circle, in which the family does not besiege God to give them [the highest] celestial glory. Telestial glory is not in their thoughts. Terrestrial glory may be all right for honorable Gentiles...but celestial glory is our aim....All that I am on this earth for is to get celestial glory."[10]

In conclusion, the relationship between *general* and *individual* salvation may be seen in the following summary statement by James Talmage in his work *Jesus the Christ*:

> ...general salvation, in the sense of redemption from the effects of the Fall, comes to all without their seeking it; but...individual salvation or rescue from the effects of personal sins is to be required by each for himself by faith and good works.[11]

As we have seen, in addition to the first and inferior kind of redemption there is also a second and full redemption. This is a fully conditional salvation, entirely based upon good works, personal merit, and strict obedience to what Mormons term "Gospel law."

## Individual Redemption: True Salvation

While *general* redemption merely assures resurrection to one of two lower kingdoms of "damnation," true salvation affords resurrection to the highest kingdom, the celestial kingdom. It is this salvation alone which is crucial to Mormons, which forgives all sin, and which determines whether one has the opportunity for deification. This salvation is not by grace at all. McConkie teaches, "Salvation in the celestial kingdom of God, however, is not salvation by grace alone. Rather, it is salvation by grace coupled with obedience to the laws and ordinances of the gospel."[12] There are three heavens within the celestial kingdom, but only in the highest heaven do Mormons actually attain godhood. Again, this is the salvation all Mormons seek, for it constitutes the possibility of becoming a god. Here is full salvation by which Mormons may earn eternal sexual rights to produce never-ending spirit offspring and kingdoms in which to rule them.

Mormons do not believe that they become gods immediately after death. They must continue to accumulate personal merit and attain divine attributes through aeons of effort and progression in the postmortem state. They believe that if they are successful, ultimately, they will become gods.

But these doctrines must be *believed* in order for one to actually achieve true salvation. For example, in order to be exalted, one must believe that God is an exalted man: "God revealed himself to Adam by this name to signify that he is a Holy Man, a truth which man must know and comprehend if he is to become like God and inherit exaltation."[13] Further, the doctrine of exaltation is vitally integrated with the doctrines of celestial marriage (temple marriage) and the concept of eternal increase, or having children in eternity. These doctrines must also be accepted for one to have the possibility of exaltation.

Thus, in the most alluring way possible, Mormonism cements loyalty to its doctrines. The promises of eternal marriage, eternal sexual pleasure, eternal family, and eternal godhood itself are offered to those who truly believe.

Nevertheless, in the celestial kingdom as well, we find a distinction between *immortality* and *eternal life*. Those who do not gain eternal life do not become gods, and have only another form of immortality. Along with those in the two lower kingdoms, individuals in the two lower levels of the highest (celestial) kingdom are only "angels" who will serve those more worthy Mormons who have become gods or attained exaltation. Thus, Mormonism teaches that in this sense, even those in the celestial kingdom may be considered "damned" because they have not inherited *full* salvation—godhood and eternal increase.[14] As McConkie explains:

> Even those in the celestial kingdom, however, who do not go on to exaltation, will have immortality only and not eternal life. Along with those of the telestial and terrestrial worlds they will be "ministering servants, to minister for those who are worthy of a far more, and an exceeding, and an eternal weight of glory." They will live "separately and singly" in an unmarried state "without exaltation, in their saved condition, to all eternity" (*D&C*, 132:16,17). Salvation in its true and full meaning is synonymous with exaltation or eternal life and consists in gaining an inheritance in the highest of the three heavens within the celestial kingdom. With few exceptions this is the salvation of which the scriptures speak. It is the salvation which the saints [Mormons] seek....This full salvation is obtained in and through the continuation of the family unit in eternity, and those who obtain it are gods (*D&C*, 131:1-4; 132)....If it had not been for Joseph Smith and the restoration, there would be no salvation.[15]

Again, to be "damned" in Mormonism is to have a *limit* placed on one's eternal progression. "Those who inherit the telestial glory, the terrestrial glory, and even lower degrees in the celestial glory *will all be damned*, for there are boundaries set beyond which they can never pass, throughout all eternity."[16] Thus, "Damnation means a limit to eternal progression."[17]

Whatever else Mormonism teaches, the only true salvation in Mormonism is attaining the highest portion of the celestial kingdom—which is the same as becoming a god. To be saved in Mormon theology is to become of like nature with God the Father. As McConkie emphasizes:

> With three or four possible exceptions all of the revelations of all the ages speak of salvation as being wholly, completely, and totally synonymous with eternal or everlasting life, with exaltation in the highest heaven of the celestial world, with attaining Godhood and being like God the Eternal Father.[18]

Thus the student manual *Doctrines of the Gospel* teaches Mormons, "Each one of you has it within the realm of his possibility to develop a kingdom over which you will preside as its king and god. You will need to develop yourself and grow in ability and power and worthiness, to govern such a world with all of its people."[19]

And,

> It is the blessed privilege of resurrected beings who attain an exaltation in the celestial kingdom [the highest portion] to enjoy the glory of endless increase, to become the parents of generations of spirit offspring, and to direct their development through probationary stages analogous to those through which they themselves have passed.[20]

In conclusion, the Mormon church teaches that salvation comes only through the Mormon church and that it comprises various conditions of existence after death. Worthy Mormons will attain exaltation or deification in the highest heaven within the celestial kingdom. With their celestial wife or wives, they will have spirit children forever and rule worlds upon worlds. All others are "damned," which means they inherit a servant status in lesser kingdoms with successively worse restrictions and/or punishments, but "kingdoms" nonetheless. Mormons agree that progression is possible within each of the two lower kingdoms, but they debate whether or not progression from one kingdom to another is possible.

This is the Mormon concept of salvation. It has nothing whatever to do with the biblical doctrine of salvation, which teaches four things:

1. Christ *alone* wrought full and complete salvation on the cross (Ephesians 1:7; Colossians 2:13; Hebrews 10:14).

2. *Full* salvation can be freely received by anyone merely by receiving Christ as his or her personal Savior from sin (John 1:12; 3:16; 5:24; 6:47).

3. Salvation is *not* a lengthy process of becoming the same as God, but rather, it involves men and women who, as God's redeemed children, honor and enjoy Him and experience eternal life with Him forever (Revelation 21:1-7; 1 John 2:25).

4. Salvation is *wholly* by grace, not by works in any sense (Ephesians 2:8,9). Works are the logical product of salvation, not its cause.

Nevertheless, Mormons argue that they accept and promote the biblical doctrine of salvation by grace. But a closer look at their scriptures and statements from their leaders reveals otherwise—that's the focus of our next chapter.

# Chapter 8

# Mormonism, God's Grace, and Man's Works

~

Mormonism vigorously claims that it believes in the biblical teaching of salvation by grace. One Mormon promotional brochure declares, "Salvation by grace is one of the glorious doctrines of Christ."[1] In his apologetic text defending the assertion that Mormons are Christians, Dr. Stephen E. Robinson goes out of his way to argue that both the Mormon scriptures and the Mormon church do in fact believe that salvation is *wholly by grace*.

Because approaches like these so easily confuse both Mormons and uninstructed Christians concerning the nature of the Mormon religion, we shall begin our analysis with Dr. Robinson's book *Are Mormons Christians?* Significantly, Robinson assigns this discussion of grace to his section of "Lesser Arguments" as to why critics think Mormonism should not be classified as Christian. But relegating so vital an issue as salvation by grace to the status of a "lesser argument" is itself indicative of the Mormon confusion over the biblical doctrine of salvation.

Nevertheless, Robinson makes the following claims against the critics of Mormonism:

One sometimes hears that Latter-day Saints are not Christians because all true Christians believe in salvation by grace, while the Mormon believes in salvation by works....*this idea of salvation by works...has nothing to do with LDS doctrine*....The charge that this is what Latter-day Saints believe *badly misrepresents the LDS position.*[2]

However, it is not the critics who are engaging in distortion here. It is the Mormon church and its apologists who distort matters and equivocate. Robinson further argues, "The charge that Latter-day Saints believe in salvation by works *is simply not true.* That human beings can save themselves by their own efforts is *contrary* to the teachings of the *Book of Mormon*, which eloquently states the doctrine of salvation by grace."[3]

But Dr. Robinson is wrong. The *Book of Mormon* does not "eloquently" state the *biblical* doctrine of salvation by grace—far from it. Thus, in defending his views, the best Dr. Robinson can do is cite a few weak, if not entirely irrelevant, scriptures from the *Book of Mormon* (Mosiah 2:21,24; 5:7,8; 2 Nephi 2:3-8; 25:23; Alma 5:14,15; Ether 12:27; Moroni 10:32,33). Even the strongest of these passages (2 Nephi 2:3-8) is not considered as teaching salvation by grace through faith according to Mormon prophets, presidents, and doctrinal theologians—at least not in any orthodox Christian or biblical sense.

Thus, when Mormonism speaks of "salvation by grace" or maintains that salvation does not come by "keeping the law," it means something different from what Christians mean by these terms. As noted earlier, for Mormons "salvation by grace" is the means of general redemption or merely a physical resurrection from the dead—not true or complete Mormon salvation. Further, the Mormon argument that men are not saved by "keeping the law" only refers to *Mosaic* law. Mormons know full well that they demand that people keep all the requirements of the "Gospel law" for true salvation—requirements far more severe than the Mosaic law.

Mormons argue that the Apostle Paul condemned only the belief in keeping the *Mosaic* law as a means to salvation; he never condemned the belief in keeping the *Gospel* law as a means to salvation. In other words, when Mormons claim they do not teach salvation by works, what they mean is that they do not teach that salvation comes through *Mosaic* works—the ceremonial law as found in Leviticus, for example.[4] But other works, what Mormonism calls "Gospel" works, *are* necessary for salvation. Understanding this Mormon distinction between Gospel law and Mosaic law is crucial:

> Did not Paul say that salvation came by faith alone, without works? Yes, he most assuredly did; and he also said that the works he was talking about were the performances [ceremony] of the Mosaic Law. [5]

Theologian McConkie explains that because the Mosaic law is now abrogated, God has substituted a better law in its place—the Gospel law—and that keeping this law is essential for salvation:

> In effect Paul is saying that the law of Moses was good in its day, that God gave it for a purpose, but that now it is dead, and in place thereof God has given a higher law *to which all men must now turn for salvation*....Now, Paul philosophizes, *since he obeys* the higher gospel law, he cannot be condemned for failure to keep the lesser Mosaic standard....But even after the gospel law is imprinted in his mind, carnal desires persist; *and if they are not subdued, he is not justified.*[6]

The Mormon church must maintain this distinction so that it may be claimed that when Paul rejected "law keeping" as a way of salvation, he was referring *only* to the ceremonial law of Moses and not the moral law itself. But Mormonism is wrong. In Galatians 2 and 3 it is the *moral* law of God, not the ceremonial law, which Paul says *cannot* be a way of salvation, since "the law" requires—even demands—man to be sinlessly perfect (Galatians 3:10-12). Because no one is, or ever can be, sinlessly perfect (Romans 3:10-17), all men who approach God by moral law keeping are condemned (Romans 3:19; 4:6,15). Further, Paul never stated—anywhere—that he successfully kept the "Gospel law"; to the contrary, he said he could *not* keep it (Romans 7; Philippians 3).

Thus, the Mormon distinction between Mosaic and Gospel law is not only arbitrary, but false. The Mosaic law and Gospel law are "one" law as far as moral requirements before God are concerned. For example, Jesus' teaching on "Gospel law" in the Sermon on the Mount simply amplifies and extends the teachings of the Mosaic law. Jesus came to fulfill the law of Moses, both in His life and actions. And certainly if Christ came to fulfill the law of Moses, then His personal emphasis on moral law over ceremonial law indicates the moral nature of the law of Moses.

Jesus emphasized the true meaning of the Mosaic law. When God said, "Thou shalt not kill," it involved an attitude of the heart as well. Just as lusting after a woman was committing adultery in the heart, so hatred was murder in the heart, and whether in the heart or in the act, both violated the moral law of God (Matthew 5:20-28). This inner sense of the law was evident in the Mosaic law itself (Exodus 20:17).

Thus, when Mormonism attempts to make a distinction between Mosaic and Gospel law, it is not doing justice to the underlying moral unity of those laws. It cannot claim that when New Testament Scripture speaks of the "law of Moses" it refers primarily or only to the "lower teachings" of Moses— the "carnal commandments" of "ordinances and performances" in Leviticus, Exodus, etc.[7]

Since it is biblically true that the Mosaic law included the moral law of God, one cannot imply that if the ceremonial aspects of the Mosaic law are now ended, then the moral aspects of the Mosaic law have no authority over us. God's moral law does not change, nor the human inability to keep it.

And as we have abundantly documented, Mormons do hope to attain salvation by keeping the moral law. But the claim to be able to keep the "higher" moral law of God (the Gospel law) not only denies scriptural teaching, it also makes the atonement of Christ unnecessary, for "if righteousness comes through the Law, then Christ died needlessly" (Galatians 2:21), and "if a Law had been given which was able to impart life, then righteousness would indeed have been based on Law" (Galatians 3:21). Obviously, then, such a law was never given.

Righteousness does not come through moral law because Christ did *not* die needlessly; the law *cannot* impart eternal life because it has no *power* to do so. These facts based on biblical truth undermine the central pillar of Mormonism: that salvation comes through actually keeping the moral law of God.

In trusting their own righteousness for salvation, Mormons will never be saved, let alone be exalted as gods. Unfortunately, they will only be condemned as unforgiven and unrepentant sinners.

It is significant that, in his arguments about salvation by grace, Robinson cites only the *Book of Mormon*. He never cites *Doctrine and Covenants*, which is the Mormon scripture that most accurately reflects current Mormon beliefs and from which Mormon doctrines were originally derived. Robinson never once mentions that *Doctrine and Covenants* adamantly and repeatedly teaches salvation by works. One can only wonder why.

Further, Robinson at times betrays his own awareness that a problem exists with his definition of grace.

> Some critics may object that the Latter-day Saints do not insist that we are saved by grace alone...but *the fundamental LDS belief regarding grace and works is well within the spectrum of traditional Christianity*, with strong affinities to the Wesleyan position. While not every Christian will agree with *this specific LDS concept of grace*, the Latter-day Saints have never believed in salvation by any other means—*and especially not by individual works....The LDS scriptures are clear—we are saved by grace*.[8]

But again, what does Mormonism mean by the word *grace*? Not the Christian or biblical meaning, as we will show in a moment.

Further, to say that Mormon teaching on grace and works "is well within the spectrum of traditional Christianity" is about as gross a misrepresentation of Mormon belief, Christian belief, and historical Christian theology as can be found. Further, if Mormonism really teaches salvation by grace, how did literally every Mormon president and prophet, theologian and layman end up so confused, all of them staunchly maintaining that salvation is by works? We will document this as well.

Indeed, one of the few Mormon doctrines that has never been altered, suppressed, or simultaneously affirmed and denied is the doctrine that salvation *is* by personal merit and works of righteousness. Mormonism teaches that personal salvation is *never* a free gift secured by grace through faith alone, as the Bible teaches. Rather, it is secured by personal merit through zealous good works and impeccable law keeping. As in the theology of traditional Armstrongism and many other cults, "the Gospel" is not the idea of having one's sins forgiven through exercising faith in Christ's atonement; it is earning salvation by good works and becoming a god in the process. Thus, the biblical doctrine of salvation by grace through faith alone is one teaching the Mormon church never has tolerated, and never will tolerate.[9]

From the beginning the Mormon prophets and their gods have emphasized that such an idea is an "abomination." This is why Mormon theologians reject this doctrine so passionately—they are zealously obeying their gods as quoted in their scriptures. Let us give you a few illustrations of what Mormons really believe about salvation by grace, or justification by faith.

In his Articles of Faith, James Talmage refers to "a most pernicious doctrine—that of justification by belief alone."[10] We are further told that "the sectarian [Christian] dogma of justification by faith alone has exercised an influence for evil" and leads to "vicious extremes."[11] Theologian McConkie called it a "soul-destroying doctrine."[12] The tenth president and prophet,

Joseph Fielding Smith, emphasized that "Mankind [is] damned by [the] 'faith alone' doctrine" and "we must emphatically declare that men must obey these [Gospel] laws if they would be saved."[13]

Likewise, Mormon apostle LeGrand Richards declared:

> One erroneous teaching of many Christian churches is: By faith alone we are saved. This false doctrine...would teach man that no matter how great the sin, a confession [of faith in Christ as personal savior] would bring him complete forgiveness and salvation.[14]

And the early Mormon apostle Orson Pratt is just as definite:

> Faith alone will not save men; neither will faith and works save them, unless they are [works] of the right kind....True faith and righteous works are essential to salvation; and without both of these no man ever was or ever can be saved....There are some who believe that faith alone, unaccompanied by works, is sufficient for justification, sanctification, and salvation.... [They]...are without justification—without hope —without everlasting life, and will be damned, the same as unbelievers.[15]

## The Mormon Teaching on Salvation

### Examining the Terms

Before we continue our discussion, it is important to recall that Mormonism consistently redefines or reinterprets biblical or Christian terminology in order to make it conform to its own unbiblical standards (see p. 292). In order to fully understand what Mormons believe salvation to be, we have to know how they have redefined the following key terms: *grace, justification, the new birth, salvation, gift, repentance,* and *sanctification*. Notice how all these terms (and many others) are redefined to incorporate works salvation.

## 1. The term grace *incorporates works.*

As we noted in chapter 7, for Mormons "salvation by grace" merely refers to being resurrected from the dead. But one's place of residence in eternity is determined wholly by good works. Second, according to Mormonism, salvation by grace is merely an infusing of grace based on good works. This is similar to the Roman Catholic doctrine wherein grace itself becomes a "work," so that as men increase in personal righteousness, more and more "grace" is granted them. In other words, "grace" is secured from God only on the basis of individual merit and personal righteousness. Thus, Bruce McConkie explains how the Mormon God grants grace:

> Grace is granted to men proportionately as they conform to the standards of personal righteousness that are part of the gospel plan.[16]

Further,

> Grace, which is an outpouring of the mercy, love, and condescension of God...[is] received—not without works, not without righteousness, not without merit—but by obedience and faith![17]

This is why McConkie, emphasizing the *false* definition of grace in classical Christian belief, argues:

> Many Protestants...erroneously conclude that men are saved by grace alone without doing the works of righteousness.[18]

Thus, Mormonism teaches that grace *alone* cannot possibly save anyone. Mormons are to save themselves, "with the help of the Lord." This brings us to the next significant aspect of the Mormon concept of grace—that Christ's death, alone, did *not* forgive sin, but it did grant the possibility of salvation through good works. (See chapter 6.)

Mormonism teaches that the atonement of Christ provides men the opportunity to earn their own salvation by "trusting in the Lord" to help them attain a personal righteousness that fulfills all the requirements and laws of the Gospel:

> Complete salvation, which is full and eternal life, results from man's full endeavor to conform to the laws of life, the gospel of the Lord Jesus Christ. That is why we often say that men save themselves with the aid of the Lord.[19]

Sterling M. McMurrin is E.E. Ericksen Distinguished Professor of History at the University of Utah. In his study of Mormon theology, he shows how the Mormon definition of grace incorporates a doctrine of works:

> Mormon theology is not without a doctrine of grace, but it undertakes to conform that doctrine to the belief in merit....The orthodox position that there is no salvation except by the atonement through Jesus Christ is thoroughly affirmed. But...the meaning of the atonement is that by the grace of God through Christ it is made possible for man, who is by nature neither corrupt nor depraved, to merit his salvation by free obedience to the law.[20]

In other words, Mormonism teaches a concept of grace— but one that bears no resemblance whatever to the biblical teaching.

## 2. *The term* justification *incorporates works.*

Biblically speaking, *justification* is the act of God that declares a sinner righteous entirely apart from works and predicated only upon his/her faith in the atoning death of Christ for their sins. (See pages 153-160 for documentation on this.) But in Mormon theology the concept of justification is inextricably bound with conditions of personal merit and righteousness. According to the Mormon church, justification does *not* declare one perfectly righteous before God; it only gives one the opportunity to earn righteousness before God. Notice McConkie's reformulation: "The very atoning sacrifice itself was wrought out by the Son of God so that men might be justified, that is, so they could *do the things* which will give them eternal life in the celestial realm (*D&C*, 20:21-30, emphasis added)."[21]

What are some of those "things" necessary for salvation in the celestial heaven? Consider the following discussion of justification as provided by McConkie. Here we clearly see that Mormons have no understanding of the biblical definition of justification:

> What is lacking in the sectarian [Christian] world is a true knowledge of the law of justification. Simply stated, that law is this: "All covenants, contracts, bonds, obligations, oaths, vows, performances, connections, associations, or expectations" (*D&C*, 132:7), in which men must abide to be saved and exalted...must be entered into and performed in righteousness so that the Holy Spirit can justify the candidate for salvation in what has been done (1 Ne. 16:2; Jac. 2:13,14; Alma 41:15; *D&C*, 98; 132:1,62)....As with all other doctrines of salvation, justification is available because of the atoning sacrifice of Christ, but it becomes operative in the life of an individual only on conditions of personal righteousness.[22]

In other words, Mormon justification 1) only gives one the opportunity to earn salvation, and 2) is completed only after the individual has met all of the severe requirements of law keeping. This is why the *Doctrines of the Gospel: Student Manual* emphasizes that "justification comes [both] through faith in Jesus Christ and through individual righteousness." And it proceeds to supply a list of specific requirements, such as overcoming evil, keeping oneself unspotted from the world, and so on, that Mormons must meet in order to be "justified before God."[23]

### 3. The term new birth incorporates works.

The tenth president and prophet of the Mormon church, Joseph Fielding Smith, taught that even "the new birth is also a matter of obedience to law."[24] Smith was echoing the teachings of the *Book of Mormon* (Alma 5:14-30), which declares that to be "born again" a person has to fulfill a number of prerequisites, such as being blameless before God, having an absence of pride and envy, etc. In other words, the new birth is a spiritual *process* secured by good works, not a one-time event secured by faith in Christ. Commenting on this same passage of scripture, McConkie declares that its guidelines enable Mormons "to determine whether and to what extent they have overcome the world, which is the exact extent to which they have in fact been born again."[25]

Biblically, of course, being born again is something that happens in an instant—it is not a process. Scripture repeatedly refers to the fact that every believer has already been (past tense) born again, simply by faith in Jesus (1 Peter 1:3,23; Titus 3:5, cf. John 3:16; 5:24; 6:47).

### 4. The term salvation incorporates works.

In a discussion of the subject of salvation in his work *The Miracle of Forgiveness*, former president and prophet Spencer W. Kimball emphasizes that terms must not be misunderstood—a reference to supposedly false Christian teaching:

> Of course we need to understand terms. If by the word "salvation" is meant the mere salvation or redemption from the grave, the "grace of God" is sufficient. But if the term "salvation" means returning to the presence of God with eternal progression, eternal increase, and eventual godhood, for this one certainly must have the "grace of God," as it is generally defined, plus personal purity, overcoming of evil, and the good "works"

made so important in the exhortations of the
Savior and his prophets and apostles....Immor-
tality [resurrection] has been accomplished by the
savior's sacrifice. Eternal life [exaltation or god-
hood] hangs in the balance awaiting the works of
men.[26]

### 5. The term *gift* incorporates works.

Even the meaning of the word *gift* is redefined, at least as
far as salvation is concerned. Here we see that a gift is not
something freely given; rather, it is something that must be
earned. The apostle LeGrand Richards asserts: "Nevertheless,
to obtain these 'graces,' and the gift of 'eternal salvation,' we
must remember that this gift is [given] only to 'all them that
obey him.' "[27] Thus, as McConkie emphasizes, "One thing only
comes as a free gift to men—the fact of the atoning sacrifice.
All other gifts must be earned. That is, God's gifts are
bestowed upon those who live the law entitling them to
receive whatever is involved."[28] Notice how McConkie
employs the word *gift* to denote the idea of incorporating
works:

> What *price* must men pay for this precious gift
> [of salvation]? Not conformity to Mosaic stan-
> dards...but the price of faith, faith in the Lord
> Jesus Christ, faith that includes within itself
> enduring works of righteousness, *which faith
> cannot so much as exist unless and until* men con-
> form their lives to gospel standards.[29]

Certainly Mormonism has little concept of what a gift is.
Any dictionary definition of the word *gift* will indicate that it
is something given, not something earned. A man does not tell
his wife that he is giving her a gift of flowers on the condition
that she wash his car. A gift is a gift. Mormonism has perverted
the most important gift of all—salvation—by requiring that
men attempt the impossible feat of earning it.

## *6. The term* repentance *incorporates works.*

In Mormonism, the term *repentance* means nothing less than strict obedience to law rather than the biblical meaning of turning from one's sins. After a discussion of all the requirements and commandments that must be fulfilled until the end of one's life in order to achieve salvation, Spencer Kimball comments that many people do not understand repentance properly. "They are not 'doing the commandments,' hence they do not repent."[30] In other words, repentance equals obedience. In fact, "Repentance must involve an all-out, total surrender to the program of the Lord," which amounts to everything Mormonism says is necessary to salvation. Indeed, a "transgressor is not fully repentant who neglects his tithing, misses his meetings, breaks the Sabbath, fails in his family prayers, does not sustain the authorities of the Church, breaks the *Word of Wisdom* [church regulations], does not love the Lord nor his fellowman....God cannot forgive unless a transgressor shows a true repentance which spreads to all areas of his life....'Doing the commandments' includes the many activities required of the [Mormon] faithful."[31]

## *7. The term* sanctification *incorporates works.*

Similarly distorting the biblical concept of sanctification (meaning to be "set apart" to God), *Doctrines of the Gospel: Student Manual* teaches that to be sanctified is to be sinless:

> Members of the Church of Jesus Christ are commanded to become sanctified....*To be sanctified is to become holy and without sin*....Sanctification is attainable because of the atonement of Jesus Christ, but *only if we obey his commandments*.... Sanctification is the state of saintliness, a state attained *only by* conformity to the laws and ordinances of the gospel.[32]

But biblically, sanctification involves three aspects. First, we are (past tense) "set apart" to Christ at the moment of regeneration or saving faith. Second, we are progressively being sanctified as we grow in the grace, knowledge, and obedience of our Lord, and third, we are fully sanctified—that is, fully set apart to God and His purposes—when we become glorified at the moment of our going to be with Him. The first and third of these aspects are entirely by grace, whereas Mormonism makes all of sanctification a matter of works.

These are only a few of the Mormon reformulations of theological terms. They should be kept in mind in any discussion with individual Mormons. Now, we proceed to document, in some detail, the Mormon reliance upon good works.

### Examining the Theology

In order to show how thoroughly Mormonism teaches salvation by works, we have divided the following material into four basic sections:

1. The teaching of Mormon scriptures;
2. The teaching of Mormon presidents and prophets;
3. The teaching of Mormon theologians and church leaders; and
4. A listing of specific requirements held to be necessary to achieving Mormon salvation.

We will discuss these in turn. Since this section is deliberately lengthy for purposes of documentation, you may wish to read only those sections that are of immediate relevance at this time.

### 1. Do the Mormon scriptures teach that salvation is by works?

Even though Mormon leaders such as Dr. Robinson have claimed that the Mormon scriptures teach that salvation is by grace, the Mormon scriptures say otherwise.

The *Book of Mormon* teaches works salvation. For example:

*Alma 7:16 teaches works salvation:*

And whosoever doeth this [is water baptized], and keepeth the commandments of God from thence forth, the same...shall have eternal life.

_Mosiah 5:8,9 teaches works salvation:_

...All you that have entered into the covenant with God that ye should be obedient unto the end of your lives....Whosoever doeth this shall be found at the right hand of God.

_2 Nephi 9:23,24 teaches works salvation:_

And he [God] commandeth all men that they must repent, and be baptized in his name, having perfect faith in the Holy One of Israel, or they cannot be saved in the kingdom of God. And if they will not repent and believe in his name, and be baptized in his name, and endure to the end, they must be damned; for the Lord God, the Holy One of Israel, has spoken it.

_3 Nephi 27:14,15,17,21,22 teaches works salvation:_

[Jesus is allegedly speaking: men will] stand before me, to be judged of their works, whether they be good or whether they be evil....That they may be judged according to their works....He that endureth not unto the end, the same is he that is also hewn down and cast into the fire, from whence they can no more return, because of the justice of the father....Verily, verily, I say unto you, this is my gospel; and ye know the things that ye must do in my church; for the works which ye have seen me do that shall ye also do....Therefore, if ye do these things blessed are ye, for ye shall be lifted up at the last day.

Mormons almost universally cite these passages as evidence that salvation must come by works and *not* by grace.

For example, Jack Weyland, a member of the Rapid City, South Dakota Stake Mission presidency, refers to these last verses, noting that they present the true definition of the "gospel" of Jesus Christ. In answering the question, "When nonmembers say we're not Christians, what is the best way to respond?" he comments that Christians don't think Mormons are saved because "we don't subscribe to their notions of the doctrine of grace." Then, after discussing why the Mormon doctrine of grace incorporates works, he comments on the passages just cited:

> It is unfortunate that nonmembers do not have the *Book of Mormon's* definition of the gospel of Jesus Christ, a definition given by the Savior Himself in 3 Nephi 27. Here the Savior described what constitutes true Christianity.[33]

He then observes that for salvation "we have much work to do as followers of Jesus Christ, works that require more than just acceptance of him as the Savior and Redeemer."[34]

A Mormon believes he is saved "by grace" only after he first meets all the numerous requirements outlined for him according to the Mormon church. If he is successful in fulfilling all these requirements to the end of his life, *then* he believes he is saved by "grace."

Thus, the *Book of Mormon's* true teaching on salvation is given in 2 Nephi 25:23: "For we know that it is by grace that we are saved, *after all we can do*" (emphasis added). In Mormon theology, then, we see once again that grace does not *provide* salvation; it only makes earning it possible.

*Doctrine and Covenants* also teaches salvation by works and not by grace. For example:

*Doctrine and Covenants, 7:37 teaches salvation by works:*

> Be faithful, keep my commands and ye shall inherit the kingdom of heaven.

*Doctrine and Covenants, 18:46 teaches salvation by works:*

> If you keep not my commandments you cannot be saved in the kingdom of my father.

*Doctrine and Covenants, 130:20,21 teaches salvation by works:*

> There is a law, irrevocably decreed in heaven before the foundations of this world, upon which all blessings are predicated—and when we obtain any blessing from God, it is by obedience to that law upon which it is predicated.

*Doctrine and Covenants, 132:12 teaches salvation by works:*

> I am the Lord thy God; and I give unto you this commandment—that no man shall come unto the father but by me or by my word, which is my law, sayeth the Lord.

The above are only a few of the citations from Mormon scriptures teaching salvation by personal merit.

## 2. Do Mormon presidents and prophets teach that salvation is by works?

From Joseph Smith onward, literally every Mormon president and prophet—without exception—has strenuously maintained that salvation comes only by good works and personal merit. Below we supply examples:

*The first president and prophet of the Mormon church, Joseph Smith, taught works salvation.*

Joseph Smith was the author of the Mormon church's standard doctrinal confession known as the thirteen Articles of Faith. Point 3 teaches that men are saved "by obedience to the laws and ordinances of the gospel."[35] Elsewhere Smith wrote, "I...spoke to the people, showing them that to get salvation we must not only do some things, but *everything* which God has commanded."[36] Further, "If...all God's people were saved by keeping the commandments of God, we, if saved at all, shall be saved upon the same principle."[37]

*Brigham Young, the second president and prophet of the Mormon church, taught works salvation.*

The following citations are taken from the selection on "obedience" in the text *Discourses of Brigham Young*. The numbers after the quotations refer to *Journal of Discourses* (vol. 13, p. 21), where the original sermon (which Young himself classified as "scripture"—see p. 218) is found:

> I cannot save you. I can tell you how to save yourselves, but you must do the will of God (10:317). How shall we know what to do? By obedience to every requirement of the Gospel (8:148) ....Strict obedience to the truth will alone enable people to dwell in the presence of the Almighty (7:55). The Lord has sent forth his laws, commandments, and ordinances to the children of men, and requires them to be strictly obeyed (16:31).[38]

In this same text, citing *Journal of Discourses* 3:132 and 1:312:

> Though our interest is one as a people, yet remember, salvation is an individual work; it is every person for himself....There are those in this Church who calculate to be saved by the righteousness of others. They will miss their mark....I am the only person that can possibly save myself.[39]

Young also taught:

> Unless we believe the Gospel of Christ and obey its ordinances we have no promise of the life to come....It is a fact that all who receive eternal life and salvation will receive it on no other conditions

than believing in the Son of God and obeying the principles that he has laid down.[40]

Finally, Young taught that strict obedience even in extremely minor matters (such as making one's own clothes) was necessary in order to become a "saint."[41]

*Wilford Woodruff, the fourth president and prophet of the Mormon church, taught works salvation.*

Woodruff commented that "the labours of the saints are for their own salvation, and not to enrich the Lord."[42] Further:

> I want the brethren to understand this one thing, that our tithing, our labour, our works are not for the exaltation of the almighty, but they are for us....In paying our tithing, in obeying every law that is given to exalt us and to do us good, is all for our individual benefit...which leads to salvation and eternal life.[43]

*Joseph Fielding Smith, the tenth president and prophet of the Mormon church, taught works salvation.*

Smith emphasized that "obedience to law is the order throughout the universe."[44] Commenting on James 2:10, he stresses the *extent* of the obedience to law required for salvation:

> Therefore each who enters the kingdom must of his own free will accept all of the laws and be obedient to them, finding himself in complete accord with all. Anything short of this would cause confusion. Therefore the words of James are true. Unless a man can abide strictly in complete accord, he cannot enter there, and in the words of James, he is guilty of all. In other words, if there is one divine law that he does not keep he is barred from participating in the kingdom....So in the

celestial kingdom, we must be worthy in every point, or we fail to receive the blessing. The Kingdom of God must exist in absolute unity. Every law must be obeyed, and no member of the Church can have a place there unless he is in full accord.[45]

*Spencer W. Kimball, the twelfth president and prophet of the Mormon Church, teaches works salvation.*

In his *The Miracle of Forgiveness,* this theme is emphasized again and again. For example, chapter 15 is titled "Keeping God's Commandments Brings Forgiveness." He says,

Jesus Christ, our Redeemer and Savior, has given us our [spiritual] map—a code of laws and commandments whereby we might attain perfection and, eventually, godhood....The Church of Jesus Christ of Latter-day Saints is the sole repository of this priceless program in its fullness, which is made available to those who accept it.[46]

Thus, he teaches, "All transgressions must be cleansed, all weaknesses must be overcome, before a person can attain perfection and godhood."[47]

Kimball emphasizes that good works enable one "to pile up credits against the accumulated errors and transgressions" that one commits.[48] Characteristically, he attacks the biblical teaching of salvation by grace through faith alone:

One of the most fallacious doctrines originated by Satan and propounded by man is that man is saved alone by the grace of God; that belief in Jesus Christ alone is all that is needed for salvation....Church members are fortunate indeed to have [Mormon] scriptures brought forth in this age which clarify this and other doctrinal questions beyond all doubt.[49]

*Ezra Taft Benson, former Mormon president and prophet, teaches works salvation.*

He follows in the footsteps of his predecessors when he says,

> We accept quite literally the savior's mandate: "Be ye therefore perfect, even as your father which is in heaven is perfect."[50]

And,

> Immortality [resurrection] is a free gift to all men because of the resurrection of Jesus Christ. Eternal life [Mormon salvation] is the quality of life enjoyed by our Heavenly Father. Those who fully comply with his commandments believe the promise that they will have this quality of life.[51]

And finally,

> God, our Heavenly Father, governs his children by law. He has instituted laws for our perfection. If we obey his laws, we receive the blessings pertaining to those laws....A spiritual person obeys all the Lord's commandments.[52]

### 3. Do Mormon theologians and church leaders teach that salvation is by works?

We are aware of no Mormon theologian or church leader who teaches that salvation is by grace in the biblical sense. Even the strongest "defense" of Mormonism as teaching salvation by grace—that of Dr. Robinson cited earlier—is equivocation at best. If Dr. Robinson were really teaching salvation by grace through faith alone according to the Bible, he would certainly be excommunicated from the Mormon church. Below we cite examples of Mormon leaders who emphasize over and over that salvation occurs only by personal righteousness.

*James Talmage* is certainly one of the most respected Mormon leaders. He refers to "the absolute requirement of individual compliance with the laws and ordinances of His [Jesus'] gospel as the means by which salvation may be attained."[53]

The late *Bruce McConkie* is perhaps the leading doctrinal theologian within Mormonism. He emphasizes literally hundreds of times throughout his writings that salvation comes only by works and never by grace in a biblical sense.

For example, his three-volume *Doctrinal New Testament Commentary* contains hundreds of statements demanding works salvation, so much so that any Mormon with any real awareness of God's holiness and his own sinfulness could easily be driven to despair:

> For salvation comes by obedience to the laws upon which its receipt is predicated and in no other way....Paul is the apostle of good works, of personal righteousness, of keeping the commandments, of pressing forward with a steadfastness in Christ, of earning the right to eternal life by obedience to the laws and ordinances of the gospel.[54]

> Salvation is available because of the atonement, but it is gained through personal righteousness, as Paul proclaims again and again....Since salvation consists in having the character, perfections, and attributes of Deity, and since all things are governed and controlled by law, it is a self-evident truth that some people are nearer to gaining eternal life than are others.[55]

Notice his other comments on the Apostle Paul:

> Paul is the great expounder of the doctrine that through God's grace salvation is available to those who keep the commandments after baptism.... Paul deals with obedience; pure, diamond, unadulterated obedience; obedience to the whole law

of God; not a presumptuous, self-serving hope that salvation comes through Christ, without more on man's part than a whispered confession of belief; but obedience, obedience, obedience, obedience.[56]

McConkie goes even further: "Salvation comes by obedience to the whole law of the whole gospel....Thus, *a man may be damned for a single sin*....Obedience to the whole law is required for salvation."[57]

Predictably, like all Mormon leaders, he explicitly denounces the Christian teaching concerning salvation by grace through faith:

[The Apostle John] now announces how it is possible to know God. It is by obedience to the laws and ordinances of the gospel! And in no other way! Which is to say, among other things: There is not one scintilla of spiritual sense in the sectarian [Christian] supposition that salvation is gained simply by saying: "I accept Jesus as my personal savior." Since the very fact of knowing God, in the ultimate and full sense [exaltation or becoming God], consists of thinking what he thinks, saying what he says, doing what he does, and of being like him, thus having exaltation or godhood—it follows that saved souls must advance and progress until they acquire his character, perfections, and attributes, until they gain his eternal power, until they themselves become gods.*[58]

Finally, the *Doctrines of the Gospel: Student Manual*, which contains quotations from numerous Mormon prophets and presidents, church theologians and leaders, emphasizes repeatedly in chapter 17, "Obedience, a Law of Heaven," that salvation comes only through personal merit. Obedience is defined as "complete subjection to God and his commands."[59]

---

* Similar statements to those above are found in *DNTC*, 2:41-44,212,215,220,240-260,274,282,290, etc.; 3:66,86,87,138,175-248,252,254,258-260,266,284-286; and throughout his *Mormon Doctrine*.

Thus, "God demands strict obedience to his requirements."[60] Further, "Christ, himself, set the perfect example of obedience for his brethren." And, "To get salvation we must not only do some things, but everything which God has commanded."[61]

In *The Teachings of Spencer W. Kimball*, we are told:

> Man can transform himself and he must. Man has in himself the seeds of godhood, which can germinate and grow and develop. As the acorn becomes the oak, the mortal man becomes a god. It is within his power to lift himself by his very bootstraps from the plane on which he finds himself to the plane on which he should be. It may be a long, hard lift with many obstacles, but it is a real possibility.[62]

All of this is proof that the Mormon church teaches salvation by works. When it claims that it teaches salvation by grace, it is not only deceiving the public as to the biblical meaning of grace, but it is deceiving them concerning its own teachings as well. Having documented that the Mormon church teaches salvation wholly by works, we now proceed to discuss some of the important details of how that salvation is achieved.

Mormons believe that in order for them to achieve full salvation they must literally become perfect—absolutely sinless. However, they do not believe such a condition is attainable in this life. Rather, it must be attained at some point in the *next* life. Thus, when Mormons claim that they must eventually attain such a state of absolute perfection and 100 percent compliance with every iota of God's laws and requirements, they mean to fulfill such a condition quite literally. And to do so, of course, will take longer than this life allows.

Gerald N. Lund, zone administrator for the Church Educational System, comments:

> At some point, then, if we are to become like God, we must become perfect, without any flaw

or error. But must we achieve that state in this life? Here the prophets have spoken plainly.[63]

He then proceeds to quote Joseph Smith who teaches that absolute perfection "is not all to be comprehended in this world; it will be a great work to earn [more of] our salvation and exaltation even beyond the grave."[64] He also cites the tenth president and prophet, Joseph Fielding Smith:

> Salvation does not come all at once....It will take us ages to accomplish this end, for there will be greater progress beyond the grave....I believe the Lord meant just what he said: That we should be perfect, as our Father in heaven is perfect. That will not come all at once....But here we lay the foundation.[65]

Thus, Lund concludes that "[absolute literal] perfection is our eternal goal: It is what we must eventually achieve."[66]

But what are the means by which a Mormon begins to achieve his or her perfection *now*, here on earth? This takes us to our fourth point concerning the Mormon doctrine of salvation—those specific laws and requirements that are essential to begin the process of salvation.

## 4. What specific requirements are necessary to achieve salvation?

In addition to general works of righteousness that are required of Mormons in order to attain salvation, a host of other requirements are also necessary, many of which we mention below.

In fact, Mormonism goes so far as to teach that a person is actually not saved until he has perfected himself to the level of Jesus Christ! (Compare this with 1 John 5:11-13.)

> If we can find a saved being, we may ascertain without much difficulty what all others must be in order to be saved....There will be no dispute among those who believe the Bible, that it is

Christ: all will agree in this, that he is the proto-
type or standard of salvation; or in other words,
that he is a saved being....If he were anything different from what he is, he would not be saved; for
his salvation depends on his being precisely what
he is and nothing else....And no being can possess
it [salvation] but himself or one like him.[67]

The purpose of this section is not only to show the extent
of Mormonism's reliance on personal merit and effort, but also
to underscore the practical impossibility of any person ever
accomplishing all that the Mormon church claims is required
for salvation. Mormons may think they can meet the requirements listed below, but most people would consider this a
self-deception.

### Personal Revelation

Saving knowledge of God comes only by revelation from the Holy Ghost as a consequence of
obedience to the laws and ordinances of the
gospel.[68]

### Physical Labor

Temporal work is *essential to salvation*. Man
cannot be saved in idleness. It is not enough
simply to believe the great spiritual realities. We
could do that as spirits in preexistence....Work is
a commandment of the Lord.[69]

### Obedience to Leaders

Mormon people are intimidated into obeying church
leaders through fear of losing their eternal salvation:

To gain salvation the saints *must be subject* to
God's ministers. The doctrines and ordinances of
the gospel cannot be separated from those appointed to teach Christ's gospel and perform his
ordinances....It is an eternal, unvarying verity that

*salvation seekers must submit* to the direction of those whom God has placed over them in this kingdom; otherwise they *cannot be saved*....Thus when the President of the Church, the stake president, the bishop, or any duly commissioned church officer counsels those over whom he presides to follow a certain course, the Church members involved must do so *at the peril of losing their salvation.* Paul's pronouncement, as restored to its original state by the Inspired Version [a new Bible written by Joseph Smith], so specifies.[70]

## Overcoming Temptation

Overcoming temptation is an essential part of working out one's salvation.[71] If Mormons "fall into the practices and abominations of the sectarians; if they use tea, coffee, tobacco or liquor; if they fail to pay an honest tithing; if they find fault with the Lord's anointed; if they play cards; if they do anything contrary to the standards of personal righteousness required by the gospel [Mormonism]—then to that extent they are in personal apostasy...."[72]

## Intelligence or Knowledge

Because Mormons believe that "the glory of God is intelligence" (*D&C*, 93:36), they stress this subject and seek after intelligence as they work to become gods. Specifically, Mormons seek after God's own intelligence: "In our pre-earth life, as now, some spirits were more intelligent than others. Abraham recorded: '...I am the Lord thy God, I am more intelligent than they all'" (Abraham 3:19).[73] Therefore, the more "intelligence" we achieve now the fuller our salvation will be later. According to *Doctrine and Covenants*:

Whatever the principle of intelligence we attain unto in this life, it will rise with us in the resurrection. And, if a person gains more knowledge and intelligence in this life through his diligence and

obedience than another, he will have so much the
advantage in the world to come.[74]

Thus, contrary to what is said in 1 Corinthians 1:26-30, it is
being "intelligent in this life" that helps save a person. Joseph
Smith stated:

The first principles of man are self-existent
with God. God himself, finding he was in the
midst of spirits and glory, *because* he was more
intelligent, saw proper to institute laws whereby
the rest could have a privilege to advance like
himself. The relationship we have with God places
us in a situation to advance in knowledge. He has
power to institute laws to instruct the weaker
intelligences, that they may be exalted with himself, so that they might have one glory upon
another, and all that knowledge, power, glory and
intelligence, *which is requisite in order to save them in
the world of spirits....*This is good doctrine. It tastes
good....[It is] given to me by the revelation of
Jesus Christ.[75]

Mormonism is thus "gnostic" in stressing proper *knowledge* as a means of salvation:

Knowledge saves a man; and in the world of
spirits no man can be exalted but by knowledge.[76]

The principle of knowledge is the principle of
salvation.[77]

It is impossible for a man to be saved in ignorance.[78]

It [salvation] cannot be obtained without some
effort. It cannot be obtained without knowledge
of the things of God....[i.e.,] the saving principles
and ordinances by which salvation comes! [Still]
knowledge of them will not in itself save us! Obedience thereto will![79]

## Perseverance

He that would be saved must not only be sincere, but embrace the true gospel, be baptized into the true church, and continue a faithful member of the same unto the end. This is the *only way to be saved* with a full salvation.[80]

## Prayer

This course is essential if men are to be saved; *there is no salvation without prayer.*[81]

## Baptism

Without being immersed in water *no man can enter* into the fullness of Celestial glory....Many have been taught to seek forgiveness by prayer, and have been told that baptism, being only an outward ordinance, would not avail anything.... These are doctrines of false teachers, and they are the wicked traditions handed down by apostate Christendom. *Baptism is a condition of forgiveness...* cursed be that man or angel who preaches another gospel, or perverts the true gospel of Christ.[82]

## Laying on of Hands

Baptism in water for the remission of sins, and the laying on of hands for the gift of the Holy Ghost, constitute the birth of the water and of the Spirit. *This is essential to salvation....*The law governing this matter has been unalterably fixed.[83]

## Marriage/Clothing of Spirit Children

Remember that an early rationalization for Mormon teaching on polygamy was the necessity of "clothing" spirit children with physical bodies. Although most Mormons today reject polygamy (for this life), the making of bodies is still a high priority; in fact, it is essential to salvation.

No man can be saved and exalted in the kingdom of God without the woman, and no woman can reach the perfection and exaltation in the kingdom of God alone.[84]

Birth Control Is Wickedness....*It is the duty of every righteous man and woman to prepare tabernacles for all the spirits they can....*Moreover, *may we not lose our own salvation if we violate this divine law?...Those who willfully and maliciously design to break this important commandment shall be damned.*[85]

## Church Membership

Salvation is in the church, and of the church, and is obtained *only through the church.*[86]

## Tithing

The law of tithing is an eternal law...that God has instituted for the benefit of the human family, for their *salvation and exaltation.*[87]

## Temple Work

Temple work involves a variety of activities including 1) sacred rites of marriage both for the living and the dead, and 2) proxy baptism to allegedly help save the souls of the dead.[88] Thus, in Mormon temples, "Sacred ordinances, [baptism] rites, and [marriage] ceremonies are performed which pertain to salvation and exaltation."[89] These temple ordinances not only claim to seal families together for eternity, but also actually involve pagan ceremonies where the living are ritually used to redeem the dead. The Mormon publication *Gospel Principles* comments, "These ordinances and covenants are *necessary for our salvation.* They must be performed in the temples of the Lord."[90]

In this section, we will briefly discuss the Mormon doctrine of proxy baptism and marriage for the dead primarily as it relates to salvation. But we will also briefly introduce the subject of temple occultism.

## Examining a Ritual

Saving the dead is a vital work for every Mormon who wishes to attain godhood. For every committed Mormon, temple work involving rituals for the dead is an absolute requirement for salvation. Most Mormons are unaware that these rituals may involve them in occult activities that God has forbidden in the Bible (Deuteronomy 18:9-12). In attempting to save the dead, Mormons not infrequently encounter supernatural revelations from the alleged human dead or other spirits plus additional occult phenomena. Mormons reject the idea that these spirits and their revelations are spiritual deceptions intended to lead them astray from biblical truth and to give the spirits more influence over their lives. But this is exactly what can happen.

Joseph Heinerman is the author of several books discussing spiritistic manifestations and contacts within Mormon temples. Among them are *Temple Manifestations, Eternal Testimonies,* and *Spirit World Manifestations: Accounts of Divine Aid in Genealogical and Temple Work and Other Assistance To Latterday Saints.* In the preface to the latter book he notes that the inhabitants of the spirit world are anxious to accommodate Mormons in their rites for the dead:

> The inhabitants of the spirit world have received special permission to visit their mortal descendants [Mormons] and assist them and impress upon their minds the primary importance of assimilating genealogical information and performing vicarious ordinance work in the temples....Spirit world manifestations and angelic appearances have played and continue to play a major role in the upbuilding of God's kingdom [Mormonism] in these latter days.[91]

For this reason, the Mormon church requires such activity be undertaken for any Mormon who desires to please God and become a god himself. In other words, all those who desire salvation in Mormonism are required to engage in these pagan, occult practices. In *Improvement Era*, Joseph Smith is recorded as declaring, "The greatest responsibility in this world that God has laid upon us is to seek after our dead."[92] In *Times and Seasons*, Smith emphasized, "Those Saints who neglect it [baptism for the dead], in behalf of their deceased relatives, do so at the peril of their own salvation."[93] Joseph Heinerman cites both of these statements and then comments, "Work for the dead is an important determining factor in the Latter-day Saints' attempt to attain their ultimate salvation and exaltation [godhood] in the Kingdom of God."[94]

Mormons hold that their proxy baptisms for the dead are proof that they are the one true church: they do believe they are saving those who have already died. Incredibly, some Mormons allegedly teach that "through baptism for the dead [rites] the Mormons have saved more souls than Christ did when he died on the cross"![95]

Even though the Bible explicitly denies that men can perform any action on behalf of another person's salvation, or that salvation is possible after death, Mormons take this role as the "saviors" of the dead. This conviction is what accounts for one of the world's largest genealogical archives being found within the confines of the Mormon church.

But this conviction is in direct conflict with the Bible's warning that "no man can by any means redeem his brother, or give to God a ransom for him—for the redemption of his soul is costly, and he should cease trying forever" (Psalm 49:7,8). Further, the Bible also warns that salvation is not possible after death, because "it is appointed for men to die once, and after this comes judgment" (Hebrews 9:27).

But Joseph Smith and Mormonism reject these biblical teachings. Smith said of the biblical doctrine that salvation must happen in this life, "Such an idea is worse than atheism."[96] And as we have seen, he warned Mormons that failure to save their dead could mean loss of their own salvation.

So when Mormons speak of themselves as being the "saviors of men," it is specifically in regard to their saving the dead. In *The Way to Perfection*, sixth president and prophet, Joseph F. Smith, emphasized the importance of the individual Mormon becoming a savior to other men: "But greater than all this, so far as our individual responsibilities are concerned, the greatest is to become saviors, in our lesser degree which is assigned us, for the dead who have died without a knowledge of the [Mormon] gospel."[97] This concept is explained in greater detail by the tenth president and prophet, Joseph Fielding Smith, in his *Doctrines of Salvation*. Because water baptism is required for salvation, which is physically impossible for the dead, there must be a live stand-in:

> If a man cannot enter the kingdom of God without baptism, then the dead must be baptized. But how can they be baptized in water for the remission of their sins [when they are dead]?... The only way it can be done is vicariously, someone who is living acting as a substitute for the dead.
>
> When we go into the temple and act for somebody else, we are...doing for him just what he would have to do if he were [still] in mortal life. Thus, *we bring to pass his salvation*....By this means we may help to save those who have gone before and in our limited way become saviors to many people....There is no work equal to that in the temple for the dead in teaching a man to love his neighbor as himself. Jesus so loved the world that he was willing to offer himself as a sacrifice for sin that the world might be saved. We also have the privilege, in a small degree....Will not we have to answer for the blood of our dead, if we neglect these ordinances in their behalf?...If we willfully neglect the salvation of our dead, then also *we shall stand rejected of the Lord*, because we have rejected our dead (emphasis added).[98]

Thus, Joseph Fielding Smith taught that after seeking one's own salvation, "The Lord says that our greatest *individual responsibility* is to seek after our dead."[99] Why? Because Mormonism implies that its role in saving the dead is in certain respects almost as important as that of Christ's role in salvation on the cross. Mormons are saviors, in one sense, just as Christ is—by their sacrificial action they actually help forgive the sins of men in the afterlife and thus save them. Again, Joseph Fielding Smith emphasizes the importance of this work:

> The reason for this [proxy baptism] is that all the dead must be redeemed from their sins through obedience to the gospel just as the living are. It is required for us to perform this labor in their behalf....Therefore our salvation and progression depends on the salvation of our worthy dead with whom we must be joined in family ties. This can only be accomplished in our temples. The Prophet [Joseph Smith] further declared that the doctrine of salvation for the dead is the "most glorious of all subjects belonging to the everlasting gospel." The reasons for this are the great magnitude of the labor, and the fact that we have the privilege of officiating for the dead and assisting in giving to them the privileges that we also enjoy, through our obedience to the gospel....Do we Latter-day Saints fully realize the importance of the mighty responsibility placed on us in relation to the salvation of the world?[100]

In other words, if, comparatively speaking, only a few people (Mormons) have been saved historically by the death of Christ on the cross—and a much larger number of people are able to be saved by Mormonism's rites for the dead—then, in some sense, Mormonism plays a *larger* role in the salvation of the world than even Christ Himself! Mormons may or may not accept this conclusion, but it is the logical result of their doctrine.

The *Doctrines of the Gospel: Student Manual* also emphasizes the absolute necessity of engaging in close contact with the dead in order to achieve salvation. It explains that God Himself has commanded that "vicarious baptisms" be performed to enable spirits in the spirit world to receive the gospel and enter God's kingdom.[101] It further states that a spirit claiming it was the prophet Elijah appeared to Joseph Smith in the Kirtland Temple, restoring the power for men to influence the destiny of the dead.[102] Thus, "Latter-day Israel [Mormons] cannot be made perfect without doing the ordinance work for their dead, nor can the dead be made perfect without this work having been done for them."[103] These ordinances are said to "provide the dead with the opportunity to receive full salvation" or godhood. In other words, "It is through the temple that we will be able to reach our dead and not otherwise. To pray for the dead may not be of any real assistance to them. To actually help them, we must do a work for them."[104]

Mormons are further told that it is not sufficient for husband and wife to be sealed in the temple in order to guarantee that they become gods—"they must also be eternally linked with their progenitors [dead ancestors] and see that the work [proxy temple marriage] is done for those ancestors."[105] To cite Joseph Smith's *History of the Church*, "It is not only necessary that you should be baptized for your dead, but you will have to go through all the ordinances [proxy temple marriage] for them, the same as you have gone through to save yourselves."[106] Joseph Fielding Smith, in *Doctrines of Salvation*, is quoted as saying that "none is exempt from this great obligation. It is required of the apostle as well as the humblest elder....[Nothing] will...entitle one to disregard the salvation of one's dead."[107] Finally, we are told the spirits themselves are anxiously awaiting Mormon activity on their behalf. Former president and prophet Spencer W. Kimball stated, "We know that the spirit world is filled with the spirits of men who are waiting for you and me to get busy."[108]

Mormons must particularly attend to their own family history as far back as it can be traced. However, because God is no respecter of persons, they are also required to help save non-Mormons. Thus, they teach that every spirit who has not heard the gospel in this life will hear it in the next life and have the opportunity to have his or her sins forgiven through proxy baptism.[109]

Unfortunately, as we documented elsewhere in a section on Mormonism and the occult, this teaching is an open door to spiritism, especially in light of the Mormon emphasis placed upon ties to family members after death. All people are naturally close to their families, and both Mormonism and the spirit world use this fact to their advantage (see Ankerberg and Weldon, *Behind the Mask of Mormonism*, pp. 229-260).

Here we have one more tie to ancient paganism within Mormonism. Although not involving literal ancestor worship, the extreme emphasis on the dead causes an acute awareness among Mormons of their importance to their own deceased. As in pagan cultures, in Mormonism dead ancestors are dependent upon the living for advancement in the next life. Therefore, the living must serve the needs of the dead. The Tanners' comments are relevant:

> Because of this emphasis on work for the dead, one Mormon has compared the church to the ancient Egyptians. The Egyptians, of course, spent a fantastic amount of time and money building pyramids and doing other work for their dead. The *Book of Mormon* says that the false churches "rob the poor because of their fine sanctuaries" (2 Nephi 28:13), yet the Mormon Church is spending millions of dollars building beautiful temples.... The Mormon leaders are planning to build temples in a number of other countries in the near future. Most of the "endowments" performed in Mormon temples are for the dead; therefore, when we add the millions of dollars spent for temples and their upkeep to the millions spent on genealogical research, we find that the Mormons are similar to the ancient Egyptians in their attitudes toward the dead. The obsession with the dead approaches very close to ancestral worship.[110]

# The Biblical Teaching on Salvation

## Salvation Is by Faith Alone

What the Bible teaches about salvation is completely opposed to Mormon doctrine. The Bible clearly reveals that salvation does not come through personal righteousness or personal merit and good works, but only through the grace of God and the individual's faith in Christ's finished work on the cross.[111] Consider just a few Scriptures from Jesus and the New Testament. Each one teaches that salvation comes by faith—not works (emphases added).

> I tell you *the truth*, whoever hears my word and believes him who sent me *has eternal life* and *will not be condemned*; he *has crossed over* from death to life (John 5:24 NIV).

> Truly, truly, I say to you, he who believes *has eternal life* (John 6:47).

> Jesus answered and said to them, "*This* is the work of God, that you *believe* in Him whom He has sent" (John 6:29).

> Of Him all the prophets bear witness that through His name every one *who believes* in Him has received forgiveness of sins (Acts 10:43).

> For we maintain that a man is justified *by faith* apart from works of the Law (Romans 3:28).

> Just as David also speaks of the blessing upon the man to whom God reckons righteousness *apart from works*... (Romans 4:6).

> For Christ is the end of the law for righteousness to everyone who *believes* (Romans 10:4).

> But if it is by grace, it is *no longer on the basis of works*, otherwise grace *is no longer grace* (Romans 11:6).

> For by grace you have been saved through faith; and that not of yourselves, it is *the gift of God*; not as a result *of works*, that *no one* should boast (Ephesians 2:8,9).

I do not nullify the grace of God; for if righteousness comes through the Law, then Christ *died needlessly* (Galatians 2:21).

Now that *no one* is justified *by the Law* before God is evident; for, the righteous man shall live by faith. However, the Law is not of faith; on the contrary, "He who practices them shall live by them." Christ redeemed us from *the curse of the Law*, having become a curse for us—for it is written, "Cursed is everyone who hangs on a tree" (Galatians 3:11-13).

He saved us, *not on the basis of deeds which we have done in righteousness*, but *according to His mercy*, by the washing of regeneration and renewing by the Holy Spirit (Titus 3:5).

Before his conversion, the attitude of the Apostle Paul was like that of many religious people—in particular, many Mormons. He accepted the idea that God's way of salvation was through his own ability to keep the law—in this case, the law of Moses. In fact, in Philippians 3 he says that if *anyone* had a right to "confidence in the flesh," he did (verse 3), and that "as to the righteousness which is in the law" he was "found blameless" (verse 6). In Mormon theology, this would certainly earn him his exaltation.

But what was Paul's response to his own zealousness for salvation by good works and personal merit? After his salvation, how did he view his own personal righteousness? Compared to knowing Christ personally, he declares that it was all "rubbish":

> More than that, I count all things to be loss in view of the surpassing value of knowing Christ Jesus my Lord, for whom I have suffered the loss of all things, and count them but rubbish in order that I may gain Christ, and may be found in Him, *not having a righteousness of my own derived from the Law*, but that which is through faith in Christ, *the righteousness which comes from God on the basis of faith* (Philippians 3:8,9, emphasis added).

Paul puts "no confidence in the flesh" (verse 3) because he has a new understanding of God's holiness. God Himself calls even the best of our righteousness "filthy rags" (Isaiah 64:6 NIV; cf. Proverbs 16:5). Thus, Paul declares that whatever he thought was gain for him, for example, blamelessness as to the law, was but "loss" and "rubbish" compared to knowing Christ personally. In other words, all his good works and obedience to the law were *nothing* compared to his experience of salvation by faith in Christ alone (verses 7-9).

This is what Mormons need to find: the same salvation that Paul did, "for if a law had been given that could impart life, then righteousness would certainly have come by the law" (Galatians 3:21 NIV).

### The Biblical Doctrine of Justification by Faith

The doctrine of justification by faith is arguably the single most important doctrine in the Bible. Justification *is the act of God whereby He forgives the sins of believers and declares them righteous by imputing the obedience and righteousness of Christ to them through faith* (see Luke 18:9-14). Justification is without question a doctrine that is rejected and opposed by all cults and indeed all religions outside of Christianity. In his book *Know Your Christian Life: A Theological Introduction*, theologian Sinclair Ferguson discusses its importance, not only for the church but also for the Christian:

> Martin Luther, whose grasp of the gospel was better than most, once said that the doctrine of justification was the article by which the Church stands or falls. "This article," he said, "is the head and cornerstone of the Church, which alone begets, nourishes, builds, preserves and protects the Church; without it Church of God cannot subsist one hour." Luther was right. Although for our understanding of the general shape and direction of the Christian life we have suggested the doctrine of regeneration is important, the doctrine of justification is central. Not only is it the article

of the standing or falling Church, but also of the standing or falling Christian. Probably more trouble is caused in the Christian life by an inadequate or mistaken view of this doctrine than any other. When the child of God loses his sense of peace with God, finds his concern for others dried up, or generally finds his sense of the sheer goodness and grace of God diminished, it is from this fountain that he has ceased to drink. Conversely, if we can gain a solid grounding here, we have the foundation for a life of peace and joy.[112]

He then explains why this doctrine is difficult for some to accept:

The practical importance of this cannot be exaggerated. The glory of the gospel is that God has declared Christians to be rightly related to him in spite of their sin. But our greatest temptation and mistake is to try to smuggle character into his work of grace. How easily we fall into the trap of assuming that we only remain justified so long as there are grounds in our character for that justification. But Paul's teaching is that nothing we do ever contributes to our justification. So powerful was his emphasis on this that men accused him of teaching that it did not matter how they lived if God justified them. If God justifies us as we are, what is the point of holiness? There is still a sense in which this is a test of whether we offer the world the grace of God in the Gospel. Does it make men say: "You are offering grace that is so free it doesn't make any difference how you live"? This was precisely the objection the Pharisees had to Jesus' teaching![113]

Here are the characteristics that distinguish justification:

### What justification is not:

1. It is not a *reward* for anything good we have done.

2. It is not something in which we cooperate with God (it is not sanctification—i.e., growth in personal holiness).

3. It is not infused righteousness that results in good works which become the basis of justification (the Mormon and Catholic concept of justification).

4. It is not accomplished apart from the satisfaction of God's justice; i.e., it is not unjust.

5. It is not subject to degrees—one cannot be more or less justified; one can only be fully justified or fully unjustified.

## What justification is:

1. Justification is an undeserved free gift of God's mercy (Romans 3:24; Titus 3:7).

2. Justification is entirely accomplished by *God, once for all.* (It is not a process like personal sanctification, but knowledge of it does help produce sanctification.)

One of the leading theologians of our time, J.I. Packer, stated:

> This justification, though individually located at the point of time at which a man believes (Rom. 4:3; 5:1), is an eschatological once-for-all divine act, the final judgment brought into the present. The justifying sentence, once passed, is irrevocable. "The Wrath" (Rom. 5:9) will not touch the justified. Those accepted now are secure forever. Inquisition before Christ's judgment seat (Rom. 14:10-12; 2 Cor. 5:10) may deprive them of certain rewards (1 Cor. 3:15) but never of their justified status. Christ will not call into question God's justifying verdict, only declare, endorse and implement it.[114]

In other words, if God the Father *justified* us at the point of belief, is it possible the Son would ever repudiate the Father's legal declaration?

3. Justification involves an *imputed* righteousness entirely apart from works: the righteousness of God Himself has been given to the believer. It has nothing to do with a person's own righteousness (Romans 4:5,6,17-25).

It is not only that God overlooks our sin and guilt, but also that full and entire holiness is credited to our account. Bruce Milne describes the transaction this way:

> Our justification is not simply a matter of God's overlooking our guilt; our need can be met only if righteousness, full and entire holiness of character, is credited to us. This is the amazing gift of grace. Christ's law-keeping and perfect righteousness are made ours by faith in Him (1 Cor. 1:30; Phil. 3:9). It is not simply that our abysmal failure in life's moral examination is overlooked; we pass with 100%, First Class Honours! Well may Athanasius speak of "the amazing exchange" whereby, as Calvin puts it, "the Son of God though spotlessly pure took upon Himself the ignominy and shame of our sin and in return clothes us with His purity."[115]

Righteousness is imputed because the believer actually is united to Christ. In other words, because the believer is "in Christ," the righteousness of Christ is imputed to him. Justification is the subsequent legal recognition of that fact. We are declared (past tense) righteous. We *now* have perfect righteousness before God (not personally, but legally).

> By His doing you are in Christ Jesus, who became to us wisdom from God, and righteousness and sanctification, and redemption (1 Corinthians 1:30).

> He made Him who knew no sin to be sin on our behalf, that we might become the righteousness of God in Him (2 Corinthians 5:21).

In his book *God's Words: Studies of Key Bible Themes*, J.I. Packer discusses the meaning of justification and contrasts it with the Catholic and Mormon view:

> To "justify" in the Bible means to "declare righteous": to declare, that is, of a man on trial, that he is not liable to any penalty, but is entitled to all the privileges due to those who have kept the law....The Church of Rome has always maintained that God's act of justifying is primarily, if not wholly, one of making righteous, by inner spiritual renewal, but there is no biblical or linguistic ground for this view, though it goes back at least as far as Augustine. Paul's synonyms for "justify" are "reckon (impute) righteousness," "forgive (more correctly, remit) sins," "not reckon sin" (see Rom. 4:5-8)—all phrases which express the idea, not of inner transformation, but of conferring a legal status and cancelling a legal liability. Justification is a judgment passed on man, not a work wrought within man; God's gift of a status and a relationship to himself, not of a new heart. Certainly, God does regenerate those whom he justifies, but the two things are not the same.[116]

Thus, as *Baker's Dictionary of Theology* points out, every believer in Christ is now treated by God as if they are righteous (on the basis of their imputed righteousness), not as if they are sinners:

> "The righteousness of God" [i.e., righteousness from God—see Philippians 3:9] is bestowed on them as a free gift (Romans 1:17; 3:21 ff.; 5:17; cf. 9:30; 10:3-10): that is to say, they receive the right to be treated and the promise that they shall be treated, no longer as sinners, but as righteous, by the divine Judge. Thus they become "the righteousness of God" in and through Him who "knew no sin" personally but was representatively

"made sin" (treated as a sinner, and punished) in their stead (2 Corinthians 5:21). This is the thought expressed in classical Protestant theology by the phrase "the imputation of Christ's righteousness," namely, that believers are righteous (Romans 5:19) and have righteousness (Philippians 3:9) before God for no other reason than that Christ their Head was righteous before God, and they are one with Him, sharers of His status and acceptance. God justifies them by passing on them, for Christ's sake, the verdict which Christ's obedience merited. God declares them to be righteous, because He reckons them to be righteous; and He reckons righteousness to them, not because He accounts them to have kept His law personally (which would be a false judgment), but because He accounts them to be united to the one who kept it representatively (and that is a true judgment). For Paul, union with Christ is not fantasy, but fact—the basic fact indeed in Christianity; and the doctrine of imputed righteousness is simply Paul's exposition of the forensic aspect of it (see Romans 5:12ff.).[117]

4. Justification is accomplished in harmony with God's justice. It displays His holiness; it does not deny it. The only way for the sinner's justification to be truly just in God's eyes is for two requirements to be absolutely satisfied. The first is that every requirement of the law must be satisfied. The second is that the infinitely holy character of God must be satisfied. J.I. Packer comments:

The only way in which justification can be just is for the law to be satisfied so far as the justified are concerned. But the law makes a double demand on sinners: it requires both their full obedience to its precepts, as God's creatures, and their full endurance of its penalty, as transgressors. How could they conceivably meet this double demand? The answer is that it has been met already by the Lord Jesus Christ, acting in their name. The eternal Son of God was "born under the law" (Galatians 4:4) in order that he might yield double submission to the law in his people's stead. Both aspects of his submission are indicated in Paul's words: "he...became *obedient—unto* death" (Philippians 2:8). His life of righteousness culminated in his dying the death of unrighteousness according to the will of God: he bore the penal curse of the law in man's place (Galatians 3:13) to make propitiation for man's sins (Romans 3:25).

And thus, "through one act of righteousness"—the life and death of the sinless Christ—"there resulted justification of life to all men" (Romans 5:18).[118]

He concludes:

Paul's thesis is that God justifies sinners on a just ground, namely, that the claims of God's law upon them have been fully satisfied. The law has not been altered, or suspended, or flouted for their justification, but fulfilled—by Jesus Christ, acting in their name. By perfectly serving God, Christ perfectly kept the law (cf. Matthew 3:15). His obedience culminated in death (Philippians 2:8); he bore the penalty of the law in men's place (Galatians 3:13), to make propitiation for their sins (Romans 3:25). On the grounds of Christ's obedience, God does not impute sin, but imputes righteousness, to sinners who believe (Romans 4:2-8; 5:19).[119]

This is exactly what Scripture teaches—that God can be both just and the justifier of those who place their faith in Jesus:

For all have sinned and fall short of the glory of God, being justified as a gift by His grace through the redemption which is in Christ Jesus; whom God displayed publicly as a propitiation in His blood through faith. This was to demonstrate His righteousness, because in the forbearance of God He passed over the sins previously committed; for the demonstration, I say, of His righteousness at the present time, that He might be just and the justifier of the one who has faith in Jesus (Romans 3:23-26).

When the Mormon church rejects the biblical doctrine of justification through faith alone, it rejects the heart and soul of the Christian doctrine of salvation. Sadly, it insulates its own members from the glory of the Gospel and the eternal life God has so freely made available.

# Section V

# What Do the Mormons Believe About Divine Revelation?

# Chapter 9

# Mormons and the
# *Book of Mormon*

~

Mormons have always stressed that their scriptures can withstand any and all critical scrutiny. Apostle Orson Pratt even boasted that Mormons "have *more than one thousand times* the amount of evidence to demonstrate and forever establish the Divine Authority of the *Book of Mormon* than in favor of the Bible!"[1] And, "If this book be of God, it must have sufficient evidence accompanying it to convince the minds of all reasonable persons that it is a Divine revelation."[2] Further, "We defy this whole generation to bring up any testimony to condemn the truth of this book."[3] Dr. Hugh Nibley is a prominent Brigham Young University professor; some Mormons consider him one of the greatest scholars in the church. He declares, "The *Book of Mormon* can and should be tested. It invites criticism."[4] In similar fashion, the tenth Mormon president and prophet, Joseph Fielding Smith, argued, "No one can read the book with a prayerful heart and not receive the testimony that it is true. Its evidence internally and externally is overwhelming."[5]

Unfortunately, the evidence is overwhelmingly negative. From almost any angle of study, the *Book of Mormon* fails to stand up to critical examination. Indeed, this is the principal reason that Mormon leaders are increasingly claiming that the *Book of Mormon* really *can't* be proven true and that, as for Mormonism itself, one must rely upon subjective experience in prayer in order to "confirm" its alleged divine origin. This is why John W. Welch, Professor of Law and president of the Foundation for Ancient Research and Mormon Studies at Brigham Young University, quotes Mormon historian B.H. Roberts as stating, "This [power of the Holy Ghost to allegedly confirm the divine origin of the *Book of Mormon*] must ever be the chief source of evidence for the truth of the *Book of Mormon*. All other evidence is secondary to this, the primary and infallible [evidence]....[This] will ever be the chief reliance of those who accept the *Book of Mormon*, and expect to see its acceptance extended throughout the world."[6]

Former president and prophet of the church Ezra Taft Benson teaches,

> It never has been the case, nor is it so now, that the studies of the learned will prove the *Book of Mormon* true or false....God has built his own proof system of the *Book of Mormon* as found in Moroni, chapter 10, and in the testimonies of the Three and the Eight Witnesses and in various sections of *Doctrine and Covenants*. We each need to get our own testimony of the *Book of Mormon* through the Holy Ghost.[7]

Despite Benson's claim that the "studies of the learned" will never prove the *Book of Mormon* false, we suggest this is a *fait accompli*—something already done and not reversible. Below we discuss some of the facts associated with the *Book of Mormon* which disqualify it for any serious consideration as a revelation from God. These problems are in addition to the fact that we have already seen that the *Book of Mormon* contains anti-biblical teachings and could, therefore, not possibly have been inspired by the God of the Bible.

Because the *Book of Mormon* claims it is a *translation* of ancient historical records, we will emphasize evidence that collectively proves it is really only a nineteenth-century production. This not only reveals that the _Book of Mormon_ itself is a forgery—and therefore unworthy of any thinking person's trust—it also casts critical doubt upon Joseph Smith's alleged ability to "divinely translate" the other Mormon scriptures known as the _Book of Abraham_ and _Book of Moses_, both found in the _Pearl of Great Price_.

The importance of this issue cannot be overestimated. Joseph Smith's claim to be able to divinely translate ancient "scripture" is crucial to the Mormon emphasis that it is a divine revelation. If Smith was deceived on this point and it can be proven that his "translations" were either completely false or wrong on other grounds, Mormonism cannot possibly be what it claims to be.

The following material on the _Book of Mormon_ (Sections A-H) will reveal why we believe the _Book of Mormon_ was not a revelation from God. We have divided our eight sections (A-H) under two main headings, both of which suggest the essential _unreliability_ of the _Book of Mormon_:

**Division I:** Evidence that the _Book of Mormon_ is a nineteenth-century production (not a translation of ancient records), and therefore unreliable because it is a _forgery_.

A. The _Book of Mormon_'s psychic method of production, indicating it is an occult text of the nineteenth century, not a divine translation of ancient records.

B. The _Book of Mormon_'s human sources and plagiarisms, further revealing it is a nineteenth-century production, not a translation of ancient writings.

C. The _Book of Mormon_'s complete absence of archaeological verification, again showing it is a product of the nineteenth century and therefore that its claim to be a translation of ancient records is false.

D. The _Book of Mormon_'s complete lack of manuscript evidence, supplying the final reason it should not be considered an ancient text.

**Division II:** Evidence that the *Book of Mormon* is mutilated both physically and (from the perspective of Mormon teaching) doctrinally, and therefore unreliable because it is *corrupted.*

E.  The *Book of Mormon*'s textual problems—including historical, grammatical, and other changes made in the text—revealing corruption and fatal problems in the methodology and accuracy of the alleged divine translation.

F.  The *Book of Mormon*'s lack of distinctive Mormon doctrines—including even *anti*-Mormon teachings—indicating it is not even a legitimate *Mormon* text.

G.  The *Book of Mormon*'s problems of language and style, revealing additional evidence that the book was not divinely translated as claimed.

H.  The *Book of Mormon*'s "eleven witnesses" and their lack of credibility, indicating their testimony concerning its divine origin and purity cannot be trusted.

We discuss these subjects in turn.

# Division I

*Evidence that the* Book of Mormon *is a nineteenth-century production (not a translation of ancient records), and therefore unreliable because it is a forgery.*

## A. The Book of Mormon *'s psychic method of production*

We will begin our discussion by showing that the *Book of Mormon* was produced through psychic methods. Once this is established we can proceed to prove that the revelation had nothing to do with ancient history and is therefore merely a product of nineteenth-century occultism.

The Mormon church claims that Joseph Smith translated the alleged gold plates (containing the alleged historical records of the "Nephites" and "Lamanites") by the power of God using divine implements called the Urim and Thummim—which are described as two stones in silver bows fastened to a breastplate (_Book of Mormon_, introduction; testimony of Joseph Smith).

It denies the "translation" was produced by occult means through the use of a common seer stone. Nevertheless, historical documents prove that when Smith translated the alleged _Book of Mormon_ he was only engaging in his _usual_ practice of crystal gazing. For example, the testimonies of 1) Emma Smith, one of Joseph Smith's wives as well as one of the scribes; 2) William Smith, Joseph's own brother; 3) David Whitmer, one of the three key "witnesses" to the _Book of Mormon_, and many others all prove that the claims of the Mormon church are false. But if Joseph Smith was merely a common crystal gazer subject to occult fascinations, why should anyone think he was subject to divine inspiration? Further, why should anyone accept the claim of the Mormon church that his occult seer stone was really the Old Testament Urim and Thummim, when not a shred of evidence exists to substantiate such a declaration?*

In 1877, David Whitmer confessed that the alleged "Egyptian" characters on the gold plates (Nephi 1:2) and their English interpretation appeared to Joseph Smith while his face was buried inside a hat:

> I will now give you a description of the manner in which the _Book of Mormon_ was translated. Joseph Smith would put the seer stone into a hat, and put his face in the hat, drawing it closely around his face to exclude the light; and in the darkness the spiritual light would shine. A piece of something resembling parchment would appear, and on that appeared the writing. One

---

* We do not know exactly what the Old Testament Urim and Thummim were. Nevertheless, 1) they were restricted in usage to the high priest, 2) the God of the Bible "spoke" through them to reveal His will, and 3) apparently they were two separate objects, not a single stone. Thus, in each category Mormon claims are refuted. Whatever Smith used, it was not the biblical Urim and Thummim (Exodus 28:30; Numbers 27:21): 1) Joseph Smith was not an Old Testament High Priest who 2) used these implements to reveal God's will, but rather used 3) a (singular) occult seer stone to divine the "translation" of a "text" that denies God's Word (cf. Mosiah 28 preface and verse 13).

character at a time would appear, and under it was the interpretation in English. Brother Joseph would read off the English to Oliver Crowdery, who was his principal scribe, and when it was written down and repeated to Brother Joseph to see if it was correct, then it would disappear, and another character with the interpretation would appear. Thus the *Book of Mormon* was translated by the gift and power of God, and not by any power of man.[8]

(It is important to observe here that this is essentially a *mechanical dictation* theory of translation. As such, it leaves no room whatever for changes in the text. This fact will become important when we discuss the thousands of changes that have been made in the *Book of Mormon* and other Mormon scriptures.)

Whitmer further noted in an interview: "With this stone all of the present *Book of Mormon* was translated."[9]

Emma Smith, one of Joseph's wives, also revealed the occult method by which the *Book of Mormon* was produced. She confessed, "In writing for your father, I frequently wrote day after day....He sitting with his face buried in his hat, with the stone in it, and dictating hour after hour with nothing between us."[10]

It is undeniable, then, that the *Book of Mormon* was produced through a form of crystal gazing. Testimonies such as these (and others)[11] bring even some Mormons who reject the idea to conceding at least its possibility. The tenth president and prophet, Joseph Fielding Smith, opposes this view, but nevertheless confesses that "it may have been so." Apparently he had little choice but to acknowledge the possibility since he had also just confessed that the seer stone Smith owned "is now in the possession of the Church."[12]

If the *Book of Mormon* was written through occult means, this fact speaks against its divine origin. None of the Bible was ever written in such a manner. We will now prove that the supernatural information Smith allegedly received was not a translation of ancient records, but, in all likelihood, a combination of Smith's own efforts and spiritistic inspiration. Indeed, to do his "translating," Smith didn't even require the presence of the alleged gold plates:

> According to witnesses, the plates didn't even have to be present when Joseph Smith was "translating." Mormon writer Arch S. Reynolds notes that "the plates were not always before Joseph during the translation. His wife and mother state that the plates were on the table wrapped in a cloth while Joseph translated with his eyes hid in a hat with the seer stone or the Urim and Thummim. David Whitmer, Martin Harris and others state that Joseph hid the plates in the woods and other places while he was translating (_How Did Joseph Smith Translate?_ p. 21).[13]

## B. _The_ Book of Mormon _'s human sources and plagiarisms_

Mormons maintain that apart from divine revelation it would have been impossible for Joseph Smith to have written the _Book of Mormon_. They consider this one of the greatest proofs of its heavenly derivation. Unfortunately, they rarely consider other options which explain the origin of the _Book of Mormon_ far better—that it could have been, for example, a combination of Smith's natural talent and spiritistic revelation. Concerning the former, there are several possible human sources for the _Book of Mormon_ that lend doubt to Smith's claims.

Remember that the Mormon church believes that the _Book of Mormon_ is simply a divinely _translated_ account of ancient writings first inscribed on gold plates. These plates were supposedly written at least fifteen hundred years ago. They chronicled the history of the so-called "Nephite" and "Lamanite" peoples spanning a period from 600 B.C. through A.D. 421. In other words, they recorded an alleged history of the Nephites some fourteen to twenty-four hundred years *before* Joseph Smith's time.

Fawn Brodie was excommunicated from the Mormon church for her scholarly critical study on Joseph Smith, *No Man Knows My History: The Life of Joseph Smith.*[14] In this work, she cites persuasive evidence for the likelihood of a nineteenth-century origin of the *Book of Mormon.* Brodie explains why it is nearly impossible that the *Book of Mormon* could constitute a written record at least fifteen hundred years old and why it must therefore be considered a product of the nineteenth century.

For example, how likely is it that Jewish writers between 600 B.C. and A.D. 421 would discuss the social and religious issues common to nineteenth-century Christian America?

> Any theory of the origin of the *Book of Mormon* that spotlights the prophet [alone] and blacks out the stage on which he performed is certain to be a distortion.
>
> [For example,] In the speeches of the Nephi prophets one may find [discussions of] the religious conflicts that were splitting the churches in the 1820's. Alexander Campbell, founder of the Disciples of Christ, wrote in the first able review of the *Book of Mormon:* "This prophet Smith, through his stone spectacles, wrote on the plates of Nephi, in his *Book of Mormon,* every error and almost every truth discussed in New York for the last ten years. He decided all the great controversies— infant baptism, ordination, the trinity, regeneration, repentance, justification, the fall of man, the atonement, transubstantiation, fasting, penance, church government, religious experience, the call to the ministry, the general resurrection, eternal punishment, who may baptize, and even the question of Freemasonry, Republican government and the rights of man. But he is better skilled in the controversies in New York than in the geography

or history of Judea. He makes John baptize in the village of Bethabara and says Jesus was born in Jerusalem."

[Brodie continues] If one has the curiosity to read through the sermons in the book, one will be impressed with Joseph Smith's ability to argue with equal facility on both sides of a theological debate. Calvinism and Arminianism had equal status, depending upon which [Nephite] prophet was espousing the cause, and even universalism received a hearing....The theology of the *Book of Mormon*, like its anthropology, was only a potpourri ....Always an eclectic, Joseph never exhausted any theory he had appropriated. He seized a fragment here and another there and of the odd assortment built his history. As we have seen, he left unused the one hypothesis that might have helped to save the book from being made so grotesque by 20th-Century archaeological and anthropological research. This neglect was probably a result of his reading *View of the Hebrews*, which had scorned the theory expounding the Asiatic origin of the Indian.[15]

We discuss *View of the Hebrews* below. Nevertheless, why 1400- to 2400-year-old records would deal with nineteenth-century theological, social, and political disputes is certainly unknown. Unless, of course, they were not that old.

The following sources for the *Book of Mormon* indicate it is a nineteenth-century production, not the translation of ancient records Joseph Smith and Mormonism claim it to be.

## Source No. 1: Ethan Smith's View of the Hebrews

In his study *A Parallel, The Basis of the* Book of Mormon, Hal Hougey observes a number of striking similarities between the *Book of Mormon* and Ethan Smith's 1823 text *View of the Hebrews*, a book that was available to Joseph Smith.[16]

172 ～ What Do Mormons Really Believe?

In fact, the parallels between the *Book of Mormon* and *View of the Hebrews* were sufficient enough to prompt no less an authority than Mormon historian B.H. Roberts to make his own study of the issue. He concluded it *was* possible for Smith, alone, to have written the *Book of Mormon*. In the first fourteen chapters of his study, Roberts discussed similarities between the two books; the last six chapters considered the proposition that the *Book of Mormon* is of human rather than divine origin.[17]

Mormons respond by pointing out that similarity does not necessarily prove plagiarism, which, of course, is true. Nevertheless, it is the *extent* of similarity that is crucial. In addition to citing eighteen of Robert's twenty-six parallels, Hal Hougey adds an additional twenty-three. He then concludes: "While a few insignificant parallels between two books may prove nothing, a large number of parallels, many of them very striking in nature, are evidence which must honestly be considered."*[18]

### Source No. 2: The King James Bible

The King James Bible provides concrete evidence of *Book of Mormon* plagiarism. According to Dr. Anthony Hoekema, there are some 27,000 words taken from the King James Bible.[19] A few examples of these plagiarisms include:

1 Nephi chapters 20,21—Isaiah chapters 48,49

2 Nephi chapters 7,8—Isaiah chapters 50,51

2 Nephi chapters 12,24—Isaiah chapters 2–14

Mosiah chapter 14—Isaiah chapter 53

3 Nephi chapters 12,14—Matthew chapters 5–7

3 Nephi chapter 22—Isaiah chapter 54

3 Nephi chapters 24,25—Malachi chapters 3,4

Moroni chapter 10—1 Corinthians 12:1-11[20]

---

* To be fair, Smith himself may or may not have plagiarized from this book; because he was in all likelihood subject to spiritistic inspiration and the spirits themselves are known to plagiarize, he may simply have been the victim.

Anyone who compares these sections will see that Smith has apparently copied material from the King James Bible. If not, an inquiring Mormon might want to know how significant portions of the gold plates ended up containing perfect King James English a thousand years before King James English existed. If the _Book of Mormon_ was actually finished in A.D. 400, how could it contain such extensive citations from a book not to be written for another twelve hundred years?

How do Mormons respond to these facts? Some Mormons have happily claimed the translation was inspired in such a manner that Elizabethan English was provided for the convenience of those who read the King James Bible. But others, feeling the embarrassment more severely, have attempted to downplay the evidence. For example, in an inexplicable gaffe, Mormon historian B.H. Roberts claimed there were only "two or three" incidents of New Testament passages that are quoted in the _Book of Mormon_.[21] However, Jerald and Sandra Tanner, in their book, _The Case Against Mormonism_, have listed, one by one, over _four hundred_ verses and portions of verses quoted from the New Testament.[22] Elsewhere they conclude that both the Old and New Testament were important sources for the writing of the _Book of Mormon_:

> There can be no doubt that the first books of the Bible furnished a great deal of source material for the writing of the _Book of Mormon_....More than 18 chapters of Isaiah are found in the _Book of Mormon_. The Ten Commandments and many other portions of the Old Testament are also found in the _Book of Mormon_....Mark Twain said that the _Book of Mormon_ "seems to be merely a prosy detail of imaginary history, with the Old Testament for a model; followed by a tedious plagiarism of the New Testament" (_Roughing It_, 110).

> The ministry of Christ seems to have been the source of a good deal of the _Book of Mormon_.... Wesley M. Jones points out that "the ministry of St. Paul is duplicated almost exactly in the ministry of

[the Mormon character] Alma, one of Joseph's characters—even in the manner of speech and travels" (*A Critical Study of* Book of Mormon *Sources*, 14,15).

We find many New Testament verses and parts of verses throughout the *Book of Mormon*....In *Mormonism—Shadow or Reality?* we listed over 200 parallels, and in another study we had a list of 400. We have found over 100 quotations from the New Testament in the first two books of Nephi alone, and these books were supposed to have been written between 600 and 545 B.C.

Mormon writers have tried to explain why so much of the New Testament is found in the *Book of Mormon*, but we feel that their explanations are only wishful thinking. The only reasonable explanation is that the author of the *Book of Mormon* had the King James Version of the Bible. And since this version did not appear until A.D. 1611, the *Book of Mormon* could not have been written prior to that time. The *Book of Mormon*, therefore, is a modern composition and not a "record of ancient religious history."[23]

## Additional Sources

The Tanners have also supplied evidence for many other sources for the *Book of Mormon*, including Josiah Priest's *The Wonders of Nature and Providence Displayed* (Albany, NY: 1825), *The Wayne Sentinel; The Apocrypha*, a dream of Joseph Smith's father; and *The Westminster Confession and Catechism*.[24] All this is evidence that the *Book of Mormon* could not have been a translation of ancient records.*

---

* In 1977, circumstantial evidence for one more source theory appeared in Cowdrey, Davis, and Scales' *Who Really Wrote the* Book of Mormon? The theory, first proposed in 1833, asserts the *Book of Mormon* is adapted from a novel by Solomon Spalding, *Manuscript Found*, with religious material added by Sidney Rigdon.[25] However, the evidence for the theory is doubtful. In a review of the book, Wesley Walters concludes that "their proof must be regarded as highly questionable,"[26] and Jerald and Sandra Tanner also conclude in their *Did Spalding Write the* Book of Mormon?: "It is our feeling that this new theory will not stand the test of time and the more it is advocated the more damage it will do."[27] (See Brodie, *No Man Knows My History*, Select Bibliography.)

What, then, is the real source of the *Book of Mormon*? The most appropriate answer would seem to offer a combination of both human endeavor and spiritistic revelation. Given the many testimonies of Smith's occultism and use of a seer stone in the "translation," it would be difficult to completely discard the possibility of supernatural revelation. Likewise, given the numerous contemporary sources we find in the text, it is also difficult to deny Smith's own human authorship. While it is also possible that spiritistic inspiration itself may include plagiarisms or borrowings about which the medium or channeler is wholly ignorant, the fact that Smith had access to the various sources discussed would indicate the ease with which he could have made use of them.

Whatever the case, the facts we have examined so far reinforce a negative conclusion concerning the claim that the *Book of Mormon* is a divine translation of *ancient* records.

We now turn to a discussion of archaeology as further proof that the *Book of Mormon* is a nineteenth-century production.

## C. Archaeology and the Book of Mormon

If the *Book of Mormon* were truly a historical record of ancient peoples inhabiting a vast civilization in relatively recent history, it is virtually impossible that no evidence could be marshalled for the existence of such a civilization. In other words, if the *Book of Mormon* were really history, archaeological data would confirm it—just as archaeology has repeatedly confirmed biblical history and the history of other ancient cultures. But in fact, not a shred of archaeological evidence exists that the *Book of Mormon* is history.

In examining the *Book of Mormon* and the discipline of archaeology, we first need to understand the background of the alleged history taught in the *Book of Mormon*.[28]

The *Book of Mormon* claims to represent the history of three different groups of people, all of whom allegedly migrated from the Near East to Central and South America. Two of the groups supposedly traveled as far north as Mexico and North America (the *Book of Mormon*, Ether, and 1 Nephi).*

---

* Although the traditional view is that the *Book of Mormon* story covers North and South America, some modern Brigham Young University academicians, apparently attempting to coordinate *Book of Mormon* claims and geography with existing data, backpedal and accept a more limited geography.[29] (They believe, for example, that the hill Cumorah in New York was really in Southern Mexico.)

These people, the Nephites and Lamanites, were Semitic, with the most important group being led by Lehi of Jerusalem. His descendants became the Nephites. The main history of the *Book of Mormon* concerns the Nephites.

How did the alleged Nephites originate? Around 600 B.C. the family of Lehi left Jerusalem. By the time of Christ, his descendants had migrated to North America. Earlier, two of Lehi's sons, Nephi and Laman, had a dispute and the people took sides. This began two quarreling camps named after Lehi's sons: the Nephites and Lamanites. Nephi was a righteous leader, but Laman was not, which had unfortunate consequences for his descendants. Native American Indians are held by Mormons to be descendants of Laman, and, along with blacks, their dark skins are considered the sign of a curse by God (1 Nephi 12:23; 2 Nephi 5:21).

When Jesus arose in the resurrection, He allegedly came and preached to both these peoples, and they were converted. Unfortunately, a few centuries later, the Lamanites apostatized and went to war with the Nephites.

The *Book of Mormon* teaches that in A.D. 385, during the final battles that wiped out the Nephites (around A.D. 380 to 420), some 230,000 Nephites died near the hill Cumorah in New York (Mormon 6:10-15; 8:2). By A.D. 421, all the Nephites had been killed, with only the apostate Lamanites left in the land. (These were the supposed "Jewish Indians" whom Columbus discovered in 1492.)

Before this time, one Nephite historian-prophet named *Mormon* (the commander of the Nephites) had gathered all the records of his predecessors. From them he penned an abridged history of his people—allegedly written on gold plates in "reformed Egyptian." This synopsis by Mormon was largely derived from plates written by Nephi (2 Nephi 5:28-31).

Thus, Mormon wrote the supposed history of his people from about 600 B.C., when they left Jerusalem, to A.D. 385. He entrusted the plates to his son *Moroni*, who allegedly finished the history and then hid the accounts in the hill Cumorah in New York around A.D. 421. Fourteen hundred years later,

Joseph Smith was allegedly led to the same hill by the spirit of the long-deceased Moroni (the same Moroni, now a resurrected being) to discover the gold plates that Mormon had written. Thus, Mormonism claims that Smith translated the Egyptian hieroglyphics of the Jew called Mormon into English. Named after its author, it became known as the _Book of Mormon._

The story recounted in the _Book of Mormon_ certainly would have a great deal of archaeological verification if it were true. According to the _Book of Mormon,_ two entire nations developed and grew from the two migratory families. The Nephites and Lamanites (the latter were "exceedingly more numerous") spread over the face of the land and became as myriad as "the sand of the sea." They had large cities (the _Book of Mormon_ mentions thirty-eight), "nations developed," and they fought in "great _continent_-wide wars."[30] By A.D. 322 "the whole face of the land had become covered with buildings" (Mormon 1:7). Thus, the old civilizations of Mexico and Central America are claimed by Mormons to have been the people of the _Book of Mormon,_ the Nephites and Lamanites.

Nevertheless, not a shred of evidence exists to substantiate these claims—despite many vigorous archaeological excavations financed by the Mormon church. This has forced any number of non-Mormon researchers to conclude the _Book of Mormon_ is comprised primarily of myth and historical invention. For example, Dr. Walter Martin refers to "the hundreds of areas where this book defies reason or common sense."[31] Dr. Charles Crane, a professor knowledgeable on Mormon archaeology, states, "I am led to believe from my research that this is not an actual story but is a fairy tale much like Alice in Wonderland."[32] Dr. Gordon Fraser, observing that Mormons still accept their book as history, asserts that it in no way corresponds to the known facts of the ancient Americas:

> Both Mormon scientists and objective investigators have reconstructed the story of who lived where in ancient America, when they occupied certain territories, what their cultures were, and,

to a large degree, what their writing methods were. Certainly these facts were not known when Joseph Smith wrote, but this gives the Mormons of today no right to suppress the information they have found or to ignore the scientific findings of others....[in fact] the probable accuracy of the *Book of Mormon* can be evaluated by an examination of the book's records of situations, times, and places that are well-known and well documented.

If, for instance, the statements of history, geography, natural history, ethnology, and anthropology in the *Book of Mormon* almost invariably prove to be untrue, it is safe to assume that completely illogical statements in the rest of the book will follow the same pattern.[33]

Nevertheless, Mormon apologists and lay writers claim that archaeology proves that the *Book of Mormon* is true. In fact, this is a standard argument frequently used by thousands of Mormon missionaries around the world in their attempts to convert people. And, there is little doubt that many people have converted to Mormonism—trusting the claims of church members that archaeology has proven the *Book of Mormon* to be historically reliable.[34] Misinformation has also proven to be useful propaganda for Mormon believers as well:

Scores of books and pamphlets have been written by authorized writers for Mormon consumption and to be used for propaganda purposes. Mormons believe these writings because of their source. To tell a Mormon that the *Book of Mormon* has been proved by many archaeological evidences is very reassuring.[35]

For example, Ed Decker, a former Mormon of twenty years' standing, comments, "I had always been told that archaeology has proven the *Book of Mormon* to be true beyond any doubt. That...non-Mormon archaeologists had taken the *Book of Mormon* and actually used it as a guide...."[36]

Thus, Hal Hougey observes in _Archaeology and the_ Book of Mormon that most Mormons think that archaeology is on their side:

> The numerous books and articles by Latter-day Saints over the years have shown that Mormons believe that the fruits of archaeological research may properly be applied to verify the _Book of Mormon_. Dr. Ross T. Christensen, a Mormon anthropologist, agrees with this in the following quotations from the _Newsletter_ of the University Archaeological Society which has its headquarters at Brigham Young University...: "The _Book of Mormon_ is in such a key position in relation to the Latter-day Saint religion as a whole that the entire structure of the latter must stand or fall with the verification or refutation of the former....the _Book of Mormon_ is of such a nature that its validity can be submitted to a thorough and objective scientific test....If the Book's history is fallacious, its doctrine cannot be genuine....I am fully confident that the nature of the Book is such that a definitive archaeological test _can_ be applied to it."[37]

But such a definitive archaeological test has already been applied, and both the _Book of Mormon_ and Mormonism have failed. In fact, archaeology has not affirmed the _Book of Mormon_, but rather, has discredited it. The massive data accumulated by numerous archaeological excavations has failed to uncover a shred of evidence to support the _Book of Mormon_'s claims. This has recently been confessed even by some in the Mormon church.[38] Whether we consider the purported cities, rivers, crops, fabrics, animals, metals, coins, kings, wars and war implements, palaces, and so on, no evidence at all supports their existence.[39] Where are the plains of Nephaha? Or the valley of Nimrod? Where is the land of Zarahemla? Have we found coins such as the leah, shiblon, and shiblum?

Mormon researcher Gordon Fraser correctly observes that the _Book of Mormon_ has already been proven a forgery:

Mormon archaeologists have been trying for years to establish some evidence that will confirm the presence of the [Mormon] church in America. There is still not a scintilla of evidence, either in the religious philosophy of the ancient writings or in the presence of artifacts, that could lead to such a belief.

The whole array of anachronisms [historical errors] in the book stamps it as written by someone who knew nothing about ancient America and presumed that no one ever would know. It is total fiction, done by one who assumed that cultures in ancient America would probably be about the same as those of our own north eastern states in the 19th Century. While certain Mormon apologists are pledged to the task of defending the credibility of the *Book of Mormon*, because the church demands it, some professors at Brigham Young University are demanding caution concerning claims that the ruins of old temples and other artifacts found in Mexico and Central America are positive evidence of the claims of the *Book of Mormon*.

The problem has become a sticky one for Mormon scholars who would like to be investigators in depth but are forbidden by their church authorities.[40]

Although it is recognized by Christian and secular researchers alike that Mormonism's archaeological claims are invalid, this verdict has not yet been accepted by the vast majority of Mormons, whose misinformation has held them captive to distortion. In part, the problem stems from the publications of zealous but misinformed researchers who are careless or biased with their use of data in their defense of Mormonism—Dewey Farnsworth's Book of Mormon *Evidences in Ancient America*,[41] and the books of Hugh Nibley and Milton Hunter are examples.[42]

Nevertheless, Mormon church authorities continue to support such unreliable apologetic works. Thus:

> Despite the absence of archaeological support for the _Book of Mormon_, Mormons continue to produce a spate of archaeological works. Most are nonsense written by amateurs. Not until 1938 did the first Mormon earn a doctorate in archaeology, and today only a few hold this degree.[43]

As Ropp, the Tanners, and others have shown by quoting these few professional Mormon archaeologists, it is often _they_ and not the secular "enemies" of the church who have taken the church and its amateur archaeologists to task for distorting facts.[44] For example, John L. Sorenson, a former assistant professor of anthropology at Brigham Young University, complains: "As long as Mormons generally are willing to be fooled by (and pay for) the uninformed, uncritical dribble about archaeology and the Scriptures which predominates, the few LDS experts are reluctant even to be identified with the topic."*[45]

Thus, the claims of Mormons regarding various artifacts (the Lehi Tree of Life Stone, Kinderhook Plates, etc.) and ancient sites, may all be refuted by anyone willing to take the time to research the claims.[47] As Cowan observes:

> But, thus far, everything [Mormons] have pointed to as "proof" has turned out to be a forgery or else an exaggerated interpretation which cannot stand up under investigation. There has never yet been one [_Book of Mormon_] name, event, place or anything else verified through archaeological discoveries!...Dozens of biblical

---

* When one is dealing with a Mormon who maintains his archaeological "proofs," it is important to have such a person read the material by those few responsible Mormon archaeologists who insist such claims are false, as well as professional secular authorities. While the number of scholarly Mormon archaeologists is increasing, the outcome remains unchanged. The Tanners' _Archaeology and the_ Book of Mormon is one good source of such information.[46] See Resource List.

sites have been located by using the Bible as a guide—but not one has ever been found by using the *Book of Mormon*.[48]

In their book *Mormonism—Shadow or Reality?* the Tanners come to the same conclusion—that even though many claims have been made by Mormons regarding certain archaeological "discoveries," they are either bogus or misinterpreted.[49] One leading authority on New World archaeology, Michael Coe, states unequivocally that "the bare facts of the matter are that nothing, absolutely nothing, has ever shown up in any New World excavation" documenting the historicity of the *Book of Mormon*.[50]

This is highly relevant because, according to the information in the *Book of Mormon*, its alleged ancient civilizations in South and Central America are so geographically expansive they virtually demand archaeological verification:

> There are some thirty-eight cities catalogued in the *Book of Mormon*, [supplying] evidence that these were indeed mighty civilizations which should, by all the laws of archaeological research into the culture of antiquity, have left vast amounts of "finds" to be evaluated. But such is not the case as we shall show. The Mormons have yet to explain the fact that leading archaeological researchers not only have repudiated the claims of the *Book of Mormon* as to the existence of these civilizations, but have adduced considerable evidence to show the impossibility of the accounts given in the Mormon Bible.[51]

For example:

> Not one of these city sites has ever been found in South or Central America. By contrast, a great amount of evidence has been uncovered concerning the ancient cities of the Mayas and Incas who occupy these areas. The historical or

archaeological support, which should be virtually overwhelming for such a civilization as the Mormons claim, simply does not exist. In fact, the opposite is true....There is not one knowledgeable archaeologist, Mormon or non-Mormon, who will claim that there is any archaeological proof to support the *Book of Mormon*....On the other hand, *archaeologists frequently discover proof which utterly contradicts and demolishes the claims of the* Book of Mormon....Not only is there no archaeological proof to support the *Book of Mormon* history of the vast civilizations that supposedly covered all of South and Central America, but anthropologists also deny the claims in the *Book of Mormon*. Those who specialize in anthropology and genetics refute Joseph Smith's claim that the American Indians are descendants of the Israelites.[52]

But Mormon missionaries and church authorities continue to ignore such evidence.* Incredibly, they inform potential converts that the Smithsonian Institute or other prestigious professional organizations have utilized the *Book of Mormon* as an accurate archaeological guide. In fact, the Smithsonian Institute has received so many inquiries concerning this that they send out a regular form letter denying it. The first of many points it makes in refuting Mormon claims is this: "The Smithsonian Institution has never used the *Book of Mormon* in any way as a scientific guide. Smithsonian archaeologists see no direct connection between the archaeology of the New World and the subject matter of the book."[53]

In addition, the Bureau of American Ethnology of the Smithsonian Institute declares, "There is no evidence whatever of any migration of Israel to America, and likewise no evidence that pre-Columbian Indians had any knowledge of Christianity or the Bible."[54]

---

* Both *Doctrine and Covenants* and commentaries on it supply geographical maps of the various movements of the Mormon church in its early history—from New York to Missouri to Illinois to Utah, and so on. Why are no maps ever found in a *Book of Mormon*? Because there is nothing to chart.

The prestigious National Geographic Society has also denied Mormon claims:

> With regard to the cities mentioned in the *Book of Mormon*, neither representatives of the National Geographic Society nor archaeologists connected with any other institution of equal prestige have ever used the *Book of Mormon* in locating historic ruins in Middle America or elsewhere.[55]

Perhaps this is why Mormon anthropologist D.F. Green stated that he did not see how "the archaeological myths so common in our proselytizing program enhance the process of true conversion....The first myth we need to eliminate is that a *Book of Mormon* archaeology exists."[56] In other words, no *Book of Mormon* cities have ever been located; no *Book of Mormon* person, place, nation, river, or name has ever been found; no *Book of Mormon* artifacts, no *Book of Mormon* scriptures, no *Book of Mormon* inscriptions, no *Book of Mormon* gold plates have ever been recovered. Nothing that demonstrates that the *Book of Mormon* is anything other than myth or invention has *ever* been found.

As archaeological expertise and data grow, this lack of verifying evidence becomes more and more embarrassing and difficult to explain.

We are once again faced with a critical contrast between the Christian Scriptures and the Mormon scriptures, although not in theology. The antithesis between the Bible, which is accepted as a reliable archaeological guide by reputable archaeologists, and the *Book of Mormon*, which is accepted by none, is striking.

For example, even skeptical scholars can seek to disprove the Bible through archaeological investigation and yet become converted to Christianity. This was the case with archaeologist Sir William Ramsay. On the other hand, Mormon scholars who try to prove Mormonism on the basis of archaeology may wind up leaving the church. The Tanners cite the case of Thomas Stuart Ferguson, who was recognized as a "great defender of the faith," and who wrote three books on Mormonism and archaeology. He was head of the Mormon New World Archaeological Foundation, which Brigham Young University supported with funds for several fruitless archaeological expeditions.

Sir William Ramsay and Thomas Stuart Ferguson represent stark contrasts. Ferguson truly believed archaeology would prove Mormonism. Ramsay, a classical scholar and archaeologist at Oxford, was a skeptic convinced that archaeology would disprove Christianity. He had little inkling that his own excavations would prove the detailed historicity of the New Testament.

In the end, Ramsay became a committed Christian who authored some one dozen texts on the reliability of the Scriptures—based on careful, skeptical scholarship. Ferguson, on the other hand, became so disheartened that he repudiated the Mormon church's prophet.

On December 2, 1970, the Tanners received a surprise visit from Ferguson:

> He had come to the conclusion that Joseph Smith was not a prophet and that Mormonism was not true. He told us that he had spent 25 years trying to prove Mormonism, but had finally come to the conclusion that all his work in this regard had been in vain. He said that his training in law had taught him how to weigh evidence and that the case against Joseph Smith was absolutely devastating and could not be explained away.[57]

Compare this with Sir William Ramsay, who wrote that his skepticism had died: "The reversal of our judgment, then, _was complete_."[58] And he concluded, "...the New Testament is unique in the compactness, the lucidity, the pregnancy and the _vivid truthfulness_ of its expression. That is not the character of one or two only of the books that compose the Testament; it belongs in different ways to _all alike_."[59] Many of the greatest archaeologists, from William F. Albright, of Johns Hopkins, to Millar Burrows, of Yale, have stated publicly that archaeology confirms the Bible historically. No archaeologist has ever stated this for the *Book of Mormon*.

When Mormons claim there is archaeological verification for both the *Book of Mormon* and their religion, they are either uninformed or distorting the facts. The interested reader should purchase appropriate materials and prove to his own satisfaction that Mormon archaeological claims are without foundation and that therefore the *Book of Mormon* is not logically to be classified as a translation of ancient records.[60]

## D. The Book of Mormon's lack of manuscript evidence

Because of their perceived importance, the religious scriptures of most ancient peoples have been preserved, despite the sometimes incredible odds against it. Occasionally, the preservation is almost perfect. The Bible of the Jews and the New Testament of the Christians are unique in this regard.[61] But even with the Koran of the Muslims and the Hindu or Buddhist scriptures, evidence may exist to determine whether a religious document is genuine or a forgery. For example, sufficient extant manuscript evidence may exist to prove a document really is as old as it claims to be.

But this is not true for the *Book of Mormon*—even though such evidence should certainly exist given the character and influence of the Jewish people who allegedly wrote it. Thus, why the Jews would so carefully preserve the Bible and *not* the *Book of Mormon* is inexplicable.

Incredibly, Mormons often claim that the manuscript evidence for the Bible is of poor quality. But, in truth, while the manuscript evidence for the Bible is rich and abundant, that of the Mormon scriptures is nonexistent.[62] Perhaps it is also relevant to note that the discovery of the Dead Sea Scrolls' Book of Isaiah has remarkably confirmed the extant scriptural account while it has repudiated the *Book of Mormon* excerpts from Isaiah.[63]

In fact, there is no textual evidence for either the *Book of Mormon* or for any of Smith's other alleged translations of alleged ancient records.

Is there a single ancient manuscript? No. Is there even a portion of one? No. Is there even one fragment of a page? No. Can the "gold plates" from which Smith allegedly translated the *Book of Mormon* be produced? No. Were these ancient records ever cited by another writer? No. Who can explain this? No one. That the early Mormon church would ever permit the disappearance of materials of such incalculable textual (and monetary) value is simply not credible. And regardless, undoubtedly the Nephites were not in the *habit* of writing on gold plates, so certainly some additional manuscript evidence should be forthcoming. This is the source of another embarrassment to the Mormon church, for there is simply no credible reason that can explain the lack of textual materials. Thus, just as the content of the *Book of Mormon* argues for a nineteenth-century origin, not an ancient one, so does the manuscript evidence. This is true not only for the *Book of Mormon*, but also for all of Mormonism's "scripture":

> As far as historical and manuscript evidence is concerned, Joseph Smith's scriptures have absolutely no foundation. The "records of the Nephites," for instance, were never cited by any ancient writer, nor are there any known manuscripts or even fragments of manuscripts in existence older than the ones dictated by Joseph Smith in the late 1820s. Joseph Smith's "Book of Moses" is likewise without documentary support. The only handwritten manuscripts for the "Book of Moses" are those dictated by Joseph Smith in the early 1830s. The "Book of Abraham" purports to be a translation of an ancient Egyptian papyrus. However, the original papyrus is in reality the Egyptian "Book of Breathings" and has nothing to do with Abraham or his religion. Therefore, we have no evidence for the "Book of Abraham" prior to the handwritten manuscripts dictated by Joseph Smith in the 1830s. It would appear, then, that there is no documentary evidence for any of

Joseph Smith's works that date back prior to the late 1820s.[64]

In conclusion, having demonstrated that the *Book of Mormon* is a nineteenth-century production—and therefore a forgery, we will now show that the text itself has been corrupted and is therefore doubly incapable of a person's trust.

# Division II

*Evidence that the* Book of Mormon *is mutilated both textually and (from the perspective of Mormon teaching) doctrinally, and therefore unreliable because it is corrupted*

## E. Textual problems in the Book of Mormon

As noted earlier, those involved in the production of the *Book of Mormon* claimed it was divinely translated by a process equivalent to that of mechanical dictation. This has resulted in the Mormon church's belief that the entirety of the book is a divine translation. But if true, this would have prevented any need to make changes in the text, even down to the smallest detail. Thus, the original 1830 edition of the English text should have become God's Word, letter for letter. Not a single alteration should have occurred, even in grammar or spelling. But, in fact, we find literally thousands of changes. Although the vast majority are grammatical, some are clearly of substance. The Tanners have documented a significant number of such changes in *3913 Changes in the* Book of Mormon, which is a photomechanical reprint of the original 1830 edition of the Book of Mormon with the changes marked (see Resource List at back of book).

## F. The Book of Mormon's lack of distinctive Mormon doctrines: Is the Book of Mormon "Mormon"?

From the perspective of contemporary Mormon theology, the *Book of Mormon* itself must be regarded as a questionable text. Most people, including many Mormons, believe that Mormon teachings are derived principally from the *Book of*

*Mormon.* But this is not true. Mormon doctrine is derived primarily from *Doctrine and Covenants.* This is why "doctrinally the *Book of Mormon* is a dead book for most Mormons....The *Book of Mormon* teachings have little bearing upon current Mormon doctrine."[65]

The dilemma this poses for the Mormon church is a serious one. Why? Because another Mormon scripture called *Doctrine and Covenants* emphasizes that the *Book of Mormon* does contain basic or fundamental Mormon teachings. For example, according to *Doctrine and Covenants,* the *Book of Mormon* contains "the truth and the Word of God" (*D&C,* 19:26); "the *fullness* of the gospel of Jesus Christ" (that is, Mormon teachings, *D&C,* 20:9); and "the *fullness* of the *everlasting* gospel" (*D&C,* 135:3). *Doctrine and Covenants* also has Jesus claiming that the *Book of Mormon* has "the principles of my gospel" (*D&C,* 42:12) and "*all things written* concerning the foundation of my church, my gospel, and my rock" (*D&C,* 18:4; cf. 17:1-6; emphasis added; see also *Book of Mormon,* introduction).

According to *Doctrine and Covenants,* then, the *Book of Mormon* must contain at the very least most of the central doctrines of Mormon faith. But the *Book of Mormon* contains few major Mormon teachings. For example, it does not teach any of the following central Mormon principles which form the foundation of the Mormon church and its "gospel":

1. Polytheism;
2. God as the product of an eternal progression;
3. Eternal marriage;
4. Polygamy;
5. Human deification;
6. The Trinity as three separate gods;
7. Baptism for the dead;
8. Maintaining genealogical records;
9. Universalism;
10. That God has a physical body and was once a man;

11. That God organized, not created, the world;

12. Mother gods (heavenly mothers);

13. Temple marriage as a requirement for exaltation;

14. The concept of eternal intelligences;

15. Three degrees of heavenly glory (telestial, terrestrial, and celestial);

16. Salvation after death in the spirit world;

17. A New Testament era of Mormon organizational offices and functions such as the Melchizedek and Aaronic Priesthoods, Stake President, First Presidency, and so on.[66]

All this is why even some Mormon writers have noted the theological irrelevance of the *Book of Mormon* to Mormonism. For example, John H. Evans observed "how little the whole body of belief of the Latter-day Saints really depends on the revelation of the Nephite record [i.e., the *Book of Mormon*]."[67]

Some Mormons respond by saying that the above Mormon doctrines were not revealed until *after* publication of the *Book of Mormon*.[68] But this does not resolve the problem. If so, why would *Doctrine and Covenants* teach what was clearly false—that the *Book of Mormon* did contain the "fullness of the gospel" and "all things" pertaining to the foundation of the church?

With so many major Mormon doctrines entirely absent from the *Book of Mormon*, how can *Doctrine and Covenants* declare that the "Nephite" record contains the fullness of the gospel? And if it does not, how can *Doctrine and Covenants* itself be divinely inspired—or trusted? And if the same source that inspired *Doctrine and Covenants* also claimed to inspire the *Book of Mormon*, how can the *Book of Mormon* be trusted either? Finally, if all this is true, how can former president and prophet Ezra Taft Benson logically claim, "The *Book of Mormon* and *Doctrine and Covenants* testify of each other. You cannot believe one and not the other....The *Doctrine and Covenants* is by far the greatest external witness and evidence which we have from the Lord that the *Book of Mormon* is true."[69]

If, then, the authority of *Doctrine and Covenants* is placed to rest, undermined, who can maintain that its testimony concerning the *Book of Mormon* is reliable? Further, if *Doctrine and Covenants* and subjective "personal testimonies" are the *only* evidence for the genuineness of the *Book of Mormon*, why should its claims be trusted either? *Doctrine and Covenants*, then, is in serious error on a most fundamental issue and certainly cannot be considered a revelation from God even on Mormon terms. (Indeed, if *Doctrine and Covenants* cannot be a divine revelation, if the *Book of Mormon* cannot establish Mormon doctrine, and if the *Pearl of Great Price* is a proven forgery [see chapter 10], what remains of Mormon claims to having authentic, divine revelation?)

In fact, as we will see in chapter 10, the *Book of Mormon* actually *denies* Mormon doctrines. So, can a Mormon prove the *Book of Mormon* contains Mormon doctrine? No. He may attempt to prove Mormon doctrine from *Doctrine and Covenants*, but *Doctrine and Covenants* teaches he must be able to do this from the *Book of Mormon*.

And if doctrinal irrelevance were not sufficiently discouraging, there are also serious problems regarding the original text of the *Book of Mormon*.

## G. The language and style of the Book of Mormon

The Mormon church claims that the "gold plates" containing the *Book of Mormon* were penned in "reformed Egyptian." They base this belief on the *Book of Mormon* itself, which affirms, "And now, behold, we have written this record according to our knowledge, in the characters which are called among us the reformed Egyptian..." (Mormon 9:32).

But this is unlikely for several reasons. First, no such language is known to exist, and Egyptologists declare this unequivocally. For example, R.A. Parker of the Department of Egyptology at Brown University remarks, "No Egyptian writing has been found in this hemisphere to my knowledge....I do not know of any language such as Reformed Egyptian."[70]

Second, even if it were a true language, how likely is it that the allegedly Jewish Nephites would have used the Egyptian language to write their sacred scriptures? Their strong antipathy to the Egyptians and their culture makes this difficult to accept. When Jews copied their scripture, they used Hebrew.

Furthermore, just as clear evidence should exist in the Americas for the *Book of Mormon*'s claims regarding various civilizations, archaeology should also have uncovered evidence of the alleged reformed Egyptian language, for it is claimed it was a common language in the Americas fifteen hundred years ago. It is difficult to accept that the evidence for so vast a civilization could have been completely lost in fifteen hundred years, but this is what the Mormon church asks us to believe. But if modern archaeology can uncover a relatively small civilization over four thousand years old (for example, Ebla in Syria), isn't it reasonable to believe that some remnants would exist for an incomparably larger civilization a mere fifteen hundred years old?

Style is another problem for the *Book of Mormon*. Considering the Mormon claim that it is divinely translated, the first 1830 edition should have remained unchanged. But the 1830 edition has had thousands of changes, largely because its grammar was so poor. (See chapter 10 for examples.) If this book was translated by divine power, then God is certainly unfamiliar with elemental grammar. Unnecessary repetition is also a frequent occurrence. Fawn Brodie observes, "Joseph's sentences were loose-jointed, like an earthworm hacked into segments that crawl away live and whole. "Innumerable repetitions bogging down the narrative were chiefly responsible for Mark Twain's comment that the book was "chloroform in print."[71]

## H. The Eleven Witnesses

How do Mormons respond to the damaging evidence surrounding the *Book of Mormon*? For the most part, they remain silent. They are content to trust in their "personal testimony" experience and the fact that millions of others have had a similar testimony—going all the way back to the "Eleven Witnesses." Unfortunately, personal testimonies mean little when that which they attest to is already established as false. Nevertheless, the testimonies of the Eleven Witnesses is a key apologetic for promoting the *Book of Mormon*. Besides Joseph Smith, the Eleven Witnesses were the only witnesses to the "gold plates," hence their testimony is considered to be crucial.

The testimony of the Three Witnesses and the testimony of the Eight Witnesses are found in the front of every *Book of Mormon*. The Three Witnesses declare they have "seen the plates" from which the *Book of Mormon* was translated, and that it was "divinely revealed" to them that Joseph Smith's translation was correct. The Eight Witnesses declare that Joseph Smith showed them the plates as well. From such testimony, one would assume that the witnesses had physically seen the plates. But no independent testimony for such an assertion exists.

In fact, the evidence suggests they may have only *thought* they saw the plates. Fawn Brodie and others have indicated that Smith had an almost hypnotic power over other people, and keep in mind Joseph Smith's earlier-mentioned involvement with the occult. Thus there is the possibility of spiritistic visions or deception. Indeed, given the probability that mental manipulation is associated with occult involvement, it would be easy to account for the phenomenon of these men thinking they saw something that wasn't there. Similar things happen routinely in stage hypnosis, in many types of psychic encounters (such as "astral travel"and UFO "abductions") and in many other occult manifestations. Clearly, either by religious suggestion, or hypnotism (whether of human or spiritistic origin)—or by raw occult power—men can be made to see, feel, and otherwise experience things which, in fact, have no physical reality. In his commentary on Galatians, Martin Luther himself once noted that the devil had such power as to make a man swear he saw, heard, and felt such and such when, in fact, he had done no such thing.

Fawn Brodie observes:

> A careful scrutiny of the *Book of Mormon* and
> the legendary paraphernalia obscuring its origin
> discloses not only Joseph's inventive and eclectic
> nature but also his magnetic influence over his
> friends....what Crowdery in later years described
> as Joseph's "mysterious power, which even now I
> fail to fathom."...But Joseph had more than
> "second sight," which is commonplace among
> professional magicians. At an early age he had
> what only the most gifted revivalist preachers
> could boast of—the talent for making men see
> visions.[72]

Since the spirit entity calling itself "Moroni" took back the
alleged gold plates—as visiting spirits of all kinds are wont to
do with the objects they "give" to men as "proof" of the
encounter—the eleven witnesses are the only source of credibility as to the existence of the plates. Unfortunately, we discover that the witnesses' testimony itself is suspect. Brodie
again comments:

> According to the local press of the time, the
> three witnesses all told different versions of their
> experience....All three witnesses eventually quar-
> relled with Joseph and left his church.[73]

Concerning the eight witnesses, she observes, "It will be
seen that four witnesses were Whitmers and three were members of Joseph's own family. The eighth witness, Hyrum Page,
had married a Whitmer daughter. Mark Twain was later to
observe: 'I could not feel more satisfied and at rest if the entire
Whitmer family had testified.'"[74]

Brodie supplies one explanation of how the witnesses may
have "seen" the gold plates. Note that at first they saw nothing
at all:

> One of the most plausible descriptions of the
> manner in which Joseph Smith obtained these
> eight signatures [testifying to having seen the

plates] was written by Thomas Ford, Governor of Illinois, who knew intimately several of Joseph's key men after they became disaffected and left the church. They told Ford that the witnesses were "set to continual prayer, and other spiritual exercise." Then at last "he assembled them in a room, and produced a box, which he said contained the precious treasure. The lid was opened; the witnesses peeped into it, but making no discovery, for the box was empty, they said, 'Brother Joseph, we do not see the plates.' The prophet answered them, 'O ye of little faith! How long will God bear with this wicked and perverse generation? Down on your knees, brethren, every one of you, and pray God for forgiveness of your sins, and for a holy and living faith which cometh down from heaven.' The disciples dropped to their knees and began to pray in the fervency of their spirit, supplicating God for more than two hours, with fanatical earnestness; at the end of which time, looking again into the box, they were now persuaded that they saw the plates."[75]

Hence, there are several possible explanations for the alleged gold plates: spiritual intimidation, religious suggestion brought on by psychological manipulation and/or exhaustion, a spiritistically implanted vision, hypnosis, or some combination thereof. It is even slightly possible that the plates could have been temporarily apported objects, for some of the witnesses claimed to have held them.[76] But even here, a hypnotic vision or spiritistic power could have produced the same sensation.[77]

But the most damning indictment against the witnesses is their personal character and lack of credibility. It is relevant to note that "some of the most damaging statements" against the Eleven Witnesses came from the pen of Joseph Smith himself and other early Mormon leaders.[78] Some were gullible; others were psychologically unstable and religiously insecure. In other words, they "were not competent witnesses."[79]

Thus, some of the witnesses doubted their initial vision of the gold plates, as noted by Brigham Young himself.[80] More importantly, most of them later apostatized (!) and several exchanged various charges of serious immorality back and forth with Joseph Smith.[81] In the end, of the Eleven Witnesses, six (including the three key witnesses) were excommunicated from the Mormon church. Each of the three primary witnesses, all of whom later became enemies of Joseph Smith, had severely blemished records as far as their credibility was concerned.[82]

The first, Martin Harris, was described as "changeable, fickle, and puerile in his judgment and conduct."[83] Even "God" Himself—through Joseph Smith—called him a "wicked man" (D&C, 3:12,13, introductory remarks). He also appears to have been mentally unbalanced.[84] At various times, he was a Presbyterian, Quaker, Universalist, Baptist, Strangite, Mormon, Restorationer—in all, he changed his religious convictions some thirteen times.[85] At the end of his life he returned to the Mormon church.

According to Joseph Smith, Oliver Crowdery, the second of the three witnesses, was led astray by Hyrum Pages's (one of the Eight Witnesses) "seer stone" and as a result was excommunicated from the church.[86] It is disputed whether or not he ever returned, or whether he maintained until his death that Smith was a false prophet.[87] According to the Mormon *Times and Seasons* of 1841, it does appear that he, too, doubted his first testimony about the *Book of Mormon*.[88]

The last of the three witnesses, David Whitmer, never returned to the Mormon church. And he stated the following just before he died:

> If you believe my testimony to the *Book of Mormon*; if you believe that God spake to us three witnesses by his own voice, then I tell you that in June, 1838, God spake to me again by his own voice from the heavens, and told me to separate myself from among the Latter-day Saints.[89]

Whitmer maintained that the Mormon church had "gone deep into error and blindness"—for example, in accepting the new revelations found in *Doctrine and Covenants*.[90]

It is hard to understand why Mormonism continues to accept Whitmer's "testimony" as seen in the front of the *Book of Mormon* when he later testified that Mormonism had become a false religion.

It is even more difficult to believe that men of dubious character are so readily accepted at all, since the quality of any individual's testimony is so dependent upon his or her character. Even former president and prophet of Mormonism Ezra Taft Benson is forced to concede that the testimony of the Eleven Witnesses is tarnished and that even today such "wolves" continue to haunt the flock:

> Six of the original Twelve Apostles selected by Joseph Smith were excommunicated. The Three Witnesses to the *Book of Mormon* left the church. Three of Joseph Smith's counselors fell—one even helped plot his death....The wolves among our flock are more numerous and devious today than when President [J.P. Reuben] Clark made [a similar] statement [in 1949].[91]

These Mormon witnesses present a stark contrast to the twelve apostles of the New Testament, who are generally conceded to be men of integrity. But how would Christians feel if the twelve apostles were men of such uncertain character as these eleven Mormon men? How could their testimonies about Jesus ever be reliably accepted? Likewise, how can Mormons logically trust the testimony of the Eleven Witnesses?

So of what value are the eleven Mormon testimonies to the *Book of Mormon*? Of what value are dubious professions to dubious visions? Indeed, there are literally hundreds just like them—from innumerable conflicting religious sects and cults, all boasting equal conviction. Without the presence of the gold plates themselves, all that remains is the testimony of unreliable men who think they *may* have seen them. What's worse, "There are a *dozen variations* of the story of the finding and translating of the *Book of Mormon*'s golden plates, and several versions of the experiences of the Three Witnesses who claimed to have seen the plates."[92]

It is never wise to place faith in alleged revelations given under what are, at best, suspicious circumstances—especially when they deny what God has already taught in the Bible. As the Tanners comment:

> The evidence shows that they were gullible, credulous, and their word cannot always be relied upon....Some of them even gave false revelations in the name of the Lord....How can we put our trust in men who are constantly following after movements like the Shakers, Strangites, and the McLellin group? We feel that the *Book of Mormon* witnesses have been "weighed in the balance" and found wanting.[93]

## Conclusion

Given our brief survey of the *Book of Mormon*, what can we conclude? Briefly, from examining the book as a whole—its occult origin, its various sources and plagiarisms, its antibiblical teachings, the archaeological disproof, the inexplicable absence of textual data, its lack of (and even opposition to) Mormon teachings, the nonexistent Reformed Egyptian language, the embarrassing grammar, the changes that were required in the text due to the primitive nature of the first edition, and the untrustworthy testimony of the Eleven Witnesses—all the evidence points to one unavoidable conclusion: *The* Book of Mormon *is really a piece of nineteenth-century fiction.* Whatever else it is, it cannot be a divine revelation. Writing in "The Centennial of Mormonism" in *American Mercury*, Bernard De Voto correctly described it as "a yeasty fermentation, formless, aimless and inconceivably absurd."[94]

All this is why Mormon leaders are consistently forced to tell potential converts to *ignore criticism* of the *Book of Mormon* and instead rely entirely upon subjective "confirmation."

Mormons often respond to criticism with something like the following: "I don't care what they say. I don't care what the problems are. I have a burning in my bosom and I know the Mormon Church is true."[95] But if the *Book of Mormon* is truly authentic, why do Mormons everywhere claim that the only real evidence for it is subjective?

The tenth president and prophet, Joseph Fielding Smith, counseled, "Pay no attention to the criticism, but ask yourself prayerfully, if the record is not true."[96] L.S.T. Rasmussen, Professor Emeritus of Religious Education at Brigham Young University, emphasizes, "The best support for the authenticity of the *Book of Mormon* is the testimony of the Holy Spirit."[97] And, "In contrast to the indecisive nature of [the] external evidence, the Lord has provided a way to obtain decisive support for the book's authenticity: 'The Spirit of Truth....will guide [us] into all truth.' "[98]

As noted earlier, no less a figure than Mormon historian B.H. Roberts confessed that the testimony of the Holy Ghost "must ever be the chief source of evidence of the truth of the *Book of Mormon*."[99] Likewise, Steve Gilliland, director of the LDS Institute of Religion at California State University Long Beach, comments, "It's not our responsibility to try to prove it [the Mormon Gospel] or convince the other person. The only real proof is the witness of the Spirit."[100]

Unfortunately, the church's appeal to subjective evidence does no more to prove the *Book of Mormon* than does reading the book itself. To believe without any evidence is troublesome enough, but to believe in spite of the evidence is folly. But to then demand that God confirm the "truth" of the *Book of Mormon* in sanctified prayer is not only an insult to God, who knows better, but it is also sheer self-deception. This unjustified appeal to "spiritual" experience ironically leads to the same spiritual quagmire that Joseph Smith instigated on that "beautiful, clear day, early in the spring of 1820" when he started the whole business (chapter 2).

Mormons should carefully reread the *Book of Mormon*. They should read it in light of history, logic, Scripture, and common sense and see whether or not they can really believe that it represents what the Mormon church claims. If it doesn't, they should know what to do.

We cannot end this section more appropriately than with the assessments of both Mormon and non-Mormon authorities. First, Dr. Walter Martin concludes:

> The world is now in a position to judge the *Book of Mormon* on three different levels. First, the book does not correspond to what we know God has already said in His Word. Second, its internal inconsistencies, thousands of changes, and persistent plagiarization of the King James Bible decidedly remove it from serious consideration as a revelation from God. Finally, its external inconsistencies not only expose its misuse of archaeology, science, history, and language, but actually allow us to investigate its true origin.[101]

The late prophet and president of the Mormon church, Ezra Taft Benson, could not have spoken a truer word when he said,

> The *Book of Mormon* is the keystone of our religion....A keystone is the central stone in an arch. It holds all the other stones in place, and if it is removed the arch crumbles.[102]

# Chapter 10

# Documented Changes in the Mormon Scriptures

~

Standard religious bodies usually guard and protect their scriptures with unrepentant zeal. It is inconceivable that any bona fide church would permit the alteration of what it truly believed were divine scriptures, let alone alter them itself and then keep such misrepresentations secret. This would represent total irreverence and desecration before God.

But this is exactly what the Mormon church has done. The Mormon church claims as its scripture the *Book of Mormon*, *Doctrines and Covenants*, and the *Pearl of Great Price*. Dr. Walter Martin observes (the term "standard work" refers to "inspired" work):

> There isn't a single LDS-produced standard work that hasn't undergone hundreds and even thousands of changes, additions, deletions, and corrections, many of which are much more than "typographical" in nature, and all of which were done without indications or acknowledgement of the actions taken. Even granting Joseph the "right" to revise what God had told him before

(even though it is difficult to do so when we are talking about cases involving historical facts), why is there the deception associated with these changes?...Church leaders have even lied in public about these situations. Why?[1]

First, we will document that, given Mormon claims, no changes whatever should have been made in the Mormon scriptures. Second, we will document the fact of the extensive changes themselves. This will prove that even Mormon church authorities, apparently, do not consider their own scripture true, let alone sacred. Why they would then demand such allegiance from church members is apparently a mystery known only to them.

In his alleged history, Joseph Smith tells the story about the mode of translation of the gold plates. This story confirms the claim that the plates were translated "by the power of God" and therefore cannot permit even the slightest alteration.

It had been prearranged that after completion of the translation, the "three witnesses" would see the gold plates so they could bear "testimony" to them. After a time of fervent prayer in the woods, two of the three witnesses (less Harris, who allegedly saw the same vision later):

> Beheld a light above us in the air, of exceeding brightness; and behold, an angel stood before us [not in the light]. In his hands, he held the plates....he turned over the leaves, one by one, so that we could see them, and discern the engravings thereon distinctly....[then] we heard a voice from [God] out of the bright light above us, saying, "These plates have been revealed by the power of God, *and they have [now] been translated by the power of God. The translation of them which you have seen is correct*, and I command you to bear witness of what you now see and hear."[2]

This testimony is clear enough. No less an authority than God Himself had declared that the plates were translated by

His own person and power. God had also testified that the translation "is correct." And later, Jesus Christ Himself also allegedly stated of the translation, "As your Lord and your God liveth *it is true*....And, I, Jesus Christ, your Lord and your God, have spoken unto you."[3]

In light of such witnesses, it is hardly surprising that Smith himself confessed that the *Book of Mormon* was "the most correct of any book on earth."[4]

It follows, then, that if the first edition of the text was 1) translated by God's own power, 2) described as "correct," "most correct," and "true," and then 3) confirmed as such by both God and Jesus, there is simply no way it should require drastic revision, grammatical or other. A *divinely translated* text is just that, and Mormons should accept the implications. How can there possibly be errors and thousands of changes in a divinely translated text?

Some Mormons have claimed that there are no changes in the *Book of Mormon*. But this is false. Others have claimed that the changes are only minor and not really an issue. But the issue is not simply the existence of relatively minor grammatical changes, but the vast number of them. There shouldn't be even one, but there are several thousand. Further, as we will show, there are significant changes of substance.

Let us first examine the explanations or proposed "solutions" to the problem that have been offered by the Mormon church. One claim is that the printer of the *Book of Mormon* (John Gilbert) was incompetent or "unfriendly" to Mormonism, and therefore produced some errors. Unfortunately, this is not only denied by other Mormons, but it was also denied by the printer himself. Gilbert confessed he was told to typeset the material as it stood—for example, to leave in grammatical errors.[5] In any case, the errors are simply too numerous for any qualified printer to make. Considering Gilbert used a country press, the actual typographical errors in the 1830 edition were very few.

Another "solution" is that the translation *was* inerrant; it therefore infallibly translated *errors* made by its author (Mormon). In other words, God accurately translated the errors on the gold plates made by the Nephite historian Mormon. But how can an inspired translation of errant human writings be considered "the Word of God"? This means we have no way of knowing how accurate Mormon was in his history. If we know that there are *some* errors of substance, how can we guarantee that there are not many, particularly when the text we now have cannot be independently corroborated? The *Book of Mormon*'s title page, "Brief Explanation," and Nephi all declare or suggest errors (see 1 Nephi 19:6).

But again, even the claim to divine translation is suspect. Recall the translating process—Smith's face buried in a hat dictating sentences that appeared through the power of a magical seer stone. As we saw, this was the testimony of one of Joseph's wives, Emma Smith, as well as the Three Witnesses, all of whom agreed that the actual plates were often *not even present*. Nevertheless, for each sentence, "if [it was] not written correctly it remained until corrected." Only then would it disappear and a new one appear.[6] "All was as simple as when a clerk writes from dictation."[7] If this claim is true, then there should not be a single error in the text. If the claim is false, then the *Book of Mormon* could have any number of errors, serious or otherwise.

We have already cited David Whitmer's testimony that the *Book of Mormon* was produced by a process equivalent to mechanical dictation. (*Doctrine and Covenants*, chapter 9, does not negate this, as many Mormons claim.) Oliver Huntington further declared in his own journal that he heard Joseph F. Smith, the sixth prophet of the church, affirm that "Joseph did not render the writing on the gold plates into the English language in his own style of language, as many people believe, *but every word and every letter was given to him by the power of God....*If there was a word wrongly written or even a letter incorrect, the writing on the stones would remain there....and when corrected the sentence would disappear as usual."[8] In other words, a perfect, inerrant translation. The Mormon theory of revelation simply will not allow for changes. As Dr. Hoekema emphasizes:

This means, then, Joseph Smith's translation differs from all other translations that have ever been made; it was inspired directly by God and is therefore errorless. This means, too, that the original manuscript of Smith's translation must be the authoritative one, since it embodies the translation as it is alleged to have come directly from God. No changes therefore may be tolerated in this original translation, since a single change would be sufficient to upset the theory that this was an errorless translation.[9]

The *1830 edition*, then, is God's Word. As the Mormon apologetic tract "The Challenge" emphasizes, "…you must have no changes in the text. The first edition as you dictated to your secretary must stand forever."[10] If Mormons can live with this claim, that is certainly their option. But perhaps they should reconsider the ethics of attempting to persuade others that no changes have ever been made in their scripture.

Some Mormons have claimed that the Three Witnesses "made up" the idea of a word-for-word translation, or that such accounts are not official, which, of course, has little to do with their truthfulness. However, even Joseph Smith himself was reported to have taught the equivalent idea of mechanical dictation.[11] So, no matter whether God *translated* errors or *inspired* errors, Mormons face a serious problem.

## Changes in the *Book of Mormon*

Jerald and Sandra Tanner have photo-reprinted the original 1830 edition of the *Book of Mormon*, noting in the current text over 3,900 changes, the majority being in spelling and grammar. Another researcher has noted a total of 11,849 changes, including capitalization, punctuation, etc., from the 1830 edition.[12] These facts prove the translation was far from perfect or "divine." And, if the issue is "inconsequential," as some Mormons claim, why did President David O. McKay attempt to suppress sales of the original editions of the Mormon scriptures? Further, why have committed Mormons said they left the church because of such errors—if the issue is really so inconsequential?[13]

Is all this why Mormon authorities eventually changed their minds?

> Finally, the Mormon church leaders became so embarrassed about the grammar that they decided to abandon the idea that God gave Joseph Smith the English that is found in the *Book of Mormon;* their new idea was that God just gave Joseph Smith the idea and that he expressed it in his own words.[14]

Unfortunately, church leaders here are denying the solemn testimony of both their prophet and their Three Witnesses. In effect, they are calling Joseph Smith and the Three Witnesses liars—or deceivers. Logically, the same charges must be brought against God and Jesus who, as we remember, also testified to the book's perfect translation. But little choice was left. Note just a few quoted portions from the first (1830) edition as cataloged by the Tanners in their *3,913 Changes in the* Book of Mormon: *A Photo Reprint of the Original 1830 Edition of the* Book of Mormon *with All the Changes Marked.* We have verified these changes by consulting our own copy of the 1830 edition, reproduced in 1958 from uncut sheets by Mormon Wilford C. Woodruff.[15]

- Diseases which was subsequent to man [i.e., to which men were subject][16]
- And whoredoms is an abomination before me: thus saith the Lord of Hosts[17]
- Wherefore, all things must needs be a compound in one....wherefore it must needs have been created for a thing of naught....And all things that in them is[18]
- Lest he should look for that which he had not ought[19]
- There he found Muloki a preaching the word[20]
- A begging for his food[21]

- They did cast up mighty heaps of earth for to get ore[22]
- But it all were vain[23]

The above are only a few of the literally thousands of places where the first edition has now been corrected. Consider these examples also: "Arrest the scriptures" has been changed to "wrested" the scriptures, "ariven" to "arrive," "respects" to "respect," "fell" to "fallen," "wrote" to "written," "exceeding afraid" to "exceedingly afraid," "began" to "begun," and so on. Hundreds upon hundreds of changes of this type as well as hundreds of cases of addition or deletion of words mean that the book could not have possibly been divinely translated as claimed.[24]

Some of the changes are not simply grammatical; they alter doctrine. For example, in 1 Nephi 20:1, an attempt is made to teach Old Testament baptismal practices by adding "out of the waters of baptism," even though this is *not* present in the original 1830 edition.[25]

In Alma 29:4 the words "[that God] yea, decreeth unto them decrees which are unalterable" is *removed*, yet it is present in the 1830 edition.[26] Hoekema concludes:

> Does it seem likely God would "inspire" a translation in which both grammatical and doctrinal corrections would have to be made? Mormons have no right to regard the grammatical errors as excusable on the grounds of Smith's lack of formal education, for this entire translation is alleged to have been made "through the gift and power of God," and is said to be "In no sense the product of linguistic scholarship."...Mormons cannot even admit a single grammatical error in Smith's original translation.[27]

As we have seen, Mormons who admit to *Book of Mormon* changes may claim that they are grammatical only and that the basic *meaning* of the text has never been changed. This is also false. For example, the 1830 edition of Mosiah 21:28 refers to King Benjamin, while modern editions read "King

Mosiah."[28] According to Mormon chronology, Benjamin was dead and so no longer king at this point (Mosiah 6:3-7; 7:1), so the divinely inspired name was changed to King Mosiah to *cover the error*. The same change was made in the book of Ether.[29]

In similar fashion in 1 Nephi 11:18, the 1830 edition (p. 25) teaches, in reference to Mary, "The virgin which thou seest, is the mother of God after the manner of the flesh."[30] However, since Mary could not have been the literal *mother* of the Mormon earth deity Elohim, modern editions read "the mother of *the son of* God" rather than "the mother of God."

The 1830 edition of 1 Nephi 11:21 reads, "Behold the lamb of God even the eternal Father!"[31] Since Mormons do not believe Jesus is the literal person of the Father, modern editions read, "Yea, even the *son of* the Eternal Father." Additional significant changes may be found in 1 Nephi 13:22; 19:20; 2 Nephi 4:12; Mosiah 29:15; Alma 37:21,24; 3 Nephi 3:23; 22:4; and other passages.

When asked about such things, many Mormons will say these changes are only lies perpetrated by "enemies" of the church. In his *Answers to Gospel Questions*, President Joseph Fielding Smith (who served as church historian from 1921 to 1970) claims the following:

> A careful check of the list of changes submitted by these critics shows there is not one change or addition that is not in full harmony with the original text. Changes have been made in punctuation and a few other minor matters that needed correction, but never has any alteration or addition changed a single original thought.[32]

But anyone who wishes can obtain a notarized copy of the 1830 edition of the *Book of Mormon* and mark these changes for themselves. All they need to do is write to Utah Lighthouse Ministry (see Resource List). President Smith is wrong.

Furthermore, as if to add insult to injury, the "inspired" translation of the *Book of Mormon* even contains *translation* errors of the King James text (e.g., Isaiah 4:5/Nephi 14:5;

Isaiah 5:25/2 Nephi 5:25). And, when it quotes the King James Version, it _includes_ the italicized words, which, of course, are not present in the original Greek and Hebrew (e.g., see Mosiah 1–4 and Isaiah 53). In a "perfect translation" done by the power of God, matters should already be perfectly lucid. Why then would God add exactly the _same_ words the King James translators happened to choose to amplify the meaning of the text? And recall that the King James translators wouldn't even be born for another thousand years.

In light of these and other facts it is incredible that Mormons say they will only accept the Christian Bible "insofar as it is translated correctly"—since it is clear they are the community having translation problems. Mormons are often critical of Christians, claiming that they have changed or removed "truths of Scripture" in order to preserve false traditions and heretical doctrines.[33] Yet Mormons make these charges without providing a shred of evidence. But Mormonism has inadvertently condemned itself, for Mormonism is the party that has changed its scriptures in literally thousands of places.

In conclusion, modern Mormons have only two choices: either 1) Smith copied mistakes that were on the alleged gold plates, or 2) the _Book of Mormon_ was not translated by divine power. Either way, the _Book of Mormon_ could contain any number of serious errors. Certainly, whatever else one may say about the _Book of Mormon_, we may say with confidence that it could not have been divinely inspired and translated. Unfortunately, from this point on, matters deteriorate precipitously.

## Changes in _Doctrine and Covenants_

The Mormon scripture known as _Doctrine and Covenants_ is clearly the most important doctrinal text for the Mormon church. The tenth president and prophet of the Mormon church, Joseph Fielding Smith, declared:

> In my judgment there is no book on earth yet come to man as important as the book known as the _Doctrine and Covenants_, with all due respect to

> the *Book of Mormon*, and the Bible and the *Pearl of
> Great Price* which we say are our standards in doc-
> trine. The book of *Doctrine and Covenants* to us
> stands in a peculiar position *above them all*....The
> Bible is [only] a history containing the doctrine
> and commandments given to the people anciently.
> That applies also to the *Book of Mormon*....But this
> *Doctrine and Covenants* contains the word of God
> to those who dwell here now. *It is our book*...it is
> worth more to us than the riches of the earth.[34]

If *Doctrine and Covenants* "stands above" the Bible and
other Mormon scriptures, then of all Mormon scripture it
should be the least tampered with—at least if respect for
things divine means something to Mormon authorities.

But if the alterations in the *Book of Mormon* are not serious
enough, consider the revisions that have been made in *Doctrine and Covenants*. At least *twenty-five thousand* words have
been removed and *three thousand* other changes have been
made in this scripture.[35]

The original edition of *Doctrine and Covenants* was published in 1833 with the title *A Book of Commandments*. This text
purportedly contained direct revelations from God to Joseph
Smith. Thus there could have been no "translation problems"
possible because Smith received word-for-word dictation of
direct divine inspiration. Even the modern introduction to
*Doctrine and Covenants* emphasizes the following: "Concerning
this publication the elders of the Church gave solemn testimony that the Lord has borne record to their souls that the
revelations were true." But strangely, in 1835 the first edition
of what came to be called *Doctrine and Covenants* appeared—
with literally *thousands* of changes made from God's earlier
revelations and commandments as given in *A Book of Commandments*. We have a copy of the 1833 text and have proven
to our own satisfaction that such changes have been made. So
may anyone else.

The Tanners explain why this is such a problem: "Of all
Mormon writing we would expect the *Doctrine and Covenants*

to be the most pure and free from revision. The reason for this is that *Doctrine and Covenants* purports to be the revelations given directly from God to Joseph Smith—not just a translation....Yet, upon careful examination, we found thousands of words added, deleted or changed. How can the Mormon leaders explain this?"[36]

They cannot. Unwilling to entirely reject their scripture, their only recourse has been to resort to subterfuge and deception. For example, they have attempted to suppress the evidence: "For many years the Mormon leaders tried to suppress *A Book of Commandments*. They would not allow us [the Tanners] to obtain photocopies of the book from Brigham Young University."[37]

Incredibly, many Mormons today will not even admit to such changes because Mormon leaders have lied to them and declared that the revelations "have remained unchanged," and that "there has been no tampering with God's word" because "there was no need for eliminating, changing, or adjusting any part to make it fit [earlier revelations]."[38]

Other Mormons who feel constrained to admit that there are vast alterations make the incredible assertion that God has the right to "change His mind" or that the scribes and publishers made thousands of errors.[39] But even other Mormons admit such ideas are absurd.[40]

What's more, the fact is that the 1835 edition has also undergone drastic alterations:

> Besides the thousands of words which were added, deleted or changed in the revelations after they were published in the *Book of Commandments* and other early publications, one whole section on marriage has been removed. Also the *Lectures on Faith*, which comprise 70 pages of the 1835 edition of the *Doctrine and Covenants*, have been completely removed from later editions....All of these alterations have been made in just a little over 140 years. Imagine what would have happened to the Bible if the churches that preserved it had altered

it at the same rate that the Mormons have altered the *Doctrine and Covenants*. We would be lucky to have anything the way it was originally written![41]

Perhaps it is easy to understand why the seventy pages comprising the *Lectures on Faith*—first published in the 1835 edition—were finally removed in 1921. This section was deleted to avoid contradictions with modern Mormon theology.[42] For example, these divine revelations declare that the Father is "a personage of spirit," which contradicts Mormonism's claim that He has a physical body.[43] They also teach that God is "omnipresent," again contradicting current Mormon doctrine.[44] *Lectures on Faith* contains many other teachings that the modern church rejects, and so it was removed. Likewise, thousands of other changes were made in *Doctrine and Covenants* whenever the need arose. Recently, the church canonized the 137th section of *Doctrine and Covenants*, omitting some two hundred words of the original divine prophecy of Joseph Smith—words containing false prophecies.[45] But are such actions credible with the church's claim to respect and honor the "Word of God"?

The interested reader may see for himself all these changes—not only in the *Book of Mormon*, but also in *Doctrine and Covenants*—by comparing photographic reprints of notarized first editions of the *Book of Mormon* and *Doctrine and Covenants*. These have been published under the title *Joseph Smith Begins His Work, Volumes 1 and 2* and are available at a minimum cost.*[46] (See Resource List.)

Significantly, recent editions of *Doctrine and Covenants* (1982, 1989) confess that *some* changes have been made:

> In successive editions of the *Doctrine and Covenants*, additional revelations or other matters of record have been added....Beginning with the 1835 edition a series of seven theological lessons was also included; these were titled the "Lectures

---

* In his book *Are the Mormon Scriptures Reliable?* Ropp lists a number of these changes with a helpful tabular comparison of *A Book of Commandments* in parallel sections (in correct order), so that the reader may observe the changes for himself.

on Faith."...these lectures have been omitted from the *Doctrine and Covenants* since the 1921 edition....It is evident that some errors have been perpetuated in past editions,...this edition contains corrections....These changes have been made so as to bring the material into conformity with the historical documents.[47]

But while being forced to admit to such changes, the Mormon church offers no explanation of them—nor an apology to church members for distorting God's Word.

## Changes in the *Pearl of Great Price*

The *Pearl of Great Price* is Mormonism's third "inspired" scripture and, again, the church maintains that no changes have been made in the sacred text. However, the *Pearl of Great Price* has had literally thousands of words deleted and hundreds added, as has been documented in the Tanners' text *Changes in the* Pearl of Great Price: *A Photo Reprint of the Original 1851 Edition of the* Pearl of Great Price *with All the Changes Marked*[48] (currently updated as *Flaws in the* Pearl of Great Price; see Resource List).

Even recent versions of the *Pearl of Great Price* (1982, 1989) confess to some changes: "Several revisions have been made in the contents as the needs of the church have required....In the present edition some changes have been made to bring the text into conformity with earlier documents."[49]

But such a confession, even if forced by data that can no longer be ignored or suppressed, gives the average Mormon no idea of the *extent* of the changes made. Let us give just one example. Page 14 of the 1851 edition requires adding 355 words, changing 63 others, and deleting 4 more to conform it to modern editions. In fact, some whole sections (for example, pages 33-35) are missing—and such examples could be multiplied with monotony.[50]

## A Look at the *Book of Abraham*

The *Book of Abraham* is a portion of the *Pearl of Great Price*, and it was supposedly written by Abraham four thousand years ago in "reformed Egyptian." Somehow it found its way into the hands of Joseph Smith, who then "divinely" translated it. Smith claimed he purchased the papyrus manuscript from a traveling Egyptologist. Of course he then translated this alleged "reformed Egyptian" text when next to nothing was known about translating Egyptian and no one could disprove the translation.

Today it can be translated accurately since a copy of the papyrus manuscript was located in 1967—and it is in a *known* Egyptian script. In fact, the *Book of Abraham* is merely a false translation of a pagan text, the Egyptian *Book of Breathings*, which is an extension of the *Egyptian Book of the Dead*, relating to the alleged journeys of the dead in the afterlife.[51]

Any number of Egyptologists have now proven that the *Book of Abraham* is a fraud. They all agree that it has nothing to do with Abraham or the *Book of Breathings*. It is thus beyond question that Smith's "divine translation" has nothing at all to do with what the Egyptian papyrus actually states. Indeed, not a "single word" of Smith's alleged translation was correct. Archaeologist Dr. Richard Fales comments, "Joseph Smith did not get right even one word in this whole translation. In fact, he took one little letter that looks like a backwards 'e' and translated it into over 76 words with seven names."[52]

Gleason Archer holds a Ph.D. in comparative literature from Harvard. He is a linguist who reads in twenty-eight different languages. He also teaches Egyptian and has been reading it since 1933.[53] He observes:

> Earlier negative verdicts of scholars like Theodule Devaria of the Louvre, and Samuel A.B. Mercer of Western Theological Seminary, and James H. Breasted of the University of Chicago and W.M. Flinders Petrie of London University (who had all been shown Smith's facsimiles) were clearly upheld by a multitude of present-day

Egyptologists. Their finding was that *not a single word* of Joseph Smith's alleged translation bore any resemblance to the contents of this document. It turned out to be a late even Ptolemaic copy in hieratic script of the Sensen Papyrus, which belongs to the same genre as the *Egyptian Book of the Dead*....Needless to say, the completely mistaken concept of Joseph Smith as to his competence in ancient Egyptian is now clearly demonstrated to be beyond debate.[54]

In other words, Smith could just as easily have translated an Egyptian cookbook and claimed his translation was an English New Testament. The *Book of Abraham* is thus either pure imagination, deliberate hoax, or spiritistic deception. Significantly, it has been rejected by the second largest organized Mormon body, the Reorganized Latter-day Saints.[55]

Yet, incredibly, the Mormon church has tried to suppress these findings while at the same time continuing to maintain the divine integrity of the *Book of Abraham* and Smith's ability to translate![56]

In the Tanners' opinion,

That the Utah Mormon leaders would continue to endorse the "Book of Abraham" in the face of the evidence that has been presented is almost beyond belief. We feel that if any person will honestly examine this matter he will see that the evidence to disprove the "Book of Abraham" is conclusive.[57]

Why is the Mormon church so reluctant to acknowledge this fabrication? Simply because it casts a fatal pall of doubt upon Smith's claims as to his ability to translate—and hence upon his other religious claims as well. Smith maintained that the *Book of Abraham* was God's word and that he had translated it for us by the "power of God." It has now proven to be a pagan text with a completely false translation. But Smith also avowed he translated the *Book of Mormon* by the "power of God." So how does anyone know that the *Book of Mormon* is not a similar fabrication?

Consider that Smith claimed that both the *Book of Abraham* and the *Book of Mormon* were translated from "reformed Egyptian." But, if the *Book of Abraham* is an example of Smith's ability to translate "Reformed Egyptian," then on what logical basis can anyone trust the *Book of Mormon*? The alleged gold plates could have contained Chinese agricultural records and it would have made no difference. Furthermore, if Smith is wrong in these crucial claims, how can anyone, especially Mormons, trust him when he tells of the first vision account, of subsequent divine revelations and manifestations—or, in fact, of anything else?

That the *Book of Abraham* is a forgery is substantiated by many scholarly works, including H. Michael Marquardt's *The Book of Abraham Papyrus Found*, and *Why Egyptologists Reject the Book of Abraham*, and "The Fall of the *Book of Abraham*" in the Tanners' book *The Changing World of Mormonism*.[58] *Why Egyptologists Reject the Book of Abraham* includes the independent, unanimous testimony of "eight of the world's greatest [recent] Egyptologists and semitists."[59] The Tanners and Walter Martin also cite several of the world's foremost modern Egyptologists, such as Klaus Baer, R.A. Parker, and J.A. Wilson in confirming that[60]

> The Mormon Church has yet to produce a single qualified Egyptologist who disagrees with those [critical] findings. Instead, what the Church has done unofficially is to promote Dr. Nibley's apologetic in an attempt to deny what archaeology, history and logic have proved untenable.[61]

Dee Jay Nelson, a Mormon lecturer, translated the book and, after doing so—like Thomas Stuart Ferguson, the Mormon archaeologist cited earlier—renounced Mormonism, convinced that the *Book of Abraham* was a forgery. In his letter of resignation to the Mormon church leadership, he stated:

> Following my translation (the first to be pub-
> lished) of the bulk of the hieratic and hieroglyphic
> Egyptian texts upon the Metropolitan-Joseph
> Smith Papyri Fragments, three of the most emi-
> nent Egyptologists now living published corrobo-
> rating translations. These amply prove the
> fraudulent nature of the _Book of Abraham_....We do
> not wish to be associated with a religious organi-
> zation which teaches lies.*[62]

Here then are the three standard works of Mormonism: the _Book of Mormon_, _Doctrine and Covenants_, and the _Pearl of Great Price_. These are the "Word of God" to Mormons. We can only ask what must be an embarrassing question: On what logical basis can Mormons trust their scriptures to be the Word of God? Every single one of the standard works has been changed in hundreds or even thousands of places—corrections, additions, deletions—all initially done without any indication or acknowledgement of such action. Why? Why have even church leaders lied about this in public? What do church leaders know that other Mormons don't? What else are they hiding? In changing their own divine revelations, did Joseph Smith and modern Mormon church leaders think they would thereby inspire confidence in the divine authority of those "revelations"? Why is it that the latest editions of the standard works "contain new and important changes in all three books"?[63] Further, if all these books actually deny what God has already revealed in the Bible, why should anyone trust them in the first place?**

In conclusion, the following chart demonstrates the scriptural problems faced by the Mormon church:

---

\* The case against the _Book of Abraham_ is not based on Nelson or his academic qualifications, as some Mormons have argued. It is based firmly on the science of Egyptology and the conclusions of leading Egyptologists.

\*\* It might be asking too much to think that men who proclaim a love for truth and yet willingly alter "God's Word" would leave their own Church history unmolested— even that of their own prophet. And it is asking too much. Numerous, detailed changes are made as seem appropriate for a particular time or circumstance.

|  | **Claim** | **Problem** |
|---|---|---|
| *Bible* | The Bible is the Word of God insofar as it is translated correctly. | The Bible is translated correctly; the *Book of Mormon*, etc., aren't. |
| *Book of Mormon* | Joseph Smith translated the *Book of Mormon* into English through the power of God as "the most correct book of any on earth." | The *Book of Mormon* is replete with changes, errors, and myth; its translation was through occult, not divine means. |
| *Doctrine and Covenants* | *Doctrine and Covenants* is a collection of modern revelations from God. | These revelations have been drastically altered, deny many teachings in the *Book of Mormon*, and are spiritistic in nature. |
| *Pearl of Great Price* | The *Pearl of Great Price* (the *Book of Moses*, the *Book of Abraham*, and certain writings of Joseph Smith) clarifies doctrine and teachings allegedly lost from the Bible and was divinely translated by Joseph Smith from an Egyptian papyrus. | The *Book of Moses* was never written by Moses. The *Book of Abraham* has been proven a fraud by the world's leading Egyptologists. Joseph Smith's ability to "divinely translate" is thoroughly discredited. |
| *Joseph Smith and Other Presidents and Prophets of the Mormon Church* | "In addition to these four books of scripture, the inspired words of our living prophets become scripture to us."[64] | Joseph Smith and the Mormon presidents and prophets historically contradict one another to such a degree that building a uniform theology is impossible. |

# Chapter 11

# Mormons and New Revelations from God

〜

A key theme of Mormon teaching is the necessity for new supernatural revelation from God. The thirteen Articles of Faith represent a condensed version of Mormonism's current doctrinal beliefs, and Article Nine declares: "We believe all that God has revealed, all that He does now reveal, and we believe that He will yet reveal many great and important things pertaining to the kingdom of God."[1]

As a result of its acceptance of new revelation, the Mormon church has added to the biblical canon three additional volumes of scripture: the *Book of Mormon*, *Doctrine and Covenants*, and the *Pearl of Great Price*. Moreover, Mormonism believes that divine revelation is necessary on two levels:

1. For the church canon (as a source of new scripture); and

2. For individual Mormon leaders and laity (as personal inspiration for daily guidance).

Let's take a closer look at these in turn.

## 1. New scripture

As far as the canon is concerned, it remains perpetually open: "The canon of Scripture is still open; many lines, many precepts are yet to be added; revelation, surpassing in importance and glorious fullness any that has been recorded, is yet to be given to the Church and declared to the world."[2]

Thus, the *Book of Mormon* teaches that the Bible does not contain the entire Word of God (2 Nephi 29:7-10) and that the person who denies additional revelation is ignorant of Christ's true gospel and lacks a proper understanding of the Scriptures (Mormon 9:7-9). But this is not what the Bible teaches. For example, when the New Testament emphasizes that the faith, or doctrine, of the church was "once for all delivered to the saints," it forcefully rejects the concept of new or post-apostolic revelation (Jude 3).

Nevertheless, the first president and prophet of the church, Joseph Smith himself, taught that any who reject the new Mormon revelations "cannot escape the damnation of hell."[3] Ezra Benson, the late president and prophet, agreed when he said, "Joseph Smith received many revelations from Jesus Christ, as have the [Mormon presidents and] prophets who have succeeded him, which means that new scripture has been given."[4]

Thus Mormonism teaches that to reject the concept of continuous revelation, as Protestantism does, is a "heresy and blasphemous denial" of God Himself.[5]

## 2. Individual revelation

On the individual level, the Mormon church teaches the necessity of personal revelation from God. That is, in addition to revealed scripture, one must also accept direct supernatural guidance from God on a daily basis. These revelations may involve such things as an audible voice from God (*D&C*, 93:1; 67:10-14), supernatural dreams, the use of "angelic" messengers, communications from the dead, or other means.[6] Without this supernatural guidance, one cannot discern truth from error or what is from God from what is from Satan. As a result, the church actively promotes the concept.[7]

Thus the late Mormon theologian Bruce McConkie teaches in his authoritative *Mormon Doctrine* that every good Mormon receives supernatural revelation and that it is the duty of Mormons to "gain personal revelation and guidance" for their personal affairs.[8]

Further, church leaders also claim that direct revelation from God is daily guiding the church: "The Spirit is giving direct and daily revelation to the presiding Brethren in the administration of the affairs of the Church (*D&C*, 102:2,9,23; 107:39; 128:11)."[9]

Unfortunately, the concept of continuous revelation places the church on the horns of a dilemma. Its doctrine requires the acceptance of new revelation, yet it has no authoritative basis by which to guard against false information. Why? Because there is no objective, unchanging standard by which to test its truth or falsehood. As we will prove later, Mormon scripture contradicts itself, as do the church's "divinely inspired" presidents and prophets (see chapter 12). Church doctrine has thus placed both laity and leadership in a precarious position: How does one determine truth? In Mormonism there is no trustworthy, objective standard by which to prove any revelation has divine authority.

What logical problem does this concept of new revelation present for Mormons? First, how can any Mormon objectively determine the real source of the inspiration, whether it is 1) divine, 2) demonic, or 3) psychological? Second, whether a person is merely deluded or actually supernaturally inspired, the "revelation" has been predefined as truth before it is even received. Third, once an openness to supernatural revelation is required, it cannot be expected that the faithful will deny any supernatural information they receive, especially if the test of its truthfulness is entirely subjective.[10]

All this is crucial for understanding how easily Mormonism was (and is) led into unbiblical teachings.

Let us illustrate the seriousness of the problem by discussing the claims of both an early and a modern Mormon prophet—Brigham Young and Ezra Taft Benson. We'll begin with Brigham Young, who was the second president and prophet of the church. Even though his sermons emphatically contradicted biblical teaching, he claimed that all his sermons were divinely inspired scripture. Young himself illustrates the crux of the problem:

> In my doctrinal teachings I have taught many things not written in any book....I have never looked into the Bible, the *Book of Mormon*, or the *Doctrine and Covenants*, or any of our Church works to see whether they agreed with them or not. When I have spoken by the power of God and the Holy Ghost, it is the truth, *it is scripture*, and I have no fears but that it will agree with all that has been revealed in every particular.[11]

Unfortunately, it did not always agree. Young had merely accepted alleged supernatural inspiration, assuming it to be divine, and concluding that it would therefore agree with other scripture. But on what logical basis can anyone think that the mere *claim* of "divine revelation" proves that it originates in God? Could it not also originate from the deceptions of a prideful heart, or even from Satan himself—particularly if it profanes God and denies and opposes what God has already said is true in His Word?

No wonder Young received revelation that was unbiblical. He naively assumed that whatever he received was "of God," never bothering to check Scripture as the standard. But time and again the Bible warns against this approach. It should not be surprising, then, that those who violated the principle outlined in Acts 17:11,12 ("examining the Scriptures daily, to see whether these things were so") might become easy targets for spiritual deception.

Nevertheless, Young believed he spoke under divine inspiration and that, therefore, his transcribed lectures were literally scripture: "I say now, when they are copied and approved by me they are as good Scripture as is couched in this Bible"[12] and, "I have never yet preached a sermon and sent it out to the children of men, that they may not call it Scripture. Let me have the privilege of correcting a sermon, and it is as good

Scripture as they deserve. The people have the oracles of God continually."[13]

In spite of some Mormons' claims to the contrary, Young's sermons were recorded accurately, so, according to him, they are to be regarded as God's Word.[14] Additional evidence that his sermons *were* regarded as scripture is provided by Mormon apostle Orson Pratt.[15]

Consider the extent of Young's own assertions for his divine inspiration and guidance. He claimed that whatever was accomplished by him was neither by his wisdom nor ability, "but it was all by the power of God, and by intelligence received from Him."[16] In the same vein he says, "I have had many revelations; I have seen and heard for myself, and know these things are true....What I know concerning God, concerning the earth, concerning government, I have received from the heavens, not through my natural ability."[17]

At this point, Mormonism has a problem in determining what constitutes a spiritual authority. Since Young claimed to have divine inspiration, the modern church cannot logically *reject* his teachings and simultaneously *maintain* his prophethood. But they *do* reject his teachings—one of which we will examine here, the "Adam-God" doctrine.

The Mormon church has long been embarrassed by an odd teaching proclaimed by Brigham Young and held by some of its early leaders. They believed that the God of this earth was not Elohim, as the modern church holds, but rather, Adam of the Garden of Eden.

Brigham Young started the controversy April 9, 1852, by stating of Adam, "He is our father and our God, and the only God with whom we have to do."[18] He further added, "There are many who know that doctrine to be true."[19] Young had no doubts on this issue; in fact, he declared that the doctrine was "the word of the Lord":

> Concerning the item of Doctrine alluded to ...that Adam is our father and God, I have to say do not trouble yourselves, neither let the Saints be troubled about the matter....If, as Elder Caffall

remarked, there are those who are waiting at the door of the Church for this objection to be removed tell such, the Prophet and Apostle Brigham Young has declared it, and *that it is the word of the Lord.*[20]

Many other Mormons, including leaders, agreed: "Adam is really God! And why not?"[21] Elder James Little remarked, "I believe in the principle of obedience; and if I am told that Adam is our father and our God, I just believe it."[22] Another observed that because President Young "says that Adam is our God—the God we worship—that most of the people believe this."[23]

Naturally, if Adam were God, then Jesus must be his son—the offspring of the sexual union of Adam and one of his celestial wives. There is plenty of evidence for this belief. Hosea Stout observed, "President B. Young taught that Adam was the father of Jesus and the only God to us."[24] Heber Kimball noted, "That first man [Adam] sent his own Son to redeem the world!"[25] An early Mormon hymnal contained the following hymn titled "We Believe in Our God," which included the phrase "Our own Father Adam, earth's Lord, as is plain....We believe in His Son Jesus Christ."[26] George Cannon, a member of the First Presidency, emphasized that "Jesus Christ is Jehovah" and that "Adam is his father and our God."[27]

These are only a few of the citations that could be listed. Mormon polygamist John Musser, the late Christian authority on Mormonism, Dr. Walter Martin, and former Mormons Jerald and Sandra Tanner cite literally dozens of similar statements that include evidence to corroborate that early Mormon leaders believed in Adam as their God.[28]

In conclusion, it *was* believed that Adam was Elohim, the father of Jesus Christ, and that he became Jesus' father through his sexual union with Mary. And although Brigham Young taught this doctrine as scripture, as he taught all his sermons were, any Mormon who teaches it today faces excommunication.

How does the church deal with this major discrepancy? In general, the church has attempted to ignore this teaching. For example, a recommended apologetic text published by the Mormon church, *A Sure Foundation: Answers to Difficult Gospel Questions,* doesn't even mention the issue. When confronted, Mormons have also denied that it was ever even taught. Bruce McConkie called it an *invention* of "cultists and other enemies of the restored truth [Mormonism]."[29]

But whether the Adam-God doctrine is vehemently denied, simply ignored, or craftily reinterpreted, no one familiar with the evidence can say that it was never a genuine teaching of Brigham Young and other early Mormon leaders—for it clearly was.

Another explanation is put forth by the tenth president and prophet of the Mormon church, Joseph Fielding Smith. He alleges that the April 9, 1852 sermon in which Brigham Young first taught this doctrine "was erroneously transcribed."[30] However, according to Dr. Walter Martin, this sermon was "written down by four Mormon scholars so there was no doubt that he said it and he signed it."[31]

If the Adam-God doctrine was somehow a scribal error, how did so many Mormons come to believe it? Once the doctrine was circulating, it is incredible to think that Young would not have stepped forth, corrected the problem, and pronounced true doctrine in the hearing of all. But even when this doctrine was causing many Mormons to leave the church, he never did this. There is no record of a retraction or correction, despite the fact that according to a formerly devout Mormon of the time, "This public declaration [of April 9, 1852] gave great offense and led to the apostasy of many."[32]

Why would Brigham Young ever permit heresy to be circulated under his name without so much as a protest? No evidence exists that Young complained his lectures were distorted by copiers. And certainly no devout Mormon scribe would seek to deliberately pervert the words of a revered prophet—words they confidently considered as coming from the mouth of God Himself! If there were a suspicion of error, would not these copiers seek clarification? Finally, how could it be a scribal error when so many other Mormon leaders accepted the teaching *because* Brigham Young himself had declared it was "God's word"? The scribal error theory is thus not credible.

Nevertheless, Joseph Fielding Smith says only "the enemies of the Church" teach such a doctrine. If so, this would make Brigham Young himself one of the "enemies of the Church." Smith asserts that "Adam is not Elohim, or the God whom we worship, who is the father of Jesus Christ."[33]

Mormon apologist Mark Peterson in *Adam: Who Is He?* also maintains the scribal error theory.[34] He too confesses that "Adam was not Deity" and that "to say that Adam is God is, of course, opposed utterly and completely to the Scriptures as well as to our Articles of Faith."[35]

But no one argues that this teaching is currently held. The question is, did early Mormon authorities hold to this doctrine? And if so, doesn't this mean they too were "opposed utterly and completely to the Scriptures...[and] the Articles of Faith"?

Mormons who are more frank with the evidence at least concede that Brigham Young made some strange statements. An example of this is Dr. Stephen Robinson, chairman of the Department of Ancient Scripture at Brigham Young University. He confesses—a bit sheepishly—that Brigham Young "made some remarks about the relationship between Adam and God that Latter-day Saints have never been able to understand."[36] Noting that Young's teachings on Adam not only conflict with Young's other teachings but also with those of the modern church as well, he asks, "So how do Latter-day Saints deal with the phenomenon? We don't; we simply set it aside. It is an anomaly."[37]

Dr. Robinson seems to imply this was *only* a teaching of Brigham Young and that, besides, it is a largely irrelevant issue. Further, he says that whatever Brigham Young taught, it was never a doctrine of the church because it was never presented to the church for a sustaining vote. Finally, he falsely charges critics with distorting what Brigham Young really taught:

According to them [critics] Brigham Young taught that Adam, the husband of Eve and the father of Cain, is identical to that Elohim who is God, the father of spirits and the father of Jesus Christ. But for Latter-day Saints this interpretation has always been simply impossible. It contradicts the LDS scripture; it contradicts the teachings of Joseph Smith; it contradicts other statements by Brigham Young...it contradicts the teachings of all the prophets since Brigham Young.

Latter-day Saints have never believed that Brigham Young taught the "Adam-God theory" as explained in anti-Mormon literature, and that whether Brigham Young believed it or not, the "Adam-God theory" as proposed and interpreted by non-Mormons simply cannot be found in the theology of the Latter-day Saints. I do not believe it; my parents do not believe it; and neither did their parents before them. Yet, there are few anti-Mormon publications that do not present this "Adam-God theory," the doctrinal creation of our opponents, as one of the most characteristic doctrines of the Latter-day Saints. This is certainly misrepresentation; I believe it is also dishonest.[38]

In other words, he also claims that Brigham Young never really taught the doctrine, but that even if he did, it isn't current doctrine.

But we know of no responsible Christian apologist who has ever maintained that the Adam-God teaching is the current doctrine of the modern church. But Young did call it "the word of the Lord," and the Mormon church has rejected it. Further, over twenty years later, in 1873, Brigham Young remarked concerning this teaching, "How much unbelief exists in the minds of the Latter-day Saints about one doctrine which I revealed to them and which God revealed to me."[39] Thus, we do not think Dr. Robinson is correct when he implies the issue is unimportant or irrelevant. We already documented that Young himself claimed all his sermons were scripture. If so, how can the modern church logically reject the teaching? But if he was wrong, how can the modern church uphold him as a true authority from God? And if Young contradicts both himself and the modern church, so much the worse for the credibility of both.

As we can see from the above-cited example, the church's doctrine of supernatural guidance has thus proven to be its Achilles' heel. It has always maintained that its presidents and prophets were spiritual authorities because they were divinely inspired—then turned around and denied their teachings whenever convenient. But if the church leadership does not respect its own prophets, why should any other Mormon? How do Mormon leaders respond?

Mormon authorities claim that Mormon doctrines are official only if they are found in the standard works of the church—the Bible, the *Book of Mormon*, *Doctrine and Covenants*, and the *Pearl of Great Price*—or if they are sustained by the Mormon church in general conference. They can thus claim that the writings of the Mormon presidents and prophets are *not* scripture or not *necessarily* scripture. A prophet is only a prophet when acting as such they say.

But this approach does not solve the problem. Mormons cannot claim that their prophets' words are and are not scripture at the same time merely for convenience. They cannot deny a prophet a prophet's authority when *as a prophet* he teaches that his words are scripture.

So, was Brigham Young correct or incorrect when he claimed that his sermons were scripture? If correct, the modern church has rejected the Word of God. If incorrect, then how can anything Young taught be trusted? But doesn't the same reasoning hold true for *all* Mormon presidents and prophets?

Let's bring our discussion into the present. Consider the seven-hundred-page volume *The Teachings of Ezra Taft Benson*. Benson is a recent former president and prophet of the Mormon church. The following statement claims that *the words in this book are scripture*:

> President Ezra Taft Benson is the 13th President of The Church of Jesus Christ of Latter-day Saints. As the Prophet, Seer, and Revelator, his inspired words are considered by members of the Church *to be the word of God*. President Benson has been uniquely prepared by the Lord to serve *as His mouthpiece* to the whole world....The excerpts that make up this teaching volume have come from his speeches or public writings after he was called to the apostleship and sustained as a Prophet, Seer, and Revelator.
>
> President Benson personally reviewed the entire manuscript, as did his counselors in the First Presidency.[40]

Mormon leaders further emphasize that each of their presidents and prophets have given "living Scripture." Each one speaks with "the authority of God....God is speaking directly through him....The prophet [is] the man on the earth who is the mouthpiece for God."[41]

Obviously, if the revelations of Benson and other recent presidents and prophets *are* scripture, then logically they cannot possibly contradict the scriptural revelations of the early Mormon presidents and prophets, including Joseph Smith and Brigham Young. But because they do contradict them, the Mormon church continues to be faced with a serious predicament.

It can accept these damaging contradictions and their implications. This would either prove that a) Smith, Young, and other presidents and prophets were false prophets or b) that the presidents and prophets of the modern church are false prophets.

Or, it can simply ignore its earlier prophets and concentrate on modern "revelation." It is by this second approach that modern Mormon leaders think they have resolved the problem of contradictory theology.

But have they? If the modern Mormon church claims that it can identify which portions of its presidents' and prophets' lectures and writings are scripture, then it should do so. If it cannot, then it should not hold out this material as the Word of God to Mormon believers. If we examine Mormon revelation historically, we discover that God has changed His mind so frequently that a uniform theology cannot be built. For in so many places one revelation here denies another there, it becomes impossible to believe that God had anything to do with the Mormon church.

This is why in 1980, president and prophet Ezra Taft Benson went so far as to declare that the president of the church is the only man who can speak for God on everything and that God's new revelation actually *replaces* the old. Consider the comments of former thirty-five-year Mormon Arthur Budvarson, who quotes Benson verbatim and reports on the president's view of his own importance:

> Ezra Taft Benson…has "outlined the way to follow the (Mormon President and) Prophet." He offered fourteen fundamentals, making it perfectly clear that the President of the Mormon Church is God's prophet, and that his word is law on all issues, including politics. Mr. Benson stated in no uncertain terms that the Mormon prophet is the only man who speaks for the Lord in everything! "We are to give heed unto *all his words* as if from the Lord's own mouth." He also stated that as a prophet, the Mormon President can receive revelations on all issues. However, the President does *not* have to preface his revelations with "thus sayeth the Lord" to give scripture.[42]

Note that this prophet of the Mormon church has stated that the Mormon prophet and president does *not* have to say "thus sayeth the Lord" in order to give scripture. So, should we believe Mormon apologists when they claim that past prophets and presidents are giving scripture only when they begin with "thus sayeth the Lord"?

Budvarson then discusses Benson's approach to dealing with the thorny issue of conflicting teachings among past and present Mormon revelation. Note that the words of the president are held to have authority over the Bible as well, since it too is past revelation:

> Then too, Benson made it clear that "the living prophet is more important to the Mormon system than any dead prophet." He warned of "those who would pit the dead prophets against the living prophets, for the living prophets always take precedence." He also stated that the words of the prophet are more "vital than the Standard works" (the Bible, the _Book of Mormon, Doctrine and Covenants_ and the _Pearl of Great Price_), "for those books do not convey the word of God direct to us now, as do the words of a prophet or a man bearing the holy priesthood in our day and generation."
>
> This means that what the Mormon President says is to be regarded as "law" to the Mormon people, and even if he contradicts the Bible, the Mormon Standard works, or any past prophet of Mormonism, he is to be obeyed, since "nothing a Mormon President says can be incorrect."[43]

This is true at least until a Mormon president becomes "out of date." Then his words—words that were once God's words and binding "law"— are no longer relevant because a current Mormon president and prophet has rejected them.

In conclusion, the very basis for determining false revelation—inconsistency with an immutable standard of revealed doctrine—is rejected in Mormonism. Even the late doctrinal authority Bruce McConkie taught that what is literally God's Word and important in one generation may be wholly insignificant in another. "For the future, there are to be new revelations that will dwarf into comparative insignificance all the knowledge now revealed from heaven."[44]

The problem such teaching raises is this: How does a Mormon _know_ that the latest revelation wasn't just invented by the president and prophet for the sake of expediency? Or how does a Mormon know that it isn't a product of self-deception, or even a result of demonic inspiration? By what authoritative standard can *any* Mormon doctrine or teaching be objectively evaluated? If there is no standard, on what logical basis can *anything* a Mormon president and prophet says be trusted?

Tragically, Mormon leaders have insisted upon the complete, unquestioning trust of their followers. Theirs is an unquestioned authority; their word is binding and not open to criticism. One Web site makes this astute observation about unquestioned authority and our beliefs:

> It comes through peer pressure...sometimes it comes from an esteemed college professor. Perhaps we've been taught it from youth. However we might come to uncritically accept a world view, if we fail to search out the truth for ourselves and seek the truth from God, if we do not consider the evidence in whatever form it may come, then we allow others to dictate to us that which we must believe—and in a realm far more important than any other we could ever consider.

Any religion that permits its leaders the authority of God with no checks or balances is asking for problems. The nature of Mormon revelation since 1830 proves the point. Remember, we are not speaking here of progressive revelation—where God reveals new information that does not contradict old revelation. The New Testament is new revelation, but it never contradicts the Old Testament. Rather, it fulfills it. Jesus Himself said He came not to abolish the law and prophets, but to fulfill them (Matthew 5:17). What the Mormon church is claiming is not revelation that is *progressive*, but revelation that is *open* and ultimately *relative*. Because it is relative, it has no authority.

# Chapter 12

# Contradictory Teachings in Mormonism

~

Mormons claim they have additional scripture as "Latter-day prophets" to help them correctly understand "doctrines that have confused apostate Christianity for centuries."[1] The late president and prophet of the Mormon church, Ezra Taft Benson, emphasizes that "the [Mormon] gospel encompasses all truth; it is consistent, without conflict, eternal."[2] The response of Mormon apologist Hugh Nibley to Fawn Brodie's *No Man Knows My History* was this: "Of all churches in the world only this one has not found it necessary to readjust any part of doctrine in the last hundred years....[Mormon doctrine] remains the most stable on earth."[3] Mormons repeatedly claim that their scriptures are not contradictory and their doctrine is stable.[4] Nevertheless, if early and modern Mormon teachings are compared, one discovers they present conflicting doctrines on many key issues. As Sandra Tanner points out, Mormon "leaders have [had] to go back and rework, rewrite, cover-up, change, delete and add [material] through[out] all of their books—their histories, their Scriptures. They [also] suppress their diaries because these things show the confusion and the man-made nature of their theology and religion."[5]

## The Suppression of Information

Because Mormon theology is replete with contradiction, this has led the church to attempt to suppress information it has found embarrassing. These attempts at suppression involve the Reorganized Church as well.[6] Church leaders have apparently felt this approach was justified for at least two reasons:

1. The real Joseph Smith is not the one that the church desires to present to the world, hence suppression of true biographical data is necessary.

2. Modern Mormonism rejects many of its earlier prophets' teachings, and its earlier prophets would reject many of the teachings now approved by church leadership.

Mormon leaders have not only unconscionably suppressed important material from non-Mormon researchers, but also from their own church researchers as well![7] We refer the reader to the footnoted sources for further documentation, especially the Tanners' "Change, Censorship and Suppression" in their book *Mormonism—Shadow or Reality?* and their book *The Case Against Mormonism, Vol. 1.*[8] Even some Mormon writers have confessed to this deliberate, historical distortion:

> But the myths and myth-making persists. Striking evidence for this is found in the fact that currently one of the most successful anti-Mormon proselytizing techniques is merely to bring to light obscure or suppressed historical documents…. The reasoning of those who distort or suppress reality or alter historical manuscripts to protect the delusions of the simple believer is similar to that of the man who murders a child to protect him from a violent world.[9]

Some improvements may have been made in recent years; however, the situation is far from corrected. For example, as the Tanners observe:

A Mormon scholar told us that the journal of George Q. Cannon may never be made available because it contained so much revealing materials concerning the secret Council of Fifty. Also, the church has still not seen fit to publish the diaries of Joseph Smith and other leading Mormons. We can only hope that the Mormon people will continue to exert pressure until the diaries are printed and all the records are made available to the public.[10]

Dr. D. Michael Quinn, who, as noted earlier, received his Ph.D. in history from Yale University, has spent years in diligent study of Mormon history, including an entire "decade probing thousands of manuscripts, diaries and records of Church history."[11] As a result of his historical inquiry into Mormonism, he has produced materials that apparently have displeased church authorities. He comments, "It is discouraging to be regarded as subversive by men I sustain as prophets, seers, and revelators."[12] Nevertheless, he correctly observes that, "Historians have not created the problem areas of the Mormon past; they are trying to respond to them."[13]

He also asks a legitimate question and then comments upon the consequences of church suppression:

Why does the well-established and generally respected Mormon Church today need a protective, defensive, paranoid approach to its history?...The tragic reality is there have been occasions when Church leaders, teachers, and writers have not told the truth *they knew* about difficulties of the Mormon past, but have offered to the Saints [Mormons] instead a mixture of platitudes, half-truths, omissions, and plausible denials....A so-called "faith-promoting" Church history which conceals controversies and difficulties of the Mormon past actually undermines the faith of Latter-day Saints who eventually learn about the problems from other sources (emphasis added).[14]

236 ～ What Do Mormons Really Believe?

For these reasons, he argues, "The Mormon historian has both a religious and professional obligation not to conceal the ambivalence, debate, give-and-take, uncertainty, and simple pragmatism that often attend decisions of the prophet and First Presidency, and not to conceal the limitations, errors, and negative consequences of some significant statements of the prophet and First Presidency."[15]

In regard to the printing of historical materials that have been so damaging to the Mormon church, Dr. Quinn comments, "It is an odd situation when present general authorities criticize historians for re-printing what previous general authorities regarded not only as faith-promoting, but as appropriate for Mormon youth and the newest converts."[16]

Nevertheless, he also observed there was something of a lessening of church restriction on historical research. For example, in 1966 the critical journal *Dialogue: A Journal of Mormon Thought* was established. Also, the periodical *Brigham Young University Studies* is increasingly devoted to historical issues. Also the institutionally independent Mormon History Association, begun in 1965, has further contributed to the cause of increased exposure to the truth about Mormon history. *Sunstone* magazine and Signature Books are also worthy of note. All this is badly needed; once Mormons are frankly exposed to their true history, they will be more qualified to judge the merits of Mormon religion. (Unfortunately, from 1993–1996, many Mormon scholars were excommunicated.)

As noted, the principal reasons for suppressing historical data is to present a false portrait of Joseph Smith to the world and to cover up important contradictions and doctrinal changes. For example, the following teachings of the second president and prophet, Brigham Young, and the late doctrinal theologian, Bruce McConkie, are exactly opposite:

*Brigham Young:*

"The only men who become Gods [are exalted]…are those who enter into polygamy."[17]

"Every man who has the ability to obey and practice it [polygamy] in righteousness and [who] will not [do so] shall be damned."[18]

In making this statement, Brigham Young was merely being faithful to the Mormon scriptures: "...if ye abide not in that [everlasting] covenant [of polygamy], then ye are damned, for no one can reject this covenant and be permitted to enter into my glory" (*D&C*, 132:4). Yet the modern church teaching harmonizes with that of Bruce McConkie.

*Bruce McConkie:*

"Plural marriage is not essential to salvation or exaltation [becoming a god]....All who...engage in plural marriage in this day...will be damned in eternity."[19]

Indeed anyone who carefully examines 1) early and late editions of the *Book of Mormon, Doctrine and Covenants,* and the *Pearl of Great Price,* and 2) the teachings of Joseph Smith, Brigham Young, and other early leaders compared with those of modern prophets and presidents of the church will find conflicting doctrines. Moreover, these doctrines are those concerning God, Jesus Christ, the Holy Spirit, the virgin birth, original sin, the Trinity, polygamy, death and the afterlife, heaven and hell, exaltation, rebaptism—all of which are foundational topics of great significance.

What all Mormons, early or contemporary, do seem to agree upon is 1) the centrality of Joseph Smith, 2) salvation by works, and 3) opposition to Christianity. Beyond this, conflicting views abound.

Nevertheless, both early and modern doctrines lay equal claim to divine inspiration. Thus, as noted earlier, only if modern revelations actually cancel and supersede past ones can any Mormon ascertain God's will: "true doctrine" is then current doctrine, and God's Word of earlier days is discarded. But, then, is not the Word of God itself suspect? On what logical basis can God's revelation today be acceptable while His revelation of a century ago is rejected? However, even putting aside the early-versus-modern conflicts, there is still a problem because there are serious contradictions even among the modern Mormon scriptures. In light of the extent of this conflict, then, can any Mormon really be expected to know "true doctrine"?

The modern Mormon has no logical solution to the problems such changes in doctrine represent—just as he has no solution to the real person of Joseph Smith or the problems of changes in Mormon scriptures. This is why the response of church leadership has been an attempt to suppress knowledge from the devoted member. Thus, having false and/or insufficient information about their prophet, history, and doctrine, Mormons are incapable of independently judging the merits of their own religious convictions.

Where does that leave the average Mormon? Should he or she accept the church's claim that the early prophets *were* true prophets and hence absolutely authoritative? If so, then he or she must charge modern Mormonism (and *not* Christianity) with apostasy, for the modern church absolutely denies many of its early divine revelations.

Or should the average Mormon discard the early Mormon prophets as men who received erroneous revelations and were, therefore, false prophets—since many of their teachings are rejected today by church leadership on the basis of modern revelation? If so, then the entire Mormon church collapses, for it is based squarely upon the divine *authority* of such men.

In the end, the individual Mormon who does not retreat into subjective experiences or wishful thinking is faced with two equally unpleasant options. Either 1) the modern Mormon church is in apostasy and cannot be trusted, or 2) the early prophets were deceivers or deceived men and cannot be trusted. In either case, Mormonism is proven to be a false religion.

## Contradictions in Mormon Scripture and Theology

Again, Mormonism and its gods have always emphasized that their church offers no conflict of doctrine. Speaking in *Doctrine and Covenants*, 3:2 "God" says: "For God doth not walk in crooked paths…neither doth he vary from that which he hath said…." In the *Book of Mormon* "Jesus" warns: "Neither shall there be disputations among you concerning the points of my doctrine, as there have hitherto been" (3 Nephi 11:28).

In his *Mormon Doctrine*, Bruce McConkie, referring to the church's standard works (the Bible, *Book of Mormon*, *Doctrine and Covenants*, and the *Pearl of Great Price*), declares: "All doctrine, all philosophy, all history, and all matters of whatever nature with which they deal are truly and accurately presented.... The Lord's house is a house of order, and one truth never contradicts another."[20]

But the evidence tells us otherwise. On the following pages, you'll find a selected fraction of some of the available contradictions to be found within Mormon scripture and historical writings. We compare early Mormonism against itself, early Mormonism versus modern Mormonism, and modern Mormonism against itself. We should recall that it was the claim of President Brigham Young himself that all his sermons *were* scripture, and that most, if not all, Mormon presidents have made similar claims.

The problem is that Mormon contradictions frequently *result* from scripture ("God's doctrine") and, as Mormons emphasize, "in God's Church, the only approved doctrine is God's doctrine."[21] Below we present selected contradictions taken verbatim.

### The Doctrine of Polygamy

Plural marriage is not essential to salvation or exaltation (McConkie, *Mormon Doctrine*, 578).

For behold, I reveal unto you a new and everlasting covenant; and if ye abide not [in] that covenant, then are ye damned; for no one can reject this covenant and be permitted to enter into my glory (*D&C*, 132:4).

Now Zeezrom said: Is there more than one God? And he answered, No (*Book of Mormon*, Alma 11:28,29).

Ques. Are there more Gods than one?
Ans. Yes, many (*Catechism* by Elder John Jacques, chap. 4, p. 13 cited in "Mormonism—Can It Stand Investigation?" p. 7)

## Adam in the Garden

The *Book of Mormon*, the Bible, *Doctrine and Covenants*, and the *Pearl of Great Price* all declare that Adam's body was created from the dust of the ground, that is, from the dust of *this ground, this earth* (Joseph Fielding Smith, *Doctrines of Salvation*, 1:90).

Adam was made from the dust of an earth, but not from the dust of *this* earth (Brigham Young, *Journal of Discourses*, 3:319).

When our father Adam came into the Garden of Eden, he came into it with a celestial body (Brigham Young, *Journal of Discourses*, 1:50).

We hear a lot of people talk about Adam passing through mortality and the resurrection on another earth and then coming here to live and die again. Well, that is a contradiction of the word of the Lord, for a resurrected being does not die....*Adam had not passed through a resurrection when he was in the Garden of Eden* (Joseph Fielding Smith, *Doctrines of Salvation*, 1:91).

## The Evolution of God from Man

The Lord Omnipotent who reigneth, who was, and is from all eternity to all eternity (*Book of Mormon*, Mosiah 3:5).

There is a God in heaven, who is infinite and eternal, from everlasting to everlasting the same unchangeable God (*D&C*, 20:17).

I am going to prove it to you by the Bible....God himself was once as we are now, and is an exalted Man (Joseph Smith, *Journal of Discourses*, 6:3).

For I know that God is not a partial God, neither a changeable being; but he is unchangeable from all eternity to all eternity (*Book of Mormon*, Moroni 8:18).

## The Omniscience and Omnipotence of God

Each of these personal Gods has equal knowledge with all the rest....None of these Gods are progressing in knowledge: neither can they progress in the acquirement of any truth....

We might ask, when shall we cease to learn? I will give you my opinion about it; never never...both in time and eternity (Brigham Young, *Journal of Discourses*, 3:203).

Some have gone so far as to say that all the Gods were progressing in truth, and would continue to progress to all eternity...but let us examine, for a moment, the absurdity of such a conjecture (Pratt, *The Seer*, Aug. 1853, 117).

God is not progressing in knowledge (McConkie, *Mormon Doctrine*, 1966, 239).

Do not...say that he [God] cannot learn anymore (Brigham Young, *Deseret Weekly News* 22:309.

[God has] knowledge of all things...(Joseph Smith, *Lectures on Faith*, 44, cited in McConkie, *Mormon Doctrine*, 545).

[The teaching that] God is progressing or increasing in any of these attributes, [knowledge, faith, power, justice, judgment, mercy, truth] is false heresy (McConkie, *Mormon Doctrine*, 263).

God...is not advancing in knowledge....He *is* increasing in power (Joseph Fielding Smith, as cited in *Michael Our Father and Our God*, 27, emphasis added).

## The Fall of Man

That old serpent that did beguile our first parents, which was the cause of their fall; which was the cause of all mankind becoming carnal, sensual, devilish, knowing evil from good, subjecting themselves to the devil. Thus all mankind were lost (*Book of Mormon*, Mosiah 16:3,4).

For the natural man is an enemy to God, and has been from the fall of Adam, and will be, forever and ever, unless he yields to the enticings of the Holy Spirit (Mosiah 3:19).

[God] showed unto all men that they were lost, because of the transgression of their parents (*Book of Mormon*, 2 Nephi 2:21).

In the true gospel of Jesus Christ there is *no original sin.* (John Widstoe, *Evidences and Reconciliation*, 195, in Cowan, 75).

## Treatment of Enemies

As I remarked, we were then very pious, and we prayed the Lord to kill the mob (Apostle George A. Smith, *Journal of Discourses*, 5:107).

But behold I say unto you, love your enemies, bless them that curse you, do good to them that hate you and pray for them who despitefully use you and persecute you; that ye may be the children of your Father who is in heaven (*Book of Mormon*, 3 Nephi 12:44,45).

And may God Almighty curse our enemies (Voices: "Amen").

...And the President of the United States inasmuch as he has turned against us....He shall be cursed, in the name of Israel's God, and shall not rule over this nation....And I curse him and all his coadjustors in his cursed deeds, in the name of Jesus Christ (Heber Kimball, _Journal of Discourses_, 5:95).

God Almighty curse such men (Voices all through the congregation: "Amen!"), and women, and every damned thing there is upon the earth that may oppose this people (Heber Kimball, _Journal of Discourses_, 5:32).

The President...will die an untimely death, and God Almighty will curse him; and He will also curse his successor, if he takes the same stand....God Almighty will curse them, and I curse them in the name of the Lord Jesus Christ, according to my calling ....I pray that God my Father and his Son Jesus Christ may bring the evil upon them... (Heber Kimball, _Journal of Discourses_, 5:133).

Let every person be in subjection to the governing authorities. For there is no authority except from God, and those which exist are established by God. Therefore he who resists authority has opposed the ordinance of God; and they who have opposed will receive condemnation upon themselves (Romans 13:1,2).

First of all, then, I urge that entreaties and prayers, petitions and thanksgivings, be made on behalf of all men, for kings and all who are in authority, in order that we may lead a tranquil and quiet life in all godliness and dignity (1 Timothy 2:1,2).

### The Indwelling of God

The Lord hath said...in the hearts of the righteous doth he dwell (*Book of Mormon*, Alma 34:36).

The idea that the Father and the Son dwell in a man's heart is an old sectarian notion, and is false (*D&C*, 130:3).

### Salvation by Grace

Remember, after ye are reconciled to God, that it is only in and through the grace of God that ye are saved (*Book of Mormon*, 2 Nephi 10:24).

Fulfilling the commandments bringeth remission of sins (*Book of Mormon*, Moroni 8:25). Except ye shall keep my commandments....Ye shall in no case enter into the kingdom of heaven (*Book of Mormon*, 3 Nephi 12:20).

### God's Immutability

Mormon prophets have continuously taught the sublime truth that God the Eternal Father was once a mortal man (M.R. Hunter, *Gospel Through the Ages*, 104).

Behold I say unto you, he that denieth these things knoweth not the gospel of Christ; yea, he has not read the Scriptures; if so, he does not understand them. For do we not read that God is the same yesterday, today, and forever, and in him there is no variableness neither shadow or changing? And now if ye have imagined up unto yourselves a god who doth vary, and in whom there is shadow of changing, then have ye imagined up unto yourselves a god who is not a God of miracles (*Book of Mormon*, Mormon 9:8-10).

## The Creation of Man

God...created man, as we create our children; for there is no other process of creation in heaven, on the earth, in the earth, or under the earth, or in all the eternities that is, that were, or that ever will be (Brigham Young, *Journal of Discourses*, 11:122).

By the power of his word man came upon the face of the earth which earth was created by the power of his word. Wherefore, if God being able to speak and the world was, and to speak and man was created, O then, why is he not able to command the earth or the workmanship of his hands upon the face of it, according to his will and pleasure? (*Book of Mormon*, Jacob 4:9).

## Polygamy

I, the Lord, justified my servants Abraham, Isaac, and Jacob, as also Moses, David and Solomon, my servants, as touching the principal doctrine of their having many wives and concubines (*D&C*, 132:1).

Behold, David and Solomon truly had many wives and concubines which thing was abominable before me, saith the Lord....For there shall not any man among you have save it be one wife; and concubines he shall have none (*Book of Mormon*, Jacob 2:24,27).

Thou shalt love thy wife with all thy heart, and shalt cleave unto her and none else.... Thou shalt not commit adultery (*D&C*, 42:22,24).

We declare that we believe that man should have one wife (*D&C*, section 109 [CIX], 1866 edition).

## Salvation by Grace

"Salvation is *free*" (2 Nephi 2:4), but it must also be *purchased*; and the *price* is obedience to the laws and ordinances of the gospel. Eternal life is available *freely*, "without money and without price" (Isaiah 55:1; 2 Nephi 9:50), but it is gained only by those who *buy* it at the storehouse of the Great God who pleads with men to purchase his priceless possession (McConkie, *Doctrinal New Testament Commentary*, 3:461).

## New Revelation

God alone can add to *or diminish* from holy writ. What he has spoken, he has spoken, and none but he can alter (McConkie, *Doctrinal New Testament Commentary*, 3:593).

## God As Spirit?

The Father [is] a personage of *spirit* [meaning that he has a spiritual body which by revealed definition is a resurrected body *of flesh and bones*...] (brackets in original) (McConkie, *Doctrinal New Testament Commentary*, 2:160,161).

## Idolatry

Worship of any god rather than the true God is in fact

service to the *creature* rather than the Creator....God is an exalted *Man* from whose presence there proceeds a light and power which *fills the immensity of space* and which is called the Light of Christ or the Spirit of the Lord. In their worship of a spirit essence that *fills immensity*, the sectarians are in effect worshiping and serving the creature rather than the Creator (McConkie, *Doctrinal New Testament Commentary*, 2:218,219).

## Church Unity

[In light of more than one hundred Mormon sects historically, each one claiming to be the only true Church] Existence of the sects of Christendom is proof positive of the universal apostasy. Truth is one; Christ is not divided; *those who enjoy the Spirit all speak the same things; there are no divisions among them;* but they are "perfectly joined together in the same mind and in the same judgment" (1 Corinthians 1:10-13) (McConkie, *Mormon Doctrine*, 699).

## *Mormon Writings/Scripture and Biblical Theology: Contrasts and Denial*

Hundreds of contrasts could be listed. We list 21 representative samples.

## The Gates of Hell Prevailed

The gates of hell have prevailed and will continue to prevail over the Catholic Mother of Harlots, and over *all* her Protestant Daughters (*Pamphlets* by Orson Pratt, 112, cited by Jerald and Sandra Tanner, *Changing World*, 27).

The kingdoms of this world made war against the kingdom of God...and they prevailed against it....[It has been] overcome and nothing is left (Orson Pratt, *Journal of Discourses*, 13:125).

...I will build My church; and the gates of Hades shall not overpower it (Matthew 16:18).

## "Justification" by Polygamy

Abraham received concubines, and they bore him children; and it was accounted unto him for righteousness (*D&C*, 132:37).

For what does the Scripture say? "And Abraham believed God, and it was reckoned to him as righteousness." Now to the one who works, his wage is not reckoned as a favor but as what is due. But to the one who does not work, but believes in Him who justifies the ungodly, his faith is reckoned as righteousness, just as David also speaks of the blessing upon the man to whom God reckons righteousness apart from works (Romans 4:3-6).

## Hatred of Enemies

In Missouri we were taught to "pray for our enemies, that _God would damn them, and give us power to kill them_" (Letter, B.F. Johnson, 1903, cited in Jerald and Sandra Tanner, _Changing World_, p. 485, see _Journal of Discourses_ 5:32,95, 107,133; 7:122 for similar examples).

You have heard that it was said, "You shall love your neighbor, and hate your enemy." But I say to you, love your enemies, and pray for those who persecute you (Matthew 5:43,44).

Never pay back evil for evil to anyone. Respect what is right in the sight of all men (Romans 12:17).

## Man As Inherently Good

It is, however, universally received by professors of religion as a Scriptural doctrine that man is naturally opposed to God. This is not so. Paul says in his Epistle to the Corinthians, "But the natural man receiveth not the things of God." But I say it is the unnatural "man that receiveth not the things of God."..._The natural man is of God_ (Brigham Young, _Journal of Discourses_, 9:305)

But a natural man does not accept the things of the Spirit of God; for they are foolishness to him, and he cannot understand them, because they are spiritually appraised (1 Corinthians 2:14).

This I say therefore, and affirm together with the Lord, that you walk no longer just as the Gentiles also walk, in the futility of their mind, being darkened in their understanding, excluded from the life of God, because of the ignorance that is in them, because of the hardness of their heart (Ephesians 4:17,18).

It is not natural for men to be evil (John Taylor, 3rd President, *Journal of Discourses*, 10:50).

As it is written, "There is none righteous, not even one; there is none who understands, there is none who seeks for God; all have turned aside, together they have become useless; there is none who does good, there is not even one" (Romans 3:10-12).

## Eternal Matter

We are told by our Father in heaven that *man is eternal*; that he has always existed, and that *all life on this earth came from elsewhere* (Joseph Fielding Smith, *Doctrines of Salvation*, 1:74).

[The] only Sovereign, the King of kings and Lord of lords; who alone possesses immortality (1 Timothy 6:15,16).

"The elements are eternal" (*D&C*, 93:33); "matter or element is...eternal in nature, creation being merely the organization and reorganization of that substance" (Mc-Conkie, *Doctrinal New Testament Commentary*, 3:225); "it is an utterly false and uninspired notion to believe the world or any other thing was created out of nothing" (Mc-Conkie, *Mormon Doctrine*, 169).

By faith we understand that the worlds were prepared by the word of God, so that what is seen was not made out of things which are visible (Hebrews 11:3).

God "calls into being that which does not exist" (Romans 4:17).

By the word of the Lord the heavens were made, and by the breath of His mouth all their host....For He spoke, and it was done; He commanded, and it stood fast (Psalm 33:6,9).

## Justification by Works

Man is justified by works (McConkie, *Doctrinal New Testament Commentary*, 3:260).

For we maintain that a man is justified by faith apart from works of the Law (Romans 3:28).

By the works of the Law no flesh will be justified in His sight (Romans 3:20).

## No Original Sin

In the true gospel of Jesus Christ there is no original sin (John Widtsoe, *Evidences and Reconciliations*, 195, in Cowan, 75).

Through one transgression there resulted condemnation to all men (Romans 5:18).

## Sin Is Not Transgression of Law

It is possible to transgress a law without committing sin, as in the case of Adam (McConkie, *Mormon Doctrine*, 804).

Sin is lawlessness [the transgression of law] (1 John 3:4).

## Eternal Marriage

Marriages performed in the temples for time and eternity, by virtue of the sealing keys restored by Elijah, are called *celestial marriages*....By definition exaltation consists in the continuation of the family unit in eternity....Celestial marriage is a holy and an eternal ordinance....Its importance in the plan of salvation

For when they rise from the dead, they neither marry, nor are given in marriage, but are like angels in heaven (Mark 12:25).

and exaltation cannot be over-estimated (McConkie, *Mormon Doctrine*, 117,118).

## God in Evolution

Remember that God our Heavenly Father was perhaps once a child, and mortal like we are and rose step by step in the scale of progress (Orson Hyde, *Journal of Discourses*, 1:123).

Two of the names of God the Father are, *Man of Holiness*, and *Man of Counsel* (Moses 6:57; 7:35); that is, God is a holy Man, a Man who is perfect in counsel (McConkie, *Mormon Doctrine*, 465).

For I am God and not man (Hosea 11:9); from everlasting to everlasting, Thou art God (Psalm 90:2).

## Rejection of Christ's Deity

Jesus *became* a God...through consistent effort (M.R. Hunter, *Gospel Through the Ages*, Salt Lake City: *Deseret*, 1945, 51, in McElveen, 154).

The Word was God (John 1:1). Jesus Christ is the same yesterday and today, yes and forever (Hebrews 13:8). His goings forth are from long ago, from the days of eternity (Micah 5:2).

## Genealogical Work

Hence, genealogical research is required (McConkie, *Mormon Doctrine*, 308).

Nor to pay attention to myths and endless genealogies, which give rise to mere speculation rather than furthering the administration of God which is by faith (1 Timothy 1:4).

But shun foolish controversies and genealogies and strife and disputes about the Law; for they are unprofitable and worthless (Titus 3:9).

## Creation Order

*Pre-existence* is the term commonly used to describe the *pre-mortal existence* of the spirit-children of God the Father (Spiritual existence first, then physical) (McConkie, *Mormon Doctrine*, 589).

However, the spiritual is not first, but the natural; then the spiritual (1 Corinthians 15:46). (See context; biblically, our material existence is first, then the spiritual.)

Thus declares the LORD who stretches out the heavens, lays the foundation of the earth, and forms the spirit of man within him (Zechariah 12:1).

## The Gospel

Men either have the truths of salvation or they do not; they either possess the gospel, which is the plan of salvation, or they do not. If they have the gospel, it is in overall scope and in minutest detail, exactly what Paul had. If any part or portion of their system of religion differs from what the ancient Apostle taught and believed, what they have is in fact a perversion of the true gospel (McConkie, *Doctrinal New Testament Commentary*, 2:458).

For by grace you have been saved through faith; and that not of yourselves, it is the gift of God, not as a result of works, that no one should boast (Ephesians 2:8,9).

## The Indwelling of God

The idea that the Father and the Son dwell in a man's heart is an old sectarian notion, and is false (*D&C*, 130:3).

Jesus answered and said to him, "If anyone loves Me, he will keep My word; and My Father will love him, and We will come to him, and make Our abode with him" (John 14:23).

## Adam as God

Adam is our Father and Our God (Brigham Young, *Journal of Discourses*, 1:50).

Then to Adam He said, "...you are dust, and to dust you shall return" (Genesis 3:17,19).

## Priesthood Authority

Priesthood is the power and authority of God delegated to man on earth to act in all things for the salvation of men (McConkie, *Mormon Doctrine*, 594).

For there is one God, and one mediator also between God and men, the man Christ Jesus (1 Timothy 2:5).

## Source of Salvation

There is no salvation outside the Church of Jesus Christ of Latter-day Saints (McConkie, *Mormon Doctrine*, 670).

But as many as received Him, to them He gave the right to become children of God, even to those who believe in His name (John 1:12).

Whoever believes in the Son has eternal life; but whoever rejects the Son will not see life, for God's wrath remains on him (John 3:36 NIV).

### The Holy Spirit and Baptism

Cornelius...could not receive the gift of the Holy Ghost until after he was baptized (Joseph Smith, _Teachings_, 199).

Cornelius received "the gift of the Holy Spirit" _before_ he was baptized (Acts 10:43-48).

### The Creation

There really was no beginning because God and matter are eternal (Wallace, _Can Mormonism Be Proven Experimentally?_ 163).

In the beginning God created the heavens and the earth (Genesis 1:1).

### Death

Physical death is part of the plan of happiness our Father prepared for us (_Eternal Progression, Discussion_ 4,8).

The last enemy to be destroyed is death (1 Corinthians 15:26 NIV).

# Chapter 13

# The Track Record of Mormon Prophets

~

The legitimacy and validity of the entire Mormon church rests squarely upon its declaration that Joseph Smith was a genuine prophet of God. If he was not, then the Mormon church has been guilty of promoting a false prophet to the world for over 170 years.

Mormons themselves freely confess that upon the authority of Joseph Smith the church stands or falls. If he was a false prophet, the church cannot be genuine. This is why the issue of Smith's prophethood is so vital to Mormons. Apostle James Talmage said of Smith, "If his claims to divine appointment be false, forming as they do the foundation of the church in this last dispensation, the superstructure cannot be stable."[1] Given this, Mormon authorities have no choice but to perpetuate the claim that Joseph Smith was a true prophet and that his hundreds of prophecies were "literally fulfilled," and are therefore the "marvelous proof" of his divine appointment. For example, Bruce McConkie argues:

> By their works it shall be known whether professing ministers of religion are true or false

> prophets. Joseph Smith was a true prophet. What fruits did he leave? There is probably more evidence of his divine call and mission than of any other prophet who ever lived, Jesus himself only excepted. Joseph Smith has...uttered hundreds of prophecies which have been literally fulfilled.[2]

Joseph Smith himself emphasized that one who claims to be a true prophet of God must have his prophecies evaluated by the standard of God's Word. By his statement "the ancient Word of God" he clearly referred to biblical standards in part:

> The only way of ascertaining a true prophet is to compare his prophecies with the ancient Word of God, and see if they agree, and if they do and come to pass, then certainly he is a true prophet....When, therefore any man, *no matter who*, or how high his standing may be, utters, or publishes, anything that afterwards proves to be untrue, *he is a false prophet*.[3]

By Joseph Smith's own words, then, he is proven to be a false prophet. And by the very words of Mormon authorities the Mormon religion also is proven to be fraudulent. Not only do the many prophecies given by Joseph Smith in *Doctrine and Covenants* deny every biblical doctrine they comment upon, but Joseph Smith's specific predictions of future events have also characteristically proven wrong. While we have not studied every alleged prophecy Mormons claim for Smith, every one we did study proved false.

In 1844, while in jail, Smith was killed by an angry group of townspeople. By that time, he had uttered scores of prophecies "in the name of the Lord." But according to biblical standards, anyone who claims to be a prophet must prove himself so by establishing a perfect record of prediction, for the biblical requirement is for absolute accuracy in prophetic revelation (Jeremiah 28:9). What this means is that a single false prophecy—just one—is sufficient to establish a person as a false prophet. God Himself warned all men:

"But a prophet who presumes to speak in my name anything I have not commanded him to say, or a prophet who speaks in the name of other gods, must be put to death." You may say to yourselves, "How can we know when a message has not been spoken by the Lord?" If what a prophet proclaims in the name of the Lord does not take place or come true, that is a message the Lord has not spoken. That prophet has spoken presumptuously. Do not be afraid of him (Deuteronomy 18:20-22 NIV).

In other words, if anyone spoke in the name of the Lord (Joseph Smith), but spoke presumptuously (Joseph Smith), or in the name of other gods (Joseph Smith), and if the prophecy did not come true (Joseph Smith), that prophet was to die—as, unfortunately, Joseph Smith did in 1844. When Mormon authorities claim that Smith's prophetic record is infallible and that this proves him a true prophet, they are regrettably only continuing the well-established tradition of Mormon distortion in religious matters.

Mormons have in fact devised various ways to "explain" Smith's many false prophecies. There are so many different rationalizations that one wearies of reading them. For example, they may claim, as Smith himself did, that a prophet is only a prophet when he is acting as such—that is, presumably, when he claims to speak in the name of the Lord and is therefore under divine inspiration. Mormons claim that any errors which do exist were, therefore, given when Smith was not "acting" as a prophet.

However, since many of Smith's false prophecies _were_ given "as a prophet," when he _was_ speaking in the name of the Lord, the explanation is irrelevant.

For anyone who lets words mean what they say, the inescapable conclusion is that, according to biblical standards, Joseph Smith was a false prophet. Just as the single act of marital infidelity or a single premeditated killing makes a person an adulterer or a murderer, so a single false prophecy makes one a false prophet.[4] Joseph Smith himself agreed to that standard. In the following cases, we include examples where Smith clearly prophesied "in the name of the Lord," so there can be no mistake that the prophecy was being claimed as divine.

## Examining the Prophecies

### The Canadian Prophecy

David Whitmer (one of the three principal witnesses to the *Book of Mormon*) tells a highly relevant story that not only reveals Smith to be a false prophet, but sprouts seeds of doubt about any purported prophecy or revelation Smith claimed to receive. Just as the Mormon scriptures, in particular *Doctrine and Covenants*, contain the "feel" of occult revelation, here we also sample the flavor of spiritistic "humor."

Here is the story in Whitmer's own words:

> When the *Book of Mormon* was in the hands of the printer, more money was needed to finish the printing of it....Brother Hyrum said it had been suggested to him that some of the brethren might go to Toronto, Canada and sell the copyright of the *Book of Mormon* for considerable money: and he persuaded Joseph to inquire of the Lord about it. Joseph concluded to do so. He had not yet given up the [seer] stone. Joseph looked into the hat in which he placed the stone, and *received a revelation* that some of the brethren should go to Toronto, Canada, *and that they would sell the copyright* of the *Book of Mormon*. Hyrum Page and Oliver Crowdery went to Toronto on this mission, but *they failed entirely to sell the copyright*, returning without any money. Joseph was at my father's house when they returned. I was there also, and am *an eye-witness* to these facts. Jacob Whitmer and John

Whitmer were also present when Hyrum Page and Oliver Crowdery returned from Canada.

Well, we were all in great trouble; and we asked Joseph how it was that he had received a revelation from the Lord for some brethren to go to Toronto and sell the copyright and the brethren had utterly failed in their undertaking. Joseph did not know how it was, so he inquired of the Lord about it, and behold the following revelation came through the stone:

> _Some revelations are of God; some revelations_
> _are of man; and some revelations are of the devil._

So we see that the revelation to go to Toronto and sell the copyright was not of God [even though Smith claimed it was], but was of the devil or of the heart of man....This was a lesson for our benefit _and we should have profited by it in [the] future more than we did._

Whitmer concludes his discussion with a warning to every living Mormon:

Remember this matter brethren; it is very important....Now is it wisdom to put your trust in Joseph Smith, and believe all his revelations in the _Doctrine and Covenants_ to be of God?...I will say here, that I could tell you _other false revelations_ that came through Brother Joseph as mouthpiece (not through the stone), but this will suffice. Many of Brother Joseph's revelations were never printed. The revelation to go to Canada was written down on paper, but was never printed (emphasis added).[5]

Let's consider this account carefully. Smith and the other Mormons were obviously convinced of the divine authority of the initial revelation—or else they would never have taken the difficult journey to Canada. When the prophecy inexplicably failed, they naturally sought an answer from God (by occult means)—and what happened? They received a reply that could not help but strike dread into their hearts: "Some revelations are of God; some revelations are of man; and some revelations are of the devil." Apparently, then, there was no way to distinguish a true prophecy from a false one!

Thus, if this *false* revelation was *indistinguishable* from other revelations of Smith, how can Mormons today know that any of Smith's revelations were legitimate? And what does this fact do to the credibility of the revelations given by any Mormon president and prophet? What is worse, such revelations will never be objectively verified or validated. Why? Because the Bible itself is rejected by Mormonism as a reliable authority. For example, Mormon apostle Orson Pratt stated confidently, "Almost every verse has been corrupted and mutilated....All we have left are mutilated copies containing an incredible number of contradictory readings."[6] And he questions, "Who, in his right mind, could, for one moment, suppose the Bible in its present form to be a perfect guide? Who knows that even one verse of the whole Bible has escaped pollution so as to convey the same sense now as it did in the original?"[7]

This means that the only "Scripture" left to test such revelation by is Mormon scripture, which is itself contradictory and perpetually "open." New revelations can come at any time and be added to the canon of scripture. Whether or not they contradict earlier revelation is irrelevant. In the end, we see that no Mormon should logically place trust in any of Smith's prophecies (or any of his other revelations) because 1) they could just as easily be false as true, and 2) there is no way to tell the difference, until it is too late.

Nevertheless, we will proceed to document some of the false prophecies of Joseph Smith. Let us begin with the alleged scripture *Doctrine and Covenants*. The first false prophecy is found in chapter one, where "God" Himself promises that the prophecies in the book are all true and will come to pass:

> Search these commandments, for they are true
> and faithful, and the prophecies and promises
> which are in them *shall all be fulfilled*. What I the
> Lord have spoken, I have spoken, *and I excuse not
> myself*; and though the heavens and the earth pass
> away, my word shall not pass away, but *shall all be
> fulfilled*, whether *by mine own voice or by the voice of
> my servants, it is the same*. For behold, and lo, the
> Lord is God, and the Spirit beareth record, and *the
> record is true*, and the truth abides forever and ever.
> Amen (*D&C*, 1:37,38, emphasis added).

Note that this section of Mormon scripture claims 1) that
the commandments "are true" and that the prophecies and
promises "shall all be fulfilled"; 2) that the Mormon deity is
placing his own authority on the line when he says, "I excuse
not myself" (for having spoken them); and 3) that the prophecies "shall all be fulfilled" whether by God's own voice "or by
the voice of my servants."

These claims leave no room to maneuver: A single indisputable false prophecy anywhere in *Doctrine and Covenants*
will completely invalidate the entire book. Obviously, then,
the existence of dozens and scores of false prophecies in *Doctrine and Covenants* means that Mormons who trust this book
are being deceived. If 1) the Mormon God has spoken falsely,
and 2) "some revelations are of God; some revelations are of
men; and some revelations are of the devil," and 3) there is no
way of knowing which are which, then the logical conclusion
is that 4) Mormons should not place their trust in any of them.
We will now prove that *Doctrine and Covenants* contains false
prophecies.

### The City and Temple Prophecy

In a revelation given to Joseph Smith on September 22 and
23, 1832, "the word of the Lord" declares that both a city and
a temple are to be built "in the western boundaries of the state
of Missouri" (that is, in Independence, Missouri):

> A revelation of Jesus Christ unto his servant
> Joseph Smith, Jun[ior]....*Yea, the word of the Lord*
> concerning his church...for the gathering of his
> saints to stand upon Mount Zion, which shall be
> the city of New Jerusalem. Which *city shall be built,*
> beginning at the temple lot...*in the western bound-*
> *aries of the state of Missouri,* and dedicated by the
> hand of Joseph Smith....Verily *this is the word of the*
> *Lord,* that the city New Jerusalem shall be built by
> the gathering of saints, beginning at this place,
> even the place of the temple, which temple shall
> be reared *in this generation. For verily this genera-*
> *tion shall not all pass away* until an house shall be
> built unto the Lord, and a cloud shall rest upon it,
> which cloud shall be even the glory of the Lord,
> which shall fill the house....Therefore, as I said
> concerning the sons of Moses—for the sons of
> Moses and also *the sons of Aaron shall offer an accept-*
> *able offering and sacrifice in the house of the Lord,*
> which house shall be built under the Lord *in this*
> *generation,* upon the consecrated spot as *I have*
> *appointed* (*D&C*, 84:1-5,31, emphasis added).

This prophecy clearly teaches that a temple and a city will
be built in western Missouri in the generation of the men *then*
*living* and that it will be dedicated by the hand of Joseph Smith
himself. This temple will stand (in western Missouri) "upon
Mount Zion" and the city will be named "the city of New Jerusalem." It was to be the place Christ returned to at His Second
Coming.[8]

In *Doctrine and Covenants*, 97:19 (August 1833) and 101:17-21
(December 1833), God further declares that He is absolutely
certain as to His intent and the location of this temple: "Zion
cannot fall, nor be moved out of her place, for God is there,
and the hand of the Lord is there," and "There is none other
place appointed than that which I have appointed; neither
shall there be any other place."

It is interesting to note that on July 20, 1833, when Smith was giving this prophecy in Kirtland, Ohio—and unaware of the events taking place in Missouri—the Mormon community had already agreed to leave Missouri because of "persecution." In other words, even as Smith was giving the prophecy "in the name of the Lord," "Zion" was already being "moved out of her place."[9]

How do Mormons respond? They claim the prophecy failed because the Mormon community itself was unfaithful. However, how can Mormons credibly claim this when the church itself was being "persecuted"? Surely, if they had not been living as committed and zealous Mormons, they would never have encountered the social response they did. It was thus undoubtedly the _faithful_ Mormons who were driven from Missouri, leaving the prophecy unfulfilled. And even Mormon historians concede that when they moved to Quincy, Illinois, their promised Missouri "temple" comprised only four cornerstones.[10]

In the ensuing 170 years no temple has ever been built in western Missouri, let alone a Mormon city. Thus Joseph Smith never dedicated a temple, nor were sacrifices offered there. It was not built in "this generation," and no cloud "rested upon" the temple. This revelation alone thus contains at least _four_ false prophecies. Neither can Mormons logically claim that Zion was "reestablished" in Salt Lake City, for the December 1833 prophecy clearly says there will be "none other place" than the western boundaries of Missouri.

Nevertheless, the Mormon reaction to this prediction illustrates the basic Mormon approach to their many false prophecies. Divine predictions are vigorously maintained until proven false. Then they are rationalized. Consider the following train of events.

In spite of being driven from Missouri, the early Mormons intended to return and fulfill the prophecy. In 1861, thirty years after the prophecy was first given, Apostle George Smith emphasized, "Let me remind you that it is predicted that this generation shall not pass away till a temple shall be built, and the glory of the Lord rest upon it, according to the promises."[11]

Then in 1870, almost forty years after the prophecy, Apostle Orson Pratt stated that Mormons could expect a literal fulfillment of the prophecy as much as they do the rising and setting of the sun. Why? *"Because God cannot lie. He will fulfill all his promises.* He has spoken, it must come to pass. This is our faith!"[12]

Perhaps sensing a growing problem, the 1890 edition of *Doctrine and Covenants* (almost sixty years later) carried a footnote declaring that a generation lasted more than a hundred years.[13] This note is not found in *modern* editions of *Doctrine and Covenants*.

Again, in 1900, almost seventy years later, the fifth Mormon president and prophet, Lorenzo Snow, reiterated that Mormons would still go back and build the divinely prophesied temple.[14]

Even in 1931, ninety-nine years after the prophecy (when "that generation" would surely have been dead), the tenth president and prophet of the Mormon church, Joseph Fielding Smith, was stating his "firm belief" that the temple and city would be built. Thus, he promises that when the temple is reared, it will be by

> some of that generation who were living when this revelation was given....I have full confidence in the word of the Lord that *it shall not fail....We have not been released from this responsibility, nor shall we be. The word of the Lord will not fail....*No matter what the correct interpretation may be, the fact remains that *the city Zion*, or New Jerusalem, *will eventually be built* in Jackson County, Missouri *and the temple of the Lord will also be constructed.*[15]

Incredibly, recent editions of Smith's book (1975) continue to retain this embarrassing statement! Logically, one would think that he would have had to confess that his "full confidence in the word of the Lord" proved futile. Who could disagree with his words when he stated in a more recent text: "It is also reasonable to believe that no soul living in 1832, is still living in mortality on the earth"?[16]

It is now more than 170 years since the prophecy, and neither the temple nor the city has been built. There is no way to escape the conclusion that this prophecy is false. But, of course, since Mormonism assumes that Joseph Smith was a true prophet of God, this cannot possibly be a false prophecy. So the process of rationalization sets in. For example, Joseph Fielding Smith dealt with the problem by finally claiming that the term "generation" meant an _indefinite_ period of time and that, due to "persecution," God had "absolved the saints and postponed the day."[17]

Now everyone could relax. There never was a false prophecy.

For some reason, Mormon presidents, prophets, and leaders see "no conflict whatever" between the outcome of the prophecy just cited and the teaching of the _Book of Mormon_ in 1 Nephi 3:7, which says, "The Lord giveth no commandments unto the children of men, save he shall prepare a way for them that they may accomplish the thing which he commandeth them."

What is most disconcerting is that modern Mormons do not seem to be concerned with such an unquestionably false prophecy and refuse to recognize the implications.[18] They continue to believe, and to teach others, that _Doctrine and Covenants_ is the inerrant "word of the Lord and Joseph Smith is a true prophet of God."

### The Civil War Prophecy

The Civil War prophecy represents another false prediction. It is found in _Doctrine and Covenants_ 87:1-8, concerning a prophecy given on December 25, 1832. In his _Articles of Faith_, James Talmage refers to "the facts establishing a complete fulfillment of this astounding prophecy."[19]

However, there was no "complete fulfillment," neither was the prophecy "astounding." It was patently false. What is astounding is that Talmage applies the 1832 prophecy to World War I (1914–1918) when it has nothing at all to do with that war. Indeed, to apply the prophecy to World War I only increases the magnitude of its errors. For one thing, its own declaration requires it be applied to the "wars that will shortly come to pass, beginning…at South Carolina." The prophecy declares:

> Verily, *thus sayeth the Lord* concerning the wars that will shortly come to pass, beginning at the rebellion of South Carolina, which will eventually terminate in the death and misery of many souls; And the time will come when that war will be poured out upon *all nations*, beginning at this place.…And the Southern States will call on other nations, even the nation of Great Britain, as it is called, and they shall also call upon other nations, in order to defend themselves against other nations; and then war shall be poured out upon *all nations*.…And thus, with the sword and by bloodshed *the inhabitants of earth* shall mourn; and with famine, and plague, and earthquake, and the thunder of heaven, and the fierce and vivid lightning also, shall the *inhabitants of the earth* be made to feel the wrath, and indignation, and chastening hand of Almighty God until the consumption decreed hath made *a full end of all nations*.[20]

Joseph Smith made other predictions relating to this great war. Elsewhere he spoke another false prophecy when he declared "in the name of the Lord God" that these tumultuous events would precede the Second Coming of Jesus Christ:

> I prophecy [sic], *in the name of the Lord God*, that the commencement of the difficulties which will cause much bloodshed *previous to the coming of the Son of man* will be in South Carolina. It may probably arise through the slave question. This a voice declared to me while I was praying earnestly on the subject, December 25, 1832.[21]

But listening to "voices" can be perilous.

In looking at this prophecy, we should note several facts. First, it has been demonstrated historically that Smith could have expected a civil war, hence to write of an expected war, one that is public knowledge, is hardly "astounding." For example, "Joseph Smith was familiar with the fact that South Carolina had rebelled at the time he gave the revelation."[22] Also, "many people believed there would be a civil war before it actually took place."[23] For example, five months *previous* to Smith's "revelation," on July 14, 1832, Congress passed a tariff act, refused by South Carolina, and Andrew Jackson alerted the troops. So, even at this time, "the nation was fully expecting a Civil War to begin promptly in South Carolina."[24]

Second, even God Himself didn't seem to know whether or not this great war would arise over the issue of slavery. (He said, "It may *probably* arise through the slave question.")

Third, the revelation itself was wrong on numerous counts: 1) The war did not start until 1861, thirty years later—it did not "shortly come to pass. " 2) War was not "poured out upon all nations" but only on one nation. 3) There were no earthquakes, thunders of heaven, or lightning that struck the "inhabitants of the earth" as evidence of God's wrath. Nor did the remainder of the earth's population feel "the wrath of Almighty God." 4) There was hardly "a full end of all nations."

Finally, Smith's revelation on the war was not printed until 1851, almost twenty years *after* the revelation, and "Mormon leaders have suppressed part of Joseph Smith's diary which tended to discredit the revelation."[25] (This concerned a "dream interpretation" of the prophecy that stated that the United States Government would call on Joseph Smith to defend the "western territory" against England. Smith was already dead at the start of the Civil War, thus the interpretation was false, which cast doubt on the revelation itself.[26]) In conclusion, no one can deny that this is another false prophecy.

Brigham Young was also guilty of false prophecy relating to the Civil War. He predicted that the war would not end until it had emptied the land to allow Mormons to return to Missouri—a prediction that was never fulfilled.[27] He also predicted that the slaves would *not* be freed: "Will the present struggle free the slaves? No…they cannot do that."[28]

Joseph Smith's Civil War prophecy and his "Rocky Mountain" prophecy are considered his "most important prophecies."[29] We have seen that the first is a false prophecy; and the Tanners have documented that the latter is not worth considering in that it is a "forgery which was written after Joseph Smith's death."[30]

### The Second Coming

Along with Jehovah's Witnesses and Seventh-Day Adventists, Joseph Smith predicted that the Second Coming of Christ would occur in the latter part of the nineteenth century. In his *History of the Church*, Smith taught that the Second Coming would occur between 1890 and 1891. Thus, in 1835 he declared Christ's return would occur fifty-six years later; and in 1843 he predicted it would occur in forty-eight years. Smith claimed that the generation then living would not die "till Christ comes."[31] For example, under the date of April 6, 1843, in his *original* History (taken from Smith's diary, March 10, 1843, to July 14, 1843) one can read, "I prophecy [sic] *in the name of the Lord God*—& let it be written: that the Son of Man will not come in the heavens until I am 85 years old, 48 years hence or about 1890" (emphasis added).[32] Of course, Smith was dead within a year—and Christ still has not returned.

Some of the twelve Mormon apostles were told that they also would remain until Christ returned. For example, according to the Tanners, Lyman E. Johnson was told he would "see the Savior come and stand upon the earth with power and great glory"; and William Smith was told that he would "be preserved and remain on the earth, until Christ shall come."[33] Because of such a strong belief in the imminence of the Second Coming, Apostle Parley P. Pratt wrote in 1838:

> I will state *as a prophesy* [sic], that there will not be an unbelieving Gentile upon this continent 50 years hence; and if they are not greatly scourged, and in a great measure overthrown, within five or ten years from this date, *then the* Book of Mormon *will have proved itself false.*[34]

Perhaps not unexpectedly, the entire prophecy has been deleted from the modern versions of the *Writings of Parley P. Pratt*.

## Other Prophecies

There have been many other false prophecies throughout the history of the Mormon church, far too numerous to list. We cite only seven others for purposes of illustration:

1. In the *Book of Mormon*, in 2 Nephi 3:14, it is prophesied that "that seer" (which Mormons interpret as Joseph Smith) will be protected by God: "They that seek to destroy him shall be confounded...this promise...shall be fulfilled."

But it was not fulfilled, for "they that seek to destroy him" did in fact destroy him at a young age in 1844 when he was killed by townspeople in a gun battle in Carthage, Illinois. Smith himself had said in October 1843, "I prophesy, *in the name of the Lord God of Israel*...they never will have power to kill me till my work is accomplished, and I am ready to die."[35] But again, less than a year later, Joseph Smith was dead. And according to accounts of his death, he certainly was not yet "ready to die." While in jail, facing the prospect of confronting the angry people that would kill him, Joseph quickly wrote to his Nauvoo Legion to break into the jail and "save him at all costs."[36] Eyewitnesses noted that just before he was shot he gave the Masonic signal of distress and cried out, "Is there no help...?"—and then after he was shot came the exclamation of surprise, "Oh Lord; my God!"[37]

Furthermore, given the tremendous obstacles facing the church Joseph Smith had founded, who could reasonably say his work had been "accomplished"?

2. In *Doctrine and Covenants* (114:1), it was prophesied in the name of the Lord that David W. Patten would go on a mission one year later:

Verily *thus sayeth the Lord*: It is wisdom in my servant David W. Patten, that he settle up all his

> business...that he may perform a mission unto me next spring, in company with others, even twelve including himself, to testify of my name and bear glad tidings unto all the world.

This prophecy was given April 17, 1838. Six months later, on October 25, 1838, David W. Patten was shot and killed—he "instantly fell, mortally wounded, having received a large ball in his bowels."[38] No one can deny, then, that this is another false prophecy. But if the Mormon God is genuine, why would He prophesy that a man was to preach for Him whom He knew would shortly be killed and thus be unable to fulfill His mission? Patten's death cannot be rationalized with the claim that he was guilty of sin or apostasy because Smith's own remarks after his death claim he was a faithful Mormon until his demise.[39]

3. On May 18, 1843, in the "name of the Lord" and "in the name of Jesus Christ" Joseph Smith prophesied the complete overthrow of the United States Government. This never occurred, nor did the Government ever redress "its crimes" as Smith promised:

> President Smith, in concluding his remarks, said..."*I prophesy in the name of the Lord of Israel,* unless the United States redress the wrongs committed upon the saints in the state of Missouri and punish the crimes committed by her officers that in a few years the Government will be utterly overthrown and wasted, and there will not be so much as a potsherd left" (emphasis added).[40]

And,

> I prophesied by virtue of the holy priesthood vested in me, *and in the name of the Lord Jesus Christ,* that, if Congress will not hear our petition and grant us protection, *they shall be broken up as a government,* and God shall damn them, and there shall be *nothing* left of them—not even a grease spot.[41]

But again, Congress never granted the Mormons their petition. It correctly concluded that Mormon problems with other settlers were a result of their own religious excesses and evil practices such as polygamy, violence against non-Mormons, and their terrible doctrine of blood atonement (which taught that men could be killed to atone for their sins). In fact, the Government so increased its pressure against the polygamist activity of the church that a new "revelation" in 1890 conveniently "reversed" the polygamist doctrines that had prevented Utah's entry into the Union.

Thus, the United States Government was not "utterly overthrown and wasted," nor was there "nothing" left of it, "not even a grease spot." The United States grew to become the most powerful nation on earth.

4. In _Doctrine and Covenants_ (104:1), "Jesus" claimed that the Mormon "United Order"—the Mormon communities in Ohio and Missouri—would remain until He returned. However, the "United Order" failed and was disbanded, and over 150 years later Jesus still has not returned.

5. In the _Book of Mormon_ (Alma 7:10), it is falsely prophesied that the Messiah will be born in Jerusalem when, of course, He was born in Bethlehem. Four biblical books of history attest to Jesus' birthplace as Bethlehem: one prophet who wrote a miraculous prediction in 700 B.C., and three contemporary biographers of Jesus (Micah 5:2; Matthew 2:4-6; Luke 2:4-7; John 7:42).

6. Heber Kimball falsely prophesied that "Brother Brigham Young will become President of the United States."[42]

7. Joseph Smith's father falsely prophesied that Joseph, Jr., "should continue in the Priest's office until Christ comes."[43]

Many other false prophecies could be listed. Colleen Ralson, in _Dissecting the_ Doctrine and Covenants, lists _D&C_, 42:39; 62:6; 69:8; 84:114,115; 88:87; 97:19; 101:11,17; 103:6,7; 111:2,4-10; 112:15,19; 115:14,17; 117:12.[44] Walter Martin refers to several false prophecies in *Doctrine and Covenants* 9:22-24 (with *Doctrine and Covenants* commentary, appropriate section) and also in *Teachings of Joseph Smith* (pp. 17,18).[45] Jerald and Sandra Tanner refer to false prophecies in *Journal of Discourses* 3:228,253,262; 4:40; 5:10,93,94,164,173,174,274,275, and in other sources.[46]

## Ignoring the Deception

With so many false prophecies by Smith and other Mormons, one is tempted to assume that they were either carried away by false visions of their own mind or through spiritistic duplicity. Certainly a truthful God could not be the author of such wrong predictions.

In spite of all these false prophecies, again, Mormons do not show much concern about the issue. Apparently, this is because they have never come to grips with the biblical teaching on what God requires of a true prophet and what a false prophet really is:

> It is somewhat ironic that most Mormons are basically unimpressed by the evidence against their "prophets" concerning the many false prophecies that have issued forth from them. This behavior is so unusual because of the reverence Mormons give their Presidents as "prophets of God." Their attitude of indifference is primarily based upon ignorance and conditioning. The average Mormon is unaware of the biblical tests for a true prophet and is therefore ignorant of how to properly determine if a man is a true prophet or a false prophet. However, the greatest difficulty Mormons have is overcoming their "conditioning." They have been programmed to believe that the greatest test of a prophet is their own personal "testimony" that he is a prophet.[47]

But it must also be said that many Mormons aren't even aware of these false prophecies. For example, if one examines the _Doctrine and Covenants' Student Manual,_ an extensive five-hundred-page commentary on _Doctrine and Covenants,_ one finds that the false prophecies are either ignored or carefully reinterpreted. For example, concerning the rebuilding of the temple, the _Manual_ equivocates on the word "generation" and defines it as an indefinite period.[48] Further,

> The Lord later excused the Saints from building that temple because mobs prevented it...and because the Saints at that time had not kept the commandments as they should....The day will come, however, when the holy city of God will be established in Jackson County, Missouri, and the temple will be filled with the glory of God as envisioned by the prophets.[49]

This completely ignores the clear statements of the prophecy itself that it must be built in "this generation."

The manual's explanation of the Civil War prophecy is equally distorting. The text cites various wars around the world spanning almost a century, from 1861 to 1958. This is the alleged pouring out of wars upon "all nations" as described in the prophecy. But anyone who actually reads the prophecy can see that such an interpretation is completely false.[50] It is the end of the world itself that is predicted, and this is to happen within a set period.

But again, what else can Mormon leaders do when faced with proof of false prophecies? Being unwilling to accept the implications, which would require them to accept that Joseph Smith _was a false prophet_ and to thus have to forsake Mormonism, they have no choice but to rationalize his failures. However, in doing this, they are guilty of foisting a deliberate deception upon unsuspecting converts and the very Mormon people they claim to shepherd. The Mormon church is the epitome of the words of Jeremiah:

> Then the LORD said to me: "The prophets are prophesying lies in my name. I have not sent them or appointed them or spoken to them. They are

prophesying to you false visions, divinations, idolatries and the delusions of their own minds" (Jeremiah 14:14 NIV).

## Stating the Facts

Up to now, we have proven that the Mormon claim to divine authority is demonstrably false. The first vision account of Mormonism cannot be trusted. The *Book of Mormon* must be considered a myth. The *Book of Moses* and the *Book of Abraham* are simple frauds. Mormon authorities have made thousands of changes in their scriptures—and deliberately suppressed vital records of its early leaders from their own membership. In addition, Mormon teaching historically has such terrific internal contradictions that the church has been forced to annul all previous divine revelations through the current prophets' "revelations." Finally, the prophetic errors establishing Joseph Smith and other Mormon leaders as false prophets are there for all to see. If one can still believe that Mormonism is a divine revelation, then one can believe anything.

# SECTION VI

# WHAT DO THE MORMONS BELIEVE ABOUT CHRISTIANITY?

~

# Chapter 14

# The Mormon View of Christianity

~

In this chapter we will document the true view of Christianity held by the Mormon church, not the neighborly image they currently seek to uphold. Once we understand the true teachings of Mormonism, we can see that the friendship with Christianity is only pretended for the sake of appearance and/or evangelism. We will begin with authoritative historical teaching and then proceed to modern views. Once again, it must be stressed that the first-vision experience of Joseph Smith identifying Christianity as an "abomination" to God permanently set the stage for all subsequent beliefs relating to Christianity. The following illustrations are categorized by subject for reader convenience.

## Christians Are Unbelievers

Brigham Young dogmatically insisted that "Christians profess to believe in Jesus Christ; but, if be told the truth, not one of them really believes in him."[1] Leading church historian Brigham Henry Roberts' (1857–1933) introduction to Joseph Smith's *History of the Church* declares that those who profess belief in the great creeds of Christianity (the Nicean, Athanasian, etc.) "are wandering in the darkness of the mysticisms of the old pagan philosophies."[2] He further claims that these creeds "exhibit the wide departure—the absolute apostasy—that has taken place in respect of this most fundamental of all doctrines of religion—the doctrine of God. Truly, 'Christians' have denied the Lord that bought them, and turned literally to fables."[3]

## Christians Are Satanic False Teachers

Joseph Smith, who still remains the most influential man in Mormonism, agreed that Christian pastors, "Are of their father the devil....We shall see all the priests who adhere to the sectarian [i.e., Christian] religions of the day, with all their followers, without one exception, receive their portion with the devil and his angels."[4] In 1 Nephi, chapters 13, 14 and elsewhere, the *Book of Mormon* itself calls the Christian church "a church which is most abominable above all other churches," "the great and abominable church" founded by the devil, "the mother of abominations," and the great "whore of Babylon."[5]

In an official compilation of Joseph Smith's writings, *Teachings of the Prophet Joseph Smith*, we find the following assessments of Christianity by the founder of Mormonism:

> What is it that inspires professors of Christianity generally with the hope of salvation? It is that smooth, sophisticated influence of the devil, by which he deceives the whole world.[6]

> Respecting the Melchizedek Priesthood, the sectarians [Christians] never professed to have it; consequently they never could save anyone, and would all be damned together.[7]

> I have the truth of God, and show that 99 out of every 100 professing religious ministers are false teachers, having no authority.[8] (Cf. note[9].)

In the *Journal of Discourses*,* an official twenty-seven-volume set of authoritative speeches by early church presidents and prophets, and other leaders, we find sentiments like the following.

## Christians Are Fools and Ignorant Concerning the Things of God

The second president and prophet of the Mormon church, Brigham Young, declared:

> With regard to true theology, a more ignorant people never lived than the present so-called Christian world.[11]

> The Christian world, so called, are heathens as to their knowledge of the salvation of God.[12]

> The Christian world, I discovered…was grovelling in darkness.[13]

> While brother Taylor was speaking of the sectarian [Christian] world, it occurred to my mind that the wicked do not know any more than the dumb brutes, comparatively speaking.…We may very properly say that the sectarian [Christian] world do not know anything correctly, so far as pertains to salvation.…They are more ignorant than children.[14]

The third president and prophet of the church, John Taylor, held the same view:

---

* Mormon authorities may deny that *Journal of Discourses* is authoritative and even encourage Mormons to avoid it (e.g., *A Sure Foundation*, pp. 199-201). This is only because it contains such embarrassing material, proving the modern church is often apostate in its teachings. Nevertheless, Mormons sometimes do quote from it, as an authority, when it suits their purposes.[10] Further, the *Deseret News* 1989–1990 *Church Almanac* officially lists it under the title "Church Publication" (p. 188). When Mormons claim this material is not authoritative, not relevant for today, or not an official church publication, they are either misinformed or lying.

> We talk about Christianity, but it is a perfect pack of nonsense....And the Devil could not invent a better engine to spread his work than the Christianity of the 19th century.[15]

And,

> I consider that if I ever lost any time in my life, it was while studying the Christian theology. Sectarian [Christian] theology is the greatest tomfoolery in the world.[16]

And,

> What does the Christian world know about God? Nothing; yet these very men assume the right and power to tell others what they shall and what they shall not believe in. Why, so far as the things of God are concerned, they are the veriest fools, they know neither God nor the things of God.[17]

He also exclaimed, "What! Are Christians ignorant? Yes, as ignorant of the things of God as the brute beast."[18] Mormon apostle Orson Pratt declared that "the whole of Christendom is as destitute of Bible Christianity as the idolatrist Pagans."[19] And B.H. Roberts, noted church historian and member of the First Council of Seventy, referred to Christians as those "who are blindly led by the blind."[20]

## Christians Are Wicked

Mormon apostle Orson Pratt repeatedly emphasized the evils of Christianity:

> Will Christendom have the unblushing impudence to call themselves the people of God...? How long will the heavens suffer such wickedness to go unpunished![21]

Another evil of no small magnitude is the vast amount of false doctrines which are taught, and extensively believed, and practiced throughout Christendom. Doctrines which are calculated to ruin the soul....These soul-destroying doctrines... are taught in Christendom, and...millions have had the wickedness to believe [them]....Now what will become of all these false teachers...and what will become of the people who suffer themselves to be led by such hypocrites? They will, every soul of them, unless they repent of these false doctrines, be cast down to hell....Such heaven-daring wickedness is calculated to sink these vile impostors to the lowest hell. And unless the people repent of having received baptism and other ordinances of the Gospel at the hands of such deceivers....And embrace the fulness of the Gospel which God has revealed anew in the _Book of Mormon_....Every one of you will, most assuredly, be damned.[22]

Given this historical stance, what position does modern Mormonism take? Although the rhetoric is toned down, the same attitudes remain. We have noted that Joseph Fielding Smith, the tenth president and prophet of the church, and Bruce McConkie are acknowledged to be two of the leading doctrinal theologians of the modern Mormon church. Joseph Fielding Smith is the author of _Doctrines of Salvation_ (three volumes), _Answers to Gospel Questions_ (four volumes), and other works. Bruce McConkie is author of the three-volume _Doctrinal New Testament Commentary_ and the authoritative _Mormon Doctrine_. Smith states that "gospel truth has been perverted and defiled" by Catholicism until it became a pagan abomination and that even the Reformation "perpetuated these evils and, therefore, the same corrupted doctrines and practices were perpetuated in these Protestant organizations."[23]

In his *Mormon Doctrine*, Bruce McConkie universally condemns all non-Mormon churches. He asserts that "a perverted Christianity holds sway among the so-called Christians of apostate Christendom."[24] He also observes what he declares to be their satanic nature:

> The *Church of the Devil* and the *Great and Abominable Church* are [terms] used to identify all churches or organizations of whatever name or nature...which are designed to take men on a course that leads away from God and his laws and thus from salvation in the kingdom of God [the Mormon Church]....There is no salvation outside this one true Church, the Church of Jesus Christ.[25]

In his *Doctrinal New Testament Commentary*, McConkie alleges that Christians are the true enemies of God. Why? Because the true teachings of God "have been changed and perverted by an apostate Christendom."[26] And as a whole, modern Christians are ignorant of God's true purposes.[27] In fact, Christian doctrines are the "doctrines of devils."[28] Thus, the Christian church is part of "the great and abominable church" of the devil preparing men "to be damned."[29]

From the above statements and many others, we must conclude that Mormonism, either historically or in the present, cannot be considered neutral toward Christianity. Rather, it takes a confrontational approach, viewing Christianity as its spiritual enemy.[30]

Despite the claims of the Mormon church and the sincere conviction of Mormon people, Mormonism is not a Christian religion. From its inception, Mormonism has sought to distance itself from historic Christian faith, believing that Christianity is an apostate religion that serves to damn the souls of men.

In our final chapters, we will summarize matters and show some of the consequences of the Mormon claim to be Christian, and the deception it brings.

# Chapter 15

# What Mormons Really Mean When They Use Christian Terms

∼

It is a hapless sign of the time that tens of millions of people sincerely believe they are Christians and yet are wrong. Unfortunately, they have little idea either of the significance of the term *Christian* or what it means to be one.

The term *Christ* (Gk. *Christos*, from the Hebrew *Mashiach* or "anointed one") originally identified Jesus of Nazareth as the prophesied Jewish Messiah. Thus, to be a follower of Jesus (the) *Christ* was to be a follower of Jesus, the promised Jewish Messiah. It was to accept the truth of Jesus' own claim to be the true Messiah—the incarnate God and Savior of humanity (Isaiah 9:6; 53:1-12; John 4:26; 5:18; 10:30).[1]

In other words, to be a Christian is to be a devout follower of the biblical Jesus Christ. It is to wholeheartedly believe in what He believed—in the Bible as God's inerrant Word and in the doctrines of historic Christianity derived from God's Word. This is why the *Oxford American Dictionary* defines *Christian* as "of the doctrines of Christianity, believing in or based on these." *Christianity* is defined as "the religion based on the belief that Christ was the incarnate Son of God and on his teachings."[2]

This explains why a true Christian is one who has personally received Jesus Christ as his or her Lord and Savior and is one who leads a lifestyle based on that fact in concert with biblical teaching. Above all, Christianity involves a committed, loving relationship with the God of the Bible. It is not merely going to church on Sundays, believing in Jesus in an intellectual sense, or attempting to live "a Christian life." And, it is certainly not merely claiming to be a Christian while simultaneously rejecting Christian doctrine. Being a true Christian incorporates adherence to accurate doctrine and a godly lifestyle centered on a personal relationship with the living Jesus Christ.

No one can deny that the Mormon church deliberately seeks to be seen as a Christian religion. Indeed, to most people, Mormons appear to be genuine Christians who live their faith. Mormons express bafflement when anyone expresses the idea that they are not Christians. One Mormon Sunday school text asserts: "To members or missionaries of the Church of Jesus Christ of Latter-day Saints, it is an astonishing circumstance to find an individual who asks, with a note of disbelief in his voice, 'Are Mormons Christians?' "[3] James Talmage, one of the church's twelve apostles, states in his authoritative Articles of Faith, "The Doctrines taught by Joseph Smith, and by the Church today, are true and scriptural."[4] The former president and prophet of the Mormon church, Ezra Taft Benson, answers a resounding "yes" to the question, "Are Mormons Christians?"[5]

Jack Weyland, a member of the Rapid City, South Dakota Stake Mission Presidency, mentions that several times he has been in circumstances where someone has told him or another Mormon that they are not Christian. "And every time it happens I'm astonished. I usually respond by saying, 'but the name of the church is the Church of Jesus Christ of Latter-day Saints. Every prayer we utter is offered in his name. Every ordinance we perform we do in his name. We believe all the Bible says about him....' "[6] Dr. Harold Goodman, a Brigham Young University professor and Latter-day Saints mission president, argues, "Anyone that believes in Christ is a Christian. And we believe that we are Christians."[7]

Darl Andersen is a leader in the Mormon movement to evangelize Christians. He too expresses disbelief that anyone could possibly think that Mormonism is not Christian. He often refers to Mormons as "Mormon Christians" and says that "the very purpose of the *Book of Mormon*, as well as the life of Joseph Smith, is to proclaim Jesus Christ as Lord." But in his book he never once deals with the central issue: the teachings of Mormonism versus the teachings of the Bible. In fact, he even says, "Doctrinal arguments are [only] the evidence of ill will."[8]

Perhaps the most comprehensive defense of the idea that the Mormon religion is Christian is found in Dr. Stephen Robinson's *Are Mormons Christians?* Robinson received a Ph.D. in biblical studies from Duke University.*

Robinson agrees that the charge that Mormons are not Christians "is often the most commonly heard criticism of the LDS Church and its doctrines."[9] And he allows that "the charge that Mormons are not Christians is a serious charge indeed."[10] However, he argues:

> Most of the time the charge that the Latter-day Saints are not Christians has absolutely nothing to do with LDS belief or nonbelief in Jesus Christ, or with LDS acceptance or rejection of the New Testament as the word of God. If the term *Christian* is used, as it is in standard English to mean someone who accepts Jesus Christ as the Son of God and the Savior of the world, then the charge that Mormons aren't Christians is false.[11]

But even Robinson, despite his effort, freely concedes that Mormonism 1) rejects traditional Christian orthodoxy;[12] 2) rejects the historic orthodox view of the Trinity;[13] and 3) rejects

---

* While his book will undoubtedly convince many that Mormonism is really a Christian religion, it will be convincing only to those who are unfamiliar with how to spot logical fallacies and are ignorant in Mormon history/doctrine and biblical/historic/systematic theology.

the specific orthodox Christian teaching concerning God—confessing that Mormonism teaches that God was once a human being and that He has a tangible body.[14] Nevertheless, Robinson proceeds to express utter astonishment that Mormonism cannot be considered Christian!

Thus, wherever one cares to look within the Mormon church, one finds the label "Christian." Unfortunately, this has caused great confusion among non-Christians and even among many Christians. Millions of people today continue to hold the mistaken belief that Mormonism is a true Christian religion. The late Harry Ropp was Director of Missions to Mormons in Roy, Utah, an organization founded to "stem the flow of converts from Christian churches to Mormonism."[15] He observes that "over the past several years Mormonism has been trying to gain acceptance as a Christian denomination" and that "in recent days...the Mormons have reached their goal in the minds of many."[16] He further observes that "many Christians today accept Mormons as brothers and sisters in the faith."[17]

We also have talked with numerous Christians who see nothing at all wrong with Mormonism, believing it is simply another Christian denomination. Former Mormons Jerald and Sandra Tanner direct what is perhaps the most significant organization in the country for disseminating valuable historical materials on Mormonism. For forty years they have diligently sought to help both Mormons and Christians alike to understand what Mormonism really teaches and why it cannot be considered Christian. In a personal conversation with Sandra Tanner, she informed us that, according to her own widespread experience, the greatest problem the Christian church faces concerning Mormonism is that far too many Christians think Mormonism is a Christian religion.

Even the Navy Chief of Chaplains Rear Admiral Alvin B. Koeneman officially designated Mormon Navy chaplains as "Protestant." We have in our files a copy of a letter from the Protestant Chapel Council, Naval Air Station, Alameda, California to the Navy Chief of Chaplains RADM, Alvin B. Koeneman, Office of the Chief of Naval Operations, Department of the Navy, Washington, D.C., officially protesting this designation.

The influential Mason and father of positive thinking, Norman Vincent Peale, referred to the former Mormon president, Spencer W. Kimball, as "a godly man," noting it was correct to consider him "a prophet" and as one whose love approached that "of the Savior."[18] Occasionally, influential Mormons have even appeared on national Christian television shows presenting their faith in Mormonism as a true Christian religion.[19]

But no matter what Mormons may say or claim, they are wrong. Mormonism is not true Christianity, and true Mormons cannot, in any sense, be considered Christians. Mormon teachings are explicitly anti-Christian and, with no disrespect intended, the Mormon religion is almost as far from Christianity as one can go. The issue is an important one for Mormons because to claim to be something you are not is a deceptive practice.

Mormonism freely invites everyone to test its claims, spiritual and otherwise. Brigham Young himself urged others to "take up the Bible, compare the religion of the Latter-day Saints with it, and see if it will stand the test."[20] A modern booklet published by the Mormon church, *Apostasy and Restoration*, says, "We invite all men to test our claims to know the truth for themselves."[21] So let's further test these claims.

The Apostle John said this about Gnostics, or followers of gnosticism, who adhered to heretical teachings in the days of the early church: "They went out from us, but they were not really of us; for if they had been of us, they would have remained with us; but they went out, in order that it might be shown that they all are not of us" (1 John 2:19, see verse 26).

Similarly, since its earliest days, the Mormon church has willfully removed itself from the Christian church. Yet, Mormons demand to be called Christian. This situation became so intolerable that in July 1986 a group of evangelical Christians and former Mormons held a news conference in Salt Lake City, Utah, and subsequently presented a petition to the Mormon church asking that it stop calling itself a Christian church. According to the Mormon publication, *Deseret News*, July 15, 1986, the petition was signed by over twenty thousand persons from forty-nine states and thirty-one foreign countries.

Religious scholars and authorities on Mormonism everywhere, both Christian and non-Christian, classify Mormonism as a non-Christian religion. (Even the liberal World Council of Churches refuses to classify Mormonism as a Christian religion.)[22] Sterling M. McMurrin is E.E. Ericksen Distinguished Professor, Professor of History, Professor of Philosophy of Education, and Dean of the Graduate School at the University of Utah. In his book *The Theological Foundations of the Mormon Religion* he sets as a goal the purpose of "facilitating understanding of Mormonism."[23] Noting that Mormon theology has "a radically unorthodox concept of God," he observes that "in its conception of God as in its doctrine of man, Mormonism is a radical departure from the established theology, both Catholic and Protestant."[24]

Gordon Fraser, the author of four books on Mormonism, states in his book *Is Mormonism Christian?* "We object to Mormon missionaries posing as Christians, and our objections are based on the differences between what they are taught by their General Authorities and what the Bible teaches."[25]

The late Dr. Walter Martin, an acknowledged authority on comparative religion and biblical theology, observes in his work *The Maze of Mormonism*, "In no uncertain terms, the Bible condemns the teachings of the Mormon Church."[26]

Former Mormons turned Christians Jerald and Sandra Tanner, who have done perhaps more in-depth research into Mormonism than anyone else, declare unequivocally, "The Mormon Church is certainly not built upon the teachings of the Bible....Mormonism...is not even based on the *Book of Mormon*."[27]

In his *The Four Major Cults*, theologian Dr. Anthony Hoekema emphasizes that "we must at this point assert, in the strongest possible terms, that Mormonism does not deserve to be called a Christian religion. It is basically anti-Christian and anti-biblical."[28]

The *Evangelical Dictionary of Theology* observes that the Mormon attempt to be Christian "does little justice to either Mormon theology or the Christian tradition."[29]

Even the *Encyclopedia Britannica* classifies Mormonism as a non-Christian religion: "Mormon doctrine diverges from the orthodoxy of established Christianity, particularly in its polytheism, in affirming that God has evolved from man and that men might evolve into gods, that the Persons of the Trinity are distinct beings, and that men's souls have preexisted.... Justification is by faith and obedience to the ordinances of the Church."[30]

*The New Schaff-Herzog Encyclopedia of Religious Knowledge* comments:

> So far as the Bible is concerned, Joseph Smith and his successors have taken such liberties with its meaning, and even with its text, that it cannot be said to have any authority for a Mormon.... [The Mormon] doctrine of God, for example, is widely different from that of the Christian Church. The Mormon conception of deity rather resembles that of Buddhism. From it a system of anthropomorphisms has been developed, which far exceeds that of any Christian sect in any age....The supreme God...begot other gods. All have bodies, parts, and passions....A chief occupation of these gods is to produce souls for the bodies begotten in this and other worlds. The sex idea runs through the whole Mormon conception of the universe.[31]

*The New International Dictionary of the Christian Church* concludes: "An examination of the doctrines taught by the Mormon Church will reveal that they deny most of the cardinal teachings of the Christian faith."[32]

So, are Mormons Christians? Can a person be a Christian who rejects the Trinity and accepts polytheism, who denies that God always existed and instead maintains that God was once a man who evolved into godhood, who denies the virgin birth by the Holy Spirit, who affirms that there is a mother God, who rejects the Bible as God's only revelation to mankind, and who teaches that salvation is by law keeping instead of grace? Can Mormons logically call themselves Christian when they will not submit themselves to the words of Jesus Christ and the New Testament?

On the other hand, one cannot deny that a few encyclopedias and secular works on religion do classify Mormonism as a Christian religion or sect. That such incorrect classifications exist is testimony to the tremendous power of the Mormon church's public-relations programs.

Thus the Mormon church finds itself in a precarious spot. It apparently does not desire that its true feelings about Christianity be widely known; rather it stresses "similarities" with Christian faith whenever possible. Christians who talk with Mormons need to understand the semantic issues involved, for only then can genuine communication be established. The two charts below may be used as a starting point for discussion as to the definition of the theological terms and contrasting natures of Mormonism and Christianity.

## Mormonism vs. Christianity

### Chart A: Mormon Definitions of Biblical and Christian Terms

Mormons may use the same words that Christians use, but they use them with different, or even opposite, meanings. Unless Christians pursue the meaning of such words, and unless Mormons are frank in giving them their true Mormon definition, Christians and the public in general will continue to be confused over the religious status of Mormonism.

In any discussion with a Mormon, the following redefinition of biblical/Christian terms must be kept in mind. Although Mormons themselves may be ignorant of some of the definitions cited below, they represent true Mormon teaching according to standard Mormon theological works.

*Christianity:* sectarianism; a false and damnable apostate religion.

*God:* "Elohim"; one of innumerable self-progressing bodily deities; formerly a man, a finite creature. In early Mormon theology, Adam (of the Garden of Eden) was considered by many Mormons as the true earth deity.

*Jesus Christ:* a self-progressing deity, Jehovah of the Old Testament, and the first spirit child of Elohim and his wife.

*Holy Ghost:* a man with a spiritual body of matter.

*Trinity:* tritheistic; coordinated under general Mormon polytheism; thus the Father, Son, and Holy Ghost are separate deities.

*The Gospel:* Mormon theology.

*Born-again:* water baptism into Mormonism.

*Immortality:* Mormon salvation by grace (limited to the universal resurrection of all men).

*Atonement:* the provision God has supplied for individuals to earn their true salvation by obedience to the laws and ordinances of the Gospel.

*True salvation/eternal life/redemption:* "Exaltation" to godhood in the highest part of the celestial kingdom based upon individual good works and personal merit; exaltation incorporates ruling a new world and sexual procreation in order to produce spirit children who will eventually be embodied and inhabit that world, each then having the opportunity to be exalted.

*The Fall:* a spiritual step upward; a blessing permitting the production of physical bodies for preexistent spirits to inhabit and thus have the possibility of attaining their own exaltation or godhood.

*Death:* generally a step upward; death represents the possibility of a form of salvation (if not exaltation) for those who have never heard of Mormonism.

*Heaven:* three "kingdoms of glory" comprising various spiritual gradations.

*Hell:* generally purgatorial; possibly eternal for a very few (primarily apostate Mormons).

*Virgin birth:* the birth of Christ through a *physical* sex act between God the Father (the Mormon earth god Elohim) and Mary (hence, not a virgin birth).

*Man:* a preexistent eternal spirit with the potential to earn godhood by obedience to Mormon dictates.

*Creation:* the reorganization of eternal matter.

*The Scriptures:* the *Book of Mormon; Doctrine and Covenants;* the *Pearl of Great Price;* and the Bible "as far as it is translated correctly."

*The Bible:* an erring and often unreliable inspired record, properly interpreted only by Mormons and only in light of Mormon theology.

### Chart B: Contrasting Mormon and Christian Belief

Because Mormon theology diverges so far from Christian theology, it is easy to compare the beliefs of Mormonism with the beliefs of Christianity. Below we offer the following chart contrasting basic Mormon and Christian teaching.

| Mormonism | Christianity |
| --- | --- |
| *Bible* | *Bible* |
| Unreliable | Reliable |
| Incomplete as it is | Complete as it is |
| Adds new revelations to God's Word | Rejects new revelations |
| Unbiblical theological presuppositions utilized in interpretation | Accepted historical, grammatical principles utilized in interpretation |
| *God* | *God* |
| Tritheism/polytheistic | Trinity/monotheistic |
| Physical (evolved man) | Spirit |

| | |
|---|---|
| Finite | Infinite |
| Morally questionable | Holy |
| Organizer of eternal matter | Creator of matter from nothing |
| Sexual polygamist | Nonsexual |

| *Jesus* | *Jesus* |
|---|---|
| A god | God |
| Created | Eternal |
| Earned salvation (exaltation to godhood) | As eternal God neither salvation nor exaltation was required |
| Not virgin born | Virgin born |
| Polygamist* | Unmarried (celibate) |

| *Salvation* | *Salvation* |
|---|---|
| By works | By grace |
| Denies biblical atonement | Affirms atonement |
| Possible after death | Impossible after death |

| *Afterlife* | *Afterlife* |
|---|---|
| "Purgatorial"; three celestial kingdoms; almost universalistic | Eternal heaven or hell; no purgatory; not universalistic |

Clearly, then, for anyone to maintain that Mormonism and Christianity teach the same thing is logically, historically, and doctrinally an indefensible position.

---

* According to some early Mormon authorities.

# A Final Word

~

In this book we have evaluated the Mormon faith historically and theologically. Mormonism claims it is a Christian
religion—in fact, the only legitimate Christian religion on
earth. It claims that Joseph Smith was a genuine prophet of God
through whom true Christianity was reestablished in 1830.

However, an objective evaluation of the evidence reveals
that Mormonism is not Christian. The scriptural legacy that
Joseph Smith left to the world—as found in *Doctrine and
Covenants*, the *Book of Mormon,* and the *Pearl of Great Price*—
underscores a legacy that is anti-Christian.

In our examination of Mormon teaching we carefully compared and contrasted Mormon belief with Christian belief. We
saw that the Mormon concept of God and the God of Christianity are distinct from and opposed to one another.

Further, despite its claims to believe in Jesus Christ, we
saw that the Jesus Christ taught in the Mormon church bears
no resemblance to the biblical Christ. For example, the church
actively denies the atoning value of Christ's death, making it
little more than a stepping-stone in the quest for personal
godhood.

Concerning the church's teachings on salvation, Mormonism does not teach the biblical doctrine of salvation by grace alone. Instead, it offers the world a system of works salvation with the final hope that qualified Mormons will themselves fully become gods.

We supplied proof that the *Book of Mormon* was a nineteenth-century production and not a translation of ancient, historical records. We also cited evidence to show that it was translated by psychic means, not divine ones, and we documented its human sources and plagiarisms. Its absence of archaeological credibility was devastating.

We further discussed the *Book of Mormon*'s lack of manuscript evidence and other serious textual problems—as well as the absence of credibility of the Eleven Witnesses and their "testimony" concerning its alleged divine origin.

Unfortunately, we discovered that Mormon authorities had gravely distorted the truth about their own scriptures, their prophets, and their history, and then attempted to cover up the process. This was necessary because of the large number of embarrassments and contradictions in Mormon history, scripture, and theology.

Up through the present-day, church leaders have continually undermined their own credibility—to such an extent that individual Mormons have no logical basis upon which to trust anything they say.

## A Personal Word to Mormons

If you have stayed with us this far, perhaps you are no longer certain of the truth of Mormonism. It is our desire that you continue the process of evaluation, even if painful. The issues are too crucial for any other course of action.

But perhaps one of the most important things for Mormons to realize is that the invalidation of their own faith is not an undermining of true biblical teaching or the real Jesus Christ. The distortion of Christianity by Mormonism cannot logically be considered its disproof. In other words, if you are a Mormon who has concluded that Mormonism is not true, you should not discard the real Jesus Christ. You should begin to think in terms of deception, not rejection. If you have been deceived as to the true nature of Christian faith, you should seek out that faith in truth rather than reject it because you have been led astray. Jesus Himself said that "this is eternal life: that they may know you, the only true God, and Jesus Christ, whom you have sent" (John 17:3 NIV).

If you have concluded that Mormonism is false and would like to receive the true Jesus Christ into your life and make Him your Lord and Savior, we suggest the following prayer:

> Dear God,
>
> You know my heart now, as always. In my heart of hearts my desire is to serve You, the only true God. I now renounce the false view of You that I have promoted and ask for Your help and guidance in understanding You better. I have honestly searched my heart and it is my desire to trust in You. By searching my heart, I have recognized I cannot earn my own salvation and now realize that the hope of becoming a god is futile.
>
> I recognize this especially because I am a sinner worthy of Your judgment. I reject the pride in thinking that I could perfect myself on my own power and thereby become a god. I renounce every false view of Jesus Christ and receive the true Jesus Christ of Nazareth as presented in the Bible. I believe that this Jesus Christ is truly God, that He truly paid the penalty for my sins on the cross, and that He rose from the dead three days later. I believe that by receiving Him into my life I will now inherit eternal life. Right now I turn from my sins and from the false teachings of the Mormon church, and I receive the true Jesus Christ as my personal Lord and Savior. Help me to grow in the grace and knowledge of my true Savior Jesus Christ (2 Peter 3:18). Amen.

If you have prayed this prayer, please feel free to write us at The John Ankerberg Show and request materials that will be helpful in your new Christian life:

The John Ankerberg Show
6928 Lee Highway
Chattanooga, TN  37422-2466
www.ankerberg.com

# Select Bibliography

## Books

Ahmanson, John. *Secret History: An Eyewitness Account of the Rise of Mormonism*, translated by Gleason L. Archer. Chicago, IL: Moody Press, 1984.

Anderson, Einar. *Inside Story of Mormonism*. Grand Rapids, MI: Kregel, 1974.

Benson, Ezra Taft. *The Teachings of Ezra Taft Benson*. Salt Lake City, UT: Bookcraft, 1988.

Brodie, Fawn M. *No Man Knows My History: The Life of Joseph Smith*. 2nd ed., rev. New York: Alfred Knopf, 1976.

Brown, Robert L., and Rosemary. *They Lie in Wait to Deceive: A Study of Anti-Mormon Deception*. Edited by Barbara Ellsworth. 3 vols. Mesa, AZ: Brownsworth Publishing, 1986.

Butterworth, F. Edward. *Divine Origin of the Restoration*. Chico, CA: Cosmic Press, 1989.

Church of Jesus Christ of Latter-day Saints. *Achieving a Celestial Marriage: Student Manual*. Salt Lake City, UT: The Church of Jesus Christ of Latter-day Saints, 1976. [Texts for Courses CDFR 160 and 161.]

———. *The Book of Mormon*. Salt Lake City, UT: The Church of Jesus Christ of Latter-day Saints, 1947.

———. *The Book of Mormon: An Account Written by the Hand of Mormon upon Plates Taken from the Plates of Nephi*. Salt Lake City, UT: The Church of Jesus Christ of Latter-day Saints, 1976, 1989 eds.

———. *Book of Mormon Student Manual*. Salt Lake City, UT: Church of Jesus Christ of Latter-day Saints, n.d. [text for Religion 121-122].

———. *Come Follow Me: Melchizedek Priesthood Personal Study Guide, 1983*. Salt Lake City, UT: The Church of Jesus Christ of Latter-day Saints, 1983.

———. *Doctrine and Covenants/The Pearl of Great Price*. Salt Lake City, UT: The Church of Jesus Christ of Latter-day Saints, 1968, 1982, 1989 eds.

———. *The Doctrine and Covenants Student Manual*. Salt Lake City, UT: Church Educational System, The Church of Jesus Christ of Latter-day Saints, 1981. [Texts for Religion 324-325.]

———. *Doctrines of the Gospel: Student Manual*. Salt Lake City, UT: The Church of Jesus Christ of Latter-day Saints, 1986. [Texts for Religion 231-232.]

———. *Duties and Blessings of the Priesthood: Basic Manual for Priesthood Holders, Part A*. Salt Lake City, UT: The Church of Jesus Christ of Latter-day Saints, 1986.

———. *Duties and Blessings of the Priesthood: Basic Manual for Priesthood Holders, Part B*. Salt Lake City, UT: The Church of Jesus Christ of Latter-day Saints, 1986.

———. *Flip Charts: Uniform System for Teaching the Gospel*. Salt Lake City, UT: Church of Jesus Christ of Latter-day Saints, 1986, "Mission of the Church" reads: "Perfect the Saints. Proclaim the Gospel. Redeem the Dead."

———. *Gospel Principles*. Salt Lake City, UT: The Church of Jesus Christ of Latter-day Saints, 1988.

———. *Learn of Me: Relief Society Personal Study Guide, 2*. Salt Lake City, UT: The Church of Jesus Christ of Latter-day Saints, 1990.

———. *The Life and Teachings of Jesus and His Apostles: Course Material*. 2nd ed., rev. Salt Lake City, UT: The Church of Jesus Christ of Latter-day Saints, 1979. [Texts for Religion 211-212.]

———. *Official Report of the One Hundred Fifty-Ninth Semiannual General Conference of the Church of Jesus Christ of Latter-day Saints Held in the Tabernacle Salt Lake City, Utah, September 30 and October 1, 1989*. Salt Lake City, UT: The Church of Jesus Christ of Latter-day Saints, 1990.

————. *Official Report of the One Hundred Sixtieth Semiannual General Conference of the Church of Jesus Christ of Latter-day Saints Held in the Tabernacle Salt Lake City, Utah, March 31 and April 1, 1990.* Salt Lake City, UT: The Church of Jesus Christ of Latter-day Saints, 1990.

————. *Official Report of the One Hundred Sixtieth Semiannual General Conference of the Church of Jesus Christ of Latter-day Saints Held in the Tabernacle Salt Lake City, Utah, October 6 and 7, 1990.* Salt Lake City, UT: The Church of Jesus Christ of Latter-day Saints, 1991.

————. *Old Testament: Genesis–2 Samuel, Student Manual.* Salt Lake City, UT: The Church of Jesus Christ of Latter-day Saints, 1981. [Text for Religion 301.]

————. *Old Testament: 1 Kings–Malachi Student Manual.* 2nd ed. Salt Lake City, UT: The Church of Jesus Christ of Latter-day Saints, 1982. [Text for Religion 302.]

————. *A Sure Foundation: Answers to Difficult Gospel Questions.* Salt Lake City, UT: Deseret Book Company, 1988.

————. *Temples of the Church of Jesus Christ of Latter-day Saints.* Salt Lake City, UT: The Church of Jesus Christ of Latter-day Saints, 1988.

————. *To Make Thee a Minister and a Witness: Melchizedek Priesthood Personal Study Guide, 2.* Salt Lake City, UT: The Church of Jesus Christ of Latter-day Saints, 1990.

Cowan, Marvin W. *Mormon Claims Answered.* N.p.: Marvin W. Cowan Publisher, 1975, revised in 1989.

Cowdery, Wayne L., Howard A. Davis, and Donald R. Scales. *Who Really Wrote the Book of Mormon?* Santa Ana, CA: Vision House, 1977.

Crowther, Duane S. *Life Everlasting.* Salt Lake City, UT: Bookcraft, Inc., 1988.

Decker, Ed. *The Mormon Dilemma: The Dramatic Story of a Mormon Couple's Encounter with Truth.* Eugene, OR: Harvest House Publishers, 1990.

Decker, Ed, and Dave Hunt. *The God Makers: A Shocking Exposé of What the Mormon Church Really Believes.* Eugene, OR: Harvest House, 1984.

Deseret Sunday School Union. *The Master's Church Course, A.* Salt Lake City, UT: Deseret Sunday School Union, 1969.

*Deseret News. 1991–1992 Church Almanac.* Salt Lake City, UT: Deseret News, 1990.

*Evening and Morning Star, June 1832–Sept. 1834.* No. 1, vol. 2, no. 24. Reprint. Muhringen, West Germany: F. Wochner K.G., 1969. Microfilm.

Fraser, Gordon H. *Is Mormonism Christian?: Mormon Doctrine Compared with Biblical Christianity.* Chicago, IL: Moody Press, 1977.

————. *Joseph and the Golden Plates: A Close Look at the* Book of Mormon. Eugene, OR: Gordon H. Fraser, 1978.

————. *Sects of the Latter-day Saints (Part 1: The Reorganized Church of Jesus Christ of Latter-day Saints; Part 2: The Polygamous Sects of Mormonism).* Hubbard, OR: Gordon H. Fraser, 1978.

————. *What Does the* Book of Mormon *Teach?: An Examination of the Historical and Scientific Statements of the* Book of Mormon. Chicago, IL: Moody Press, 1964.

Hansen, Klaus J. *Quest for Empire: The Political Kingdom of God and the Council of Fifty in Mormon History.* Lincoln, NE: University of Nebraska Press, 1967.

Herald Publishing House. *Joseph Smith's "New Translation" of the Bible: A Complete Parallel Column Comparison of the Inspired Version of the Holy Scriptures and the King James Authorized Version.* Independence, MO: Herald Publishing House, 1970.

Heinerman, Joseph. *Eternal Testimonies: Inspired Testimonies of Latter-day Saints.* Salt Lake City, UT: Joseph Lyon and Associates, 1982.

————. *Spirit World Manifestations: Accounts of Divine Aid in Genealogical and Temple Work and Other Assistance to Latter-day Saints.* Salt Lake City, UT: Joseph Lyon and Associates, 1986.

Hickman, Bill. *Brigham's Destroying Angel: Being the Life, Confession and Startling Disclosures of the Notorious Bill Hickman, 1904.* Reprint. Salt Lake City, UT: Utah Lighthouse Ministry, n.d. Microfilm.

Hinckley, Gordon B. *Truth Restored: A Short History of the Church of Jesus Christ of Latter-day Saints*. Salt Lake City, UT: The Church of Jesus Christ of Latter-day Saints, 1979.

Hoekema, Anthony. *The Four Major Cults: Christian Science, Jehovah's Witnesses, Mormonism, Seventh-day Adventism*. Grand Rapids, MI: William B. Eerdmans, 1970.

Hughes, Dean. *The Mormon Church: A Basic History*. Salt Lake City, UT: Deseret Book Company, 1986.

Kimball, Spencer W. *The Miracle of Forgiveness*. Salt Lake City, UT: Bookcraft, 1989.

Marquardt, H. Michael. *The* Book of Abraham *Papyrus Found: An Answer to Dr. Hugh Nibley's Book "The Message of the Joseph Smith Papyri: An Egyptian Endowment" as It Relates to the Source of the* Book of Abraham. Sandy, UT: H. Michael Marquardt, 1975.

Martin, Walter. *The Kingdom of the Cults*. Minneapolis, MN: Bethany, 1970.

———. *The Maze of Mormonism*. Rev. ed. Santa Ana, CA: Vision House Publishers, 1978.

Matthews, Robert J. *A Bible! A Bible!: How Latter-day Revelation Helps Us Understand the Scriptures and the Savior*. Salt Lake City, UT: Bookcraft, 1990.

McConkie, Bruce. *Doctrinal New Testament Commentary, Matthew –Revelation*. 3 vols. Salt Lake City, UT: Bookcraft, 1976, 1977.

———. *Mormon Doctrine*. Salt Lake City, UT: Bookcraft, 1977.

McElveen, Floyd. *The Mormon Revelations of Convenience*. Minneapolis, MN: Bethany, 1978.

———. *Will the "Saints" Go Marching In?: A Comparison of the Mormon Faith with Biblical Christianity*. Glendale, CA: Regal, 1977, retitled *The Mormon Illusion*.

McKeever, Bill. *Answering Mormon's Questions: Simple Biblical Explanations to the Most Common Questions That Mormons Ask*. Minneapolis, MN: Bethany, 1991.

McMurrin, Sterling M. *The Theological Foundations of the Mormon Religion*. Salt Lake City, UT: University of Utah Press, 1977.

Morey, Robert A. *How to Answer a Mormon: Practical Guidelines for What to Expect and What to Reply When the Mormons Come to Your Door*. Minneapolis, MN: Bethany, 1983.

Musser, Joseph W. *Michael Our Father and Our God: The Mormon Conception of Deity As Taught by Joseph Smith, Brigham Young, John Taylor and Their Associates in the Priesthood*. Salt Lake City, UT: Truth Publishing, 1963.

Naifeh, Steven, and Gregory White Smith. *The Mormon Murders: A True Story of Greed, Forgery, Deceit, and Death*. New York: Weidenfeld & Nicholson, 1988.

Petersen, LaMar. *Hearts Made Glad: The Charges of Intemperance Against Joseph Smith the Mormon Prophet*. Salt Lake City, UT: LaMar Petersen, 1975.

Petersen, Mark E. *Adam: Who Is He?* Salt Lake City, UT: Deseret Book Company, 1976.

———. *As Translated Correctly*. Salt Lake City, UT: Deseret Book Company, 1966.

———. *The Great Prologue*. Salt Lake City, UT: Deseret Book Company, 1975.

Pratt, Orson. *The Seer*. January 1853–August 1854. Vol. 1, no. 1–Vol . 2, no. 8. Reprint. n.p., n.d., microfilm.

Quinn, D. Michael. *Early Mormonism and the Magic World View*. Salt Lake City, UT: Signature Books, 1987.

Richards, LeGrand. *A Marvelous Work and a Wonder*. Salt Lake City, UT: Deseret Book Company, 1975.

Roberts, B.H. *The Mormon Doctrine of Deity: The Roberts Van Donckt Discussion*. 1903. Reprint. Bountiful, UT: B.H. Roberts/Horizon Publishers, n.d.

Robinson, Stephen E. *Are Mormons Christians?* Salt Lake City, UT: Bookcraft, 1991.

Ropp, Harry L. *The Mormon Papers: Are the Mormon Scriptures Reliable?* Downers Grove, IL: InterVarsity Press, retitled *Are the Mormon Scriptures Reliable?* 1987.

Sackett, Chuck. *What's Going On in There?: The Verbatim Text of the Mormon Temple Rituals Annotated and Explained by a Former Temple Worker*. Thousand Oaks, CA: Sword of the Shepherd, 1982.

304 ～ What Do Mormons Really Believe?

Scott, Latayne C. *Ex-Mormons: Why We Left*. Grand Rapids, MI: Baker, 1990.

———. *The Mormon Mirage: A Former Mormon Tells Why She Left the Church*. Grand Rapids, MI: Zondervan, 1980.

Smith, Joseph. *History of the Church*. Vols. 1-6. Salt Lake City, UT: Deseret Book Company/The Church of Jesus Christ of Latter-day Saints, 1975.

*Teachings of the Prophet of Joseph Smith*. Compiled by Joseph Fielding Smith. Salt Lake City, UT: Deseret Book Company, 1977.

Smith, Joseph F. *Gospel Doctrine: Sermons and Writings of President Joseph F. Smith*. Salt Lake City, UT: Deseret Book Company, 1975.

———. *Answers to Gospel Questions*. Compiled by Joseph Fielding Smith, Jr. 4 vols. Salt Lake City, UT: Deseret Book Company, 1976.

———. *Doctrines of Salvation: Sermons and Writings of Joseph Fielding Smith*. Compiled by Bruce R. McConkie. 3 vols. Salt Lake City, UT: Bookcraft, 1976.

———. *The Way to Perfection*. Salt Lake City, UT: Deseret Book Company, 1975.

Snake River LDS Seminary District. *Is There An Answer?* Compiled by A. Lavar Thornock. Pocatello, ID: Snake River LDS Seminary District, 1968.

Spencer, James R. *Beyond Mormonism: An Elder's Story*. Grand Rapids, MI: Chosen Books, 1984.

———. *Have You Witnessed to a Mormon Lately?* Old Tappan, NJ: Fleming H. Revell, 1986.

Stenhouse, Mrs. T.B.H., *Tell It All: The Tyranny of Mormonism*. Hartford, CT: A.D. Worthington & Co., 1875.

Talmage, James E. *Jesus the Christ: A Study of the Messiah and His Mission According to Holy Scriptures Both Ancient and Modern*. Salt Lake City, UT: Deseret Book Company, 1962.

———. *The Study of the Articles of Faith: Being a Consideration of the Principal Doctrines of the Church of Jesus Christ of Latter-day Saints*. Salt Lake City, UT: The Church of Jesus Christ of Latter-day Saints, 1976.

Tanner, Jerald, and Sandra. *Archaeology and the* Book of Mormon. Salt Lake City, UT: Utah Lighthouse Ministry, 1969.

———. *Changes in Joseph Smith's History*. Salt Lake City, UT: Utah Lighthouse Ministry, n.d.

———. *Changes in the* Pearl of Great Price. Salt Lake City, UT: Utah Lighthouse Ministry, n.d.

———. *Changes in the* Pearl of Great Price: *A Photo Reprint of the Original 1851 Edition of the* Pearl of Great Price *with All the Changes Marked*. Salt Lake City, UT: Utah Lighthouse Ministry, n.d., retitled *Flaws in the* Pearl of Great Price: *A Study of Changes and Plagiarism in Joseph Smith's* Pearl of Great Price. 1991.

———. *The Changing World of Mormonism: A Behind the Scenes Look at Changes in Mormon Doctrine and Practice*. Rev. ed. Chicago, IL: Moody Press, 1981.

———. *The Case Against Mormonism*. 3 vols. Salt Lake City, UT: Utah Lighthouse Ministry, 1967–1971.

———. *Did Spaulding Write the* Book of Mormon? Salt Lake City, UT: Utah Lighthouse Ministry, 1977.

———. *Joseph Smith and Money Digging*. Salt Lake City, UT: Utah Lighthouse Ministry, 1970.

———. *Joseph Smith's Strange Account of the First Vision*. Salt Lake City, UT: Utah Lighthouse Ministry, n.d.

———. *A Look at Christianity*. Salt Lake City, UT: Utah Lighthouse Ministry, 1971.

———. *The Lucifer-God Doctrine: A Critical Look at Charges of Luciferian Worship in the Mormon Temple, with a Response to the Decker-Schnoebelen Rebuttal*. Revised and enlarged ed. Salt Lake City, UT: Utah Lighthouse Ministry, 1988.

———. *The Mormon Kingdom*. 2 vols. Salt Lake City, UT: Utah Lighthouse Ministry, 1969–1971.

———*Mormonism Like Watergate?: An Answer to Hugh Nibley*. Salt Lake City, UT: Utah Lighthouse Ministry, 1974.

———. *Mormonism—Shadow or Reality?* Enlarged ed. Salt Lake City, UT: Utah Lighthouse Ministry, 1972.

———. *3913 Changes in the* Book of Mormon: *A Photo Reprint of the Original 1830 Edition of the* Book of Mormon *with All the Changes Marked.* Salt Lake City, UT: Utah Lighthouse Ministry, n.d.

———. *Mormonism, Magic and Masonry.* Second ed. Salt Lake City, UT: Utah Lighthouse Ministry, 1988.

Tanner, Sandra, *The Bible and Mormon Doctrine.* Salt Lake City, UT: Utah Lighthouse Ministry, 1971.

Unger, Merrill, *Unger's Bible Dictionary.* Chicago, IL: Moody Press, 1975.

Walker, Williston, et al. *A History of the Christian Church.* 4th ed. New York: Charles Scribner Sons, 1985.

Wallace, Arthur. *Can Mormonism Be Proved Experimentally?* Los Angeles, CA: Arthur Wallace, 1973.

Woodruff, Wilford C. *Joseph Smith Begins His Work:* Book of Mormon. 1831. Reprint. Bountiful, UT: Wilford C. Woodruff, 1963.

Young, Brigham. *Discourses of Brigham Young.* Compiled by John A. Widtsoe. Salt Lake City, UT: Deseret Book Company, 1976.

Young, Brigham, and His Counselors, the Twelve Apostles, and Others. *Journal of Discourses.* Reported by George D. Watt. 26 vols. plus index. Liverpool, England: F.D. Richards, 1855. Reprint. Salt Lake City, UT: n.p., 1967. (We stress this is an official LDS publication, a photolithographic reprint of the exact original edition. See *Deseret News 1989–1990 Church Almanac,* p. 188.)

## Mormon Pamphlets

"The Challenge." Los Angeles, CA: The Church of Jesus Christ of Latter-day Saints, n.d.

The Church of Jesus Christ of Latter-day Saints. *Apostasy and Restoration.* Salt Lake City, UT: The Church of Jesus Christ of Latter-day Saints, 1983.

———. *Eternal Progression, Discussion 4: Uniform System for Teaching the Gospel.* Salt Lake City, UT: Church of Jesus Christ of Latter-day Saints, 1987.

———. *Eternal Progression, Study Guide 4.* Salt Lake City, UT: Church of Jesus Christ of Latter-day Saints, 1987.

———. *Faith in the Lord Jesus Christ.* Salt Lake City, UT: Deseret News Press, n.d.

———. *The Gospel of Jesus Christ, Discussion 2: Uniform System for Teaching the Gospel.* Salt Lake City, UT: Church of Jesus Christ of Latter-day Saints, 1986.

———. *The Gospel of Jesus Christ, Study Guide 2.* Salt Lake City, UT: Church of Jesus Christ of Latter-day Saints, 1986.

———. *Instructions for the Discussions: Uniform System for Teaching the Gospel.* Salt Lake City, UT: Church of Jesus Christ of Latter-day Saints, 1986.

———. *Jesus Christ Savior and Mediator of Mankind.* N.p., n.d.

———. *Living a Christlike Life, Discussion 5: Uniform System for Teaching the Gospel.* Salt Lake City, UT: Church of Jesus Christ of Latter-day Saints, 1986.

———. *Living a Christlike Life, Study Guide 5.* Salt Lake City, UT: Church of Jesus Christ of Latter-day Saints, 1986.

———. *Membership in the Kingdom, Discussion 6: Uniform System for Teaching the Gospel.* Salt Lake City, UT: Church of Jesus Christ of Latter-day Saints, 1986.

———. *Membership in the Kingdom, Study Guide 6.* Salt Lake City, UT: Church of Jesus Christ of Latter-day Saints, 1986.

———. *The Plan of Our Heavenly Father, Discussion 1: Uniform System for Teaching the Gospel.* Salt Lake City, UT: Church of Jesus Christ of Latter-day Saints, 1986.

————. *The Plan of Our Heavenly Father, Study Guide 1.* Salt Lake City, UT: Church of Jesus Christ of Latter-day Saints, 1986.

————. *Plan of Salvation.* N.p., n.d.

————. *The Prophet Joseph Smith's Testimony.* N.p., n.d.

————. *The Purpose of Life.* Salt Lake City, UT: Church of Jesus Christ of Latter-day Saints, 1983.

————. *The Restoration, Discussion 3: Uniform System for Teaching the Gospel.* Salt Lake City, UT: Church of Jesus Christ of Latter-day Saints, 1986.

————. *The Restoration, Study Guide 3.* Salt Lake City, UT: Church of Jesus Christ of Latter-day Saints, 1986.

————. *What the Mormons Think of Christ*, n.d.

————. *What the Mormons Think of Christ*, 1982.

Morgan, John. *The Plan of Salvation.* Salt Lake City, UT: The Church of Jesus Christ of Latter-day Saints, n.d.

Packer, Boyd K. *The Holy Temple.* Salt Lake City, UT: Church of Jesus Christ of Latter-day Saints, 1982.

Penrose, Charles W. *What the "Mormons" Believe: Epitome of the Doctrines of the Church of Jesus Christ of Latter-day Saints.* Salt Lake City, UT: Deseret News Press, n.d.

## Pamphlets, Booklets, Transcripts, Journals, Newsletters, Photocopies, and Letters

Adamson, Jack, and Reed C. Durham, Jr. *No Help For the Widow's Son: Joseph Smith and Masonry.* Nauvoo, IL: Martin Publishing Co., 1980.

Andersen, Darl. "Love Thy Minister, Neighbor: Worshop Outline." Photocopy.

Anderson, Kirby. *Behind the Mask of Mormonism.* Eugene, OR: Harvest House, 1992.

————. *Who Are These Good People? An Analysis of Mormonism.* Rev. ed. Dallas, TX: Probe Ministries International, 1983.

Ankerberg, John. *Former Mormons Testify.* Chattanooga, TN, 1982. Program transcript.

————. *Mormon Officials and Christian Scholars Compare Doctrines.* (Mr. K.H. Christensen, Mr. Lawrence R. Flake, Dr. James Bjornstad, Mrs. Sandra Tanner, Mr. Ed Decker, Dr. Walter Martin), Chattanooga, TN: The John Ankerberg Show, 1983. Television transcript.

————. *Mormonism Revisited* (Ed Decker with excerpts from the film *The God Makers*), Chattanooga, TN: The John Ankerberg Show, 1983. Television transcript.

Bodine, Jerry and Marian. *A Book of Commandments for the Government of the Church of Christ Organized According to Law on the 6th of April, 1830.* Independence, MO: Board of Publication, Church of Christ, 1977 (reprint of 1833 edition published by W.W. Phelps & Co. in Independence, MO: "Zion").

————. *Whom Can You Trust?* Santa Ana, CA: Christ for the Cults, 1979.

————. *Witnessing to the Mormons.* Santa Ana, CA: Christ for the Cults, 1978.

Budvarson, Arthur. *Changes in Mormonism?* La Mesa, CA: Utah Christian Tract Society.

————. *Mormonism: Can It Stand Investigation?* La Mesa, CA: Utah Christian Tract Society, n.d.

Church of Jesus Christ of Latter-day Saints. *Temples of the Church.* Salt Lake City, UT: Church Magazines/Ensign 1988.

Ex-Mormons for Jesus. *An Interview with LeGrand Richards.* Clearwater, FL: Ex-Mormons for Jesus, n.d.

Farkas, John R. *What the Mormons Really Think of Christ and the Father.* St. Louis, MO: Personal Freedom Outreach, 1988.

Fraser, Gordon. *A Manual for Christian Workers: A Workshop Outline for the Study of Mormonism.* Hubbard, OR: Gordon H. Fraser, 1978.

Geer, Thelma (Granny). *Mormonism's Salvation...By Grace or by Eternal Marriage and Sex?* Tucson, AZ: Calvary Missionary Press, n.d.

"Geraldo" TV show, June 29, 1991. Available from *Journal Graphics.* New York. (Phone: 212-732-8552.)

Hall, Andy, et al. "Mormon, Inc.: Finances and Faith." *The Arizona Republic.* June 30–July 3, 1991.

Hougey, Hal. *Archaeology and the* Book of Mormon. Concord, CA: Pacific Publishing, n.d.

———. *Archaeology and the* Book of Mormon. Rev. ed. Concord, CA: Pacific Publishing, 1976.

———. *Latter-day Saints—Where Did You Get Your Authority?* Concord, CA: Pacific Publishing, 1977.

———. *A Parallel, The Basis of the* Book of Mormon: *B.H. Roberts' "Parallel" of the* Book of Mormon *to View of the Hebrews.* Concord, CA: Pacific Publishing, 1975.

———. *Mormon Missionary Handbook—A Reprint—Accompanied by a Refutation in Parallel Columns of the Arguments Used by Mormon Missionaries.* Tucson, AZ: Roy-Co Distributors, n.d.

Kaiser, Edgar P. *How to Respond to the Latter-day Saints.* St. Louis, MO: Concordia, 1977.

Marquardt, Michael H. *The Strange Marriages of Sarah N. Whitney to Joseph Smith the Mormon Prophet, Joseph C. Kingsbury and Heber C. Kimball.* Salt Lake City, UT: Utah Lighthouse Ministry, 1973.

Martin, Walter R. *Mormonism.* Grand Rapids, MI: Zondervan, 1967.

Matthews, Robert J. *Index and Concordance for "Teachings of the Prophet Joseph Smith."* Salt Lake City, UT: Deseret Book Co., 1976.

Morley, Rev. Frank S. *What We Can Learn from the Church of Jesus Christ of Latter-day Saints by a Protestant Minister.* Salt Lake City, UT: The Church of Jesus Christ of Latter-day Saints, n.d.

Petersen, LaMar. *Problems in Mormon Text.* Concord, CA: Pacific Publishing, 1972.

Petersen, Mark E. "Which Church Is Right?" Salt Lake City, UT: Church of Jesus Christ of Latter-day Saints, 1982.

Quinn, D. Michael. *On Being a Mormon Historian (A Lecture by D. Michael Quinn, Associate Professor of History at Brigham Young University Before the Student History Association. Fall 1981).* Salt Lake City, UT: Utah Lighthouse Ministry, 1982.

Ralson, Colleen. *Color Me Confused: A Guide for Marking Your* Book of Mormon. Rev. ed. St. Louis, MO: Watchman Fellowship, 1988.

*Salt Lake City Messenger* (various issues). P.O. Box 1884, Salt Lake City, UT 84110.

Smithsonian Institution, Department of Anthropology. "Statement Regarding the Book of Mormon." Washington, D.C.: Smithsonian Institution, 1988.

*Dissecting the* Doctrine and Covenants: *A Guide for Marking Your* Doctrine and Covenants. St. Louis, MO: Watchman Fellowship, 1990.

Spaulding, F.S., and Samuel A.B. Mercer. *Why Egyptologists Reject the* Book of Abraham. Salt Lake City, UT: Utah Lighthouse Ministry, n.d.

Tanner, Jerald and Sandra. *Joseph Smith's 1826 Trial: New Discoveries Prove Court Record Authentic.* Salt Lake City, UT: Utah Lighthouse Ministry, n.d.

Taylor, Sally J., to Jerald and Sandra Tanner, September 25, 1990. Discussing the Navy Chief of Chaplain's designation of the Mormon Faith as "Protestant."

Taylor, Sally J. (Mrs. Andrew R. Taylor) et al. Letter to Rear Admiral Alvin B. Koeneman, Office of the Chief of Naval Operations, Department of the Navy, Washington D.C. from the Protestant Chapel Council Naval Air Station, Alameda, CA, protesting the designation of Mormonism as Protestant. (The U.S. Army/Air Force offer the same classification), n.d. visible on photocopy.

Whitmer, David. *An Address to All Believers in Christ by a Witness to the Divine Authenticity of the* Book of Mormon. 1887. Reprint. Concord, CA: Pacific Publishing Co., 1972.

Witte, Bob. *What's Going On Here?* Clearwater, FL: Ex-Mormons for Jesus, n.d.

———. *Where Does It Say That?: A Witnessing Resource for Christians.* Safety Harbor, FL: Ex-Mormons for Jesus, n.d.

————. *Witnessing to Mormons: Using Where Does It Say That?* Safety Harbor, FL: Ex-Mormons for Jesus Ministries, n.d.

## Newspaper and Periodical Articles

"Analysis of FBI Figure Shows S.L. [Salt Lake City] Leads U.S. in Larcenies." *The Salt Lake Tribune*, April 24, 1989.

Anderson, Vern. "Reorganized LDS Church in Turmoil After Split in Faith." *The Salt Lake Tribune*, July 9, 1990.

"Child-Abuse Cases Set Record in Utah County." *The Salt Lake Tribune*, April 23, 1988.

Dabling, Bobby B. "Attorney Says Church Can Stall Sex Cases." *The Salt Lake Tribune*, November 30, 1984.

Dart, John. "Mormon Church Passes Seven Million Mark." *Los Angeles Times*, January 6, 1990.

Davis, V. Beason appeal from the third Judicial District Court of the Territory of Idaho argued December 9-10, 1889—decided February 3, 1890 (re: bigamy and polygamy). This decision noted, "Bigamy and polygamy are crimes by the laws of all civilized and Christian countries. They are crimes by the laws of the United States, and they are crimes by the laws of Idaho. They tend to destroy the purity of the marriage relation, to disturb the peace of families, to degrade women and to debase man. Few crimes are more pernicious to the best interest of society and receive more general or more deserved punishment. To extend exemption from punishment for such crimes would be to shock the moral judgment of the community" (p. 341, Mr. Justice Field delivering the opinion of the court).

Dockstader, Julie. "Teen Suicides Becoming 'National Tragedy.'" *The Salt Lake Tribune*, October 22, 1985.

"Health of Utah Children Is Deteriorating Like Rest of U.S. Youth, Officials Warn." *The Salt Lake Tribune*, March 12, 1989.

Heber, G. Wolsey. "Who Are the Mormons?" *This People*, Spring 1990.

Jorgensen, Chris. "Task Force Begins Efforts to Treat Young Sex Offenders." *The Salt Lake Tribune*, February 27, 1989.

Lamb, David. "Salt Lake: A Worship of Order." *Los Angeles Times*, February 2, 1988.

"The Mormon Financial Empire." *Denver Post*, November 21-28, 1982.

"Mormons Testify Jesus Is the Christ." Augusta, GA: Newspaper insert, April 13, 1990.

"Most Polygamy Is in Utah, Professor Says." *The Salt Lake Tribune*, April 10, 1988.

Palmer, Anne. "Three Factors Contribute to Teenage Drug Use." *The Salt Lake Tribune*, January 26, 1987.

Renolds, Michael H. "Mormon Chaplains in the Military." *The Utah Evangel*, January–February 1992, p. 12.

Sisco, Carol. "Murder Rate of Children Ranks High: One Out of Five Victims in Utah Is Younger Than Age 15." *The Salt Lake Tribune*, August 13, 1982.

————. "Two Utah Lawmakers Sponsor Legislation to Better Protect Women from Abuse." *The Salt Lake Tribune*, January 9, 1989.

————. "Utah Must Cure Plague of Child Abuse, Says Analyst." *The Salt Lake Tribune*, January 24, 1990.

"S.L. [Salt Lake City] Crime Rate Rises 3.2% in '88." *The Salt Lake Tribune*, February 14, 1989.

Sowerby, Melinda. "The Church's New Magazine Ad Campaign Focuses on Message of Restoration." *The Salt Lake Tribune*, January 23, 1990.

"Teen Suicide Continues to Escalate." *The Salt Lake Tribune*, July 8, 1985.

Tracy, Dawn. "Study Says Utah Teens' Sex Life Mirrors U.S. Profile." *The Salt Lake Tribune*, December 25, 1987.

Zonana, Victor F. "Leaders of Mormonism Double As Overseers of a Financial Empire." *Wall Street Journal*, November 9, 1983.

# Resource List

Book List
Utah Lighthouse Ministry
Box 1884
Salt Lake City, Utah 84110
www.utlm.org

*Mormonism—Shadow or Reality?* **(1987 edition)**
*by Jerald and Sandra Tanner*
Our most comprehensive and revealing work on Mormonism. Deals with new discoveries relating to Mormon history, changes in Joseph Smith's revelations, Joseph Smith's 1826 trial for "glass looking," proof that the *Book of Mormon* is a product of the nineteenth century, changes in the *Book of Mormon*, archaeology and the *Book of Mormon*, changes in Joseph Smith's *History*, the First Vision, the Godhead, the Adam-God doctrine, the priesthood, the missionary system, false prophecy, Joseph Smith's doctrine of polygamy, polygamy after the Manifesto and in Utah today, changes in the anti-black doctrine, the rediscovery of the Joseph Smith Papyri and the fall of the *Book of Abraham*, Mormon scriptures and the Bible changes in the *Pearl of Great Price*, blood atonement among the early Mormons, the Word of Wisdom, the Council of 50, the Danites, the temple ceremony, changes in the temple ceremony and garments, the Mountain Meadows Massacre, Mormonism and money, plus hundreds of other important subjects.

*An Index to Mormonism—Shadow or Reality?*
*by Michael Briggs*

*Tract Pact*
A collection of 18 different tracts on Mormonism from various publishers.

*The Changing World of Mormonism*
*by Jerald and Sandra Tanner*
A condensed version of *Mormonism—Shadow or Reality?* Published by Moody Press. Almost 600 pages plus an index and bibliography.

*Major Problems of Mormonism*
*by Jerald and Sandra Tanner*
Thirty years of research on Mormonism distilled into a 256-page book. Covers the most important areas.

*The Bible and Mormon Doctrine*
*by Sandra Tanner*
A 33-page booklet dealing with the LDS view of man's eternal progression, modern revelation, the gospel, salvation by grace or works, the true church, preexistence, kingdoms in heaven, temple work, priesthood, and the nature of God as compared with the biblical view. A great help in understanding Mormon beliefs.

*Jerald Tanner's Testimony*
*by Jerald Tanner*
An account of why he left the Mormon church and how he found a personal relationship with Jesus Christ. Tells how he met Sandra (the great-great granddaughter of Brigham Young), how they were married, and how they set up a ministry to Mormons. Also deals with the fears and problems encountered in running such a ministry, and contains a number of personal stories.

### Evolution of the Mormon Temple Ceremony, 1842–1990
by Jerald and Sandra Tanner
Contains the *actual text* of the 1990 revision of the highly secret endowment ritual and other accounts of the ceremony dating back to 1846. Shows that Joseph Smith borrowed from Masonry in creating the ritual and that it has evolved over the years. Also shows the serious changes made in the ceremony in 1990.

### No Man Knows My History
by Fawn M. Brodie
The finest book written on the life of Joseph Smith. The Mormon writer Samuel W. Taylor remarked: "Mrs. Brodie was unchurched for the writing of it and delivered to the buffetings of Satan....It was not inaccuracy that raised the Mormon ire, but her documentation of that which we didn't wish to believe."

### The Mormon Mirage: A Former Mormon Tells Why She Left the Church
by Latayne Colvelt Scott

### Mormon Claims Answered
by Marvin Cowan
An excellent book on the teachings of Mormonism.

### Where Does It Say That?
by Bob Witte
Over 100 photos of oft-quoted pages from early LDS sources.

### Mormon Scriptures and the Bible
by Jerald and Sandra Tanner
A 53-page book dealing with such subjects as the decline of the use of the Bible in Mormon theology, the influence of Bible critics on Mormonism, the charge that the Catholics conspired to alter the Bible, a comparison of the manuscript evidence for the Bible and Mormon scriptures, Young's attempt to suppress Joseph Smith's Inspired Revision of the Bible, the way Smith ignored his own renderings, the lack of support in ancient manuscripts for Smith's "inspired" renderings, and changes in the *Pearl of Great Price*.

### A Look at Christianity
by Jerald and Sandra Tanner
Deals with the Flood, Noah's Ark, Egypt and the Bible, evidence from Palestine, the Moabite Stone, Assyrian records, the Dead Sea Scrolls, the importance of love, the destructive effects of hate, reconciliation with God, our testimony, the historicity of Jesus, manuscripts of the New Testament, early writings concerning Christianity, and more.

### Mormonism, Magic and Masonry
by Jerald and Sandra Tanner
A study of the influence of magic and Masonry on Joseph Smith and his family.

### Joseph Smith's Bainbridge, NY, Court Trials
by Wesley P. Walters
Important discoveries concerning Joseph Smith's 1826 and 1830 trials. Proves beyond all doubt that Joseph Smith was a money-digger who used a "peep stone" to find buried treasures at the very time he was supposed to be preparing himself to receive the gold plates from which the *Book of Mormon* was translated.

### Joseph Smith and Money Digging
by Jerald and Sandra Tanner
Deals with such subjects as Joseph Smith's connection with money digging; Joseph Smith's "seer stone," the use of the "seer stone" to find the *Book of Mormon* plates and its use to translate the book itself; the relationship of money digging to the story of the gold plates of the *Book of Mormon* and to the text of the book; the use of the divining rod by the Mormons; and the

revelation regarding treasure hunting. This book also contains a photographic reprint of the affidavits regarding Joseph Smith's money-digging activities, which were published by E.D. Howe in 1834.

### New Light on Mormon Origins from the Palmyra (NY) Revival
by Wesley P. Walters
A devastating blow to the First Vision story. Mormons claim that Joseph Smith was motivated to pray in the woods in 1820 due to a revival in Palmyra. Walters, however, presents evidence that there was no revival in Palmyra in 1820.

### Covering Up the Black Hole in the Book of Mormon
by Jerald and Sandra Tanner
A penetrating look at the Book of Mormon that conclusively demonstrates it was written by Joseph Smith and did not come from gold plates written by ancient Jews. Contains 74 pages of proof that Smith plagiarized extensively from the King James Version of the New Testament.

### 3913 Changes in the Book of Mormon
A photomechanical reprint of the original 1830 edition of the Book of Mormon with all the changes marked. Contains a 16-page introduction by Jerald and Sandra Tanner that proves that the changes are not in harmony with the original text.

### Joseph Smith Begins His Work, Vol. 1
A photo-reprint of the original 1830 edition of the Book of Mormon. Bound.

### Joseph Smith Begins His Work, Vol. 2
Photo-reprint of both the 1833 Book of Commandments and the 1835 edition of the Doctrine and Covenants. Bound.

### The Pearl of Great Price
Photo-reprint of the original 1851 edition.

### An Address to All Believers in Christ
by David Whitmer
One of the three witnesses to the Book of Mormon tells why he left the LDS church and how Joseph changed the revelations and fell into error. Photo-reprint of the 1887 edition.

### The Use of the Bible in the Book of Mormon and Early Nineteenth-Century Events Reflected in the Book of Mormon
by H. Michael Marquardt
A good summary of the evidence showing that the Book of Mormon is a product of the nineteenth century.

### An Examination of B.H. Roberts' Secret Manuscript
by Wesley P. Walters
An article analyzing Roberts' compilation of evidence showing that Joseph Smith could have written the Book of Mormon. Includes some photographs of Roberts' original manuscript.

### Roberts' Manuscripts Revealed
Photo reproductions of some secret manuscripts written by Mormon historian B.H. Roberts. Roberts expressed some serious doubts about the Book of Mormon and frankly admitted that Joseph Smith had a vivid enough imagination and the source material to have produced the book.

### Archaeology and the Book of Mormon
by Hal Hougey
By using quotations from well-known Mormon authors, Mr. Hougey shows that there is no real archaeological evidence to support the claims of the Book of Mormon.

*Ferguson's Manuscript Unveiled*
A significant paper on the subject of the *Book of Mormon*'s archaeology and geography. Thomas Stuart Ferguson, one of the most noted defenders of the *Book of Mormon*, was finally forced to conclude that it was "fictional."

*Did Spalding Write the* **Book of Mormon?**
*by Jerald and Sandra Tanner*
Explains why the Tanners oppose the theory that Spalding penned 12 pages of the *Book of Mormon*. Contains a photographic comparison of Spalding's handwriting with the *Book of Mormon* manuscript and a photo-reprint of Spalding's *Manuscript Found*.

*Archaeology and the* **Book of Mormon,** *1969*
*by Jerald and Sandra Tanner*
A 92-page book dealing with such subjects as the *Book of Mormon* in light of archaeological findings in the New World, the disagreement between Dr. Nibley and Dr. Jakeman over archaeology and the *Book of Mormon*, Nephite coins, the Anthon transcript, Mayan glyphs, the Paraiba text, the Kinderhook plates, the Newark stone, the Lehi Tree-of-Life stone, the problem of the *Book of Mormon's* geography, the Bat Creek inscription, Dr. Gordon's work, Adam's altar, Jewish coins in America, and many other subjects.

*View of the Hebrews*
*by Ethan Smith*
A photo-reprint of the 1825 edition; also contains parallels between *View of the Hebrews* and the *Book of Mormon* identified by the Mormon historian B.H. Roberts. Many scholars believe that Joseph Smith used this book in writing the *Book of Mormon*.

*The Golden Bible; or, the* **Book of Mormon.** *Is It From God?*
*by M.T. Lamb*
A photo-reprint of the 1887 edition. A good analysis of internal problems in the *Book of Mormon*.

*The Use of the Old Testament in the* **Book of Mormon**
*by Wesley P. Walters*
Demonstrates many errors Joseph Smith made in the *Book of Mormon*. Makes it clear that Smith was plagiarizing the King James Version of the Bible rather than translating from ancient gold plates.

*2,000 Changes in the* **Book of Mormon**
*by Lamoni Call*
A photo-reprint of Call's 1898 work. A critical study of the *Book of Mormon*.

*Latter-day Saints—Where Did You Get Your Authority?*
*by Hal Hougey*
A valuable study of Mormon priesthood.

*Joseph Smith Among the Egyptians*
*by Wesley P. Walters*
Walters, one of the top scholars on Mormon history, gives a good summary of the evidence against the *Book of Abraham*. Deals with Dr. Nibley's attempt to defend it and shows that he is in a "state of confusion" on almost every important issue.

*Joseph Smith's Egyptian Alphabet and Grammar*
A photographic reproduction of a handwritten document that was suppressed by the Mormon leaders for 130 years because it proves that Joseph Smith did not understand Egyptian and that his *Book of Abraham* is spurious. Also contains parts of two handwritten manuscripts of the *Book of Abraham*. A vital document for students of the *Book of Abraham*.

*The* **Book of Abraham** *Papyrus Found: An Answer to Dr. Hugh Nibley's Book "The Message of the Joseph Smith Papyri..."*
*by H. Michael Marquardt*
In this book Mr. Marquardt shows that Dr. Nibley has failed in his recent attempt to prove the authenticity of the *Book of Abraham.*

*Can the Browns Save Joseph Smith?*
*by Jerald and Sandra Tanner*
A rebuttal to *They Lie in Wait to Deceive.*

*The* **Book of Abraham** *Revisited*
*by H. Michael Marquardt*
A critical look at the *Book of Abraham.*

*Why Egyptologists Reject the* **Book of Abraham**
A photo-reprint of *Joseph Smith, Jr. As a Translator,* by F.S. Spalding, D.D., 1912, and *Joseph Smith As an Interpreter and Translator,* by Samuel A.B. Mercer, Ph.D. Spalding sent the *Book of Abraham* (containing the facsimiles purported to have been copied from the writing of Abraham) to eight prominent Egyptologists and Semitists and asked them to pass judgment on the "translation" made by Joseph Smith. All of these scholars denounced the *Book of Abraham* as a fraud.

*Mormon Spies, Hughes and the CIA*
*by Jerald and Sandra Tanner*
Deals with the Mullen Company (the firm that handled public relations for the Mormon church) and the Watergate break-in, the BYU spying operations, the prostitution conspiracy and the church, wiretapping and bugging, Mormons and the CIA, Robert Bennett's involvement with Hunt, Hunt's BYU spy, Bennett's cover-up, Mormons and Hughes, the possible existence of the secret Council of 50 in the church today, and many other important subjects.

*Unmasking a Mormon Spy*
*by Jerald and Sandra Tanner*
Story of a recent LDS spy, the "enemies list," infiltration into Ex-Mormons for Jesus, intelligence gathering, Mormon church security, new material on the Council of 50.

*Mormonism Like Watergate?*
*by Jerald and Sandra Tanner*
Contains an answer to Dr. Nibley's 1973 article in the *Salt Lake Tribune,* the 1831 revelation on polygamy (which commands Mormons to marry Indians to make them a "white" and "delightsome" people), and suppressed material on the anti-black doctrine. Filled with important information.

*The Strange Marriages of Sarah Ann Whitney to Joseph Smith the Mormon Prophet, Joseph C. Kingsbury and Heber C. Kimball*
*by H. Michael Marquardt*
This pamphlet proves that Joseph Smith took Sarah Ann Whitney as a secret plural wife, but performed a "pretended" marriage ceremony between her and Joseph Kingsbury to cover up his own iniquity.

*Joseph Smith and Polygamy*
*by Jerald and Sandra Tanner*
Contains a detailed study of the Mormon doctrine of plural marriage, the spiritual wife doctrine, the John C. Bennett book, the Nancy Rigdon affair, the Sarah Pratt affair, and also the Martha H. Brotherton affair. Also included is a list of 84 women who may have been married to Joseph Smith.

*Mormons and Negroes*
*by Jerald and Sandra Tanner*
Covers such subjects as the protests against BYU and the Mormon church, dissatisfaction in the church, the question of a new revelation, blacks who held the priesthood before the doctrine was changed, slavery and civil rights among the Mormons, and many other important subjects. Also included is the complete text of Apostle Mark E. Petersen's speech "Race Problems—As They Affect the Church."

**Excommunication of a Mormon Church Leader**
Contains the letter of George P. Lee.

**LDS Apostle Confesses Brigham Young Taught Adam-God Doctrine**
Contains a photographic reproduction of a 10-page letter written by Bruce R. McConkie.

**Adam Is God?**
*by Chris A. Vlachos*
A well-researched pamphlet on the Adam-God doctrine.

**Tracking the White Salamander—The Story of Mark Hofmann, Murder and Forged Mormon Documents**
*by Jerald and Sandra Tanner*
Shows how Jerald's belief that the documents were forged was confirmed by investigators. Also contains *Confessions of a White Salamander* at no extra charge.

**A Gathering of Saints: A True Story of Money, Murder and Deceit**
*by Robert Lindsey*
An excellent account of the forgeries and murders of Mark Hofmann.

**Salamander: The Story of the Mormon Forgery Murders**
*by Linda Sillitoe and Allen Roberts*
A scholarly look at Mark Hofmann and his dealings with the Mormon church.

**The Tanners on Trial**
*by Jerald and Sandra Tanner*
A detailed study of Andrew Ehat's unsuccessful attempt to stop publication of *Clayton's Secret Writings Uncovered*. A Mormon judge awarded Ehat damages, but his decision was overturned by the 10th Circuit Court of Appeals. This book has well over 100 large pages with many photographs of the original court documents. Contains fascinating testimony by some of the Mormon church's top historians. Highly recommended.

**Mormonism Exposed, Being a Journal of a Residence in Missouri from the 28th of May to the 20th of August, 1838**
*by William Swartzell*
A photo-reprint of the 1840 edition.

**An American Prophet's Record: The Diaries and Journals of Joseph Smith**
*Scott H. Faulring, ed.*
All the diaries of Joseph Smith printed in a beautiful paperback edition.

**Joseph Smith's Kirtland Revelation Book**
Introduction by Jerald and Sandra Tanner. Photographs of Joseph Smith's early revelations in handwritten form. Does not contain a typescript.

**Heber C. Kimball's Journal, November 21, 1845 to January 7, 1846**
A photographic reproduction containing some important information on the Nauvoo temple ceremony. Most of the space, however, is devoted to listing names of those who passed through temple rituals. Does not contain a typescript.

### The Lucifer-God Doctrine
*by Jerald and Sandra Tanner*
Demonstrates that some Mormon critics have gone too far in attempting to link Mormons to Satanism and witchcraft. Contains an answer to the Decker-Schnoebelen rebuttal.

### The Mormon Kingdom, Vol. 1, 1969
*by Jerald and Sandra Tanner*
Contains an account of the temple ceremony. Also discusses the changes in the ceremony and garments, the relationship to Masonry, the "oath of vengeance," the doctrine of blood atonement, baptism for the dead, the Danites, the Council of 50, the failure of the Kirtland Bank, the war in Missouri, Joseph Smith's secret ordination as king and his candidacy for president of the United States.

### The Mormon Kingdom, Vol. 2, 1971
*by Jerald and Sandra Tanner*
Deals with such subjects as the Council of 50 and how it controlled early Utah, the ordination of Mormon kings, Mormonism and money, politics in Utah, the Mountain Meadows Massacre, the Utah War, the practice of blood atonement in Utah, and Brigham Young's indictment for murder and counterfeiting.

### The Case Against Mormonism, Vol. 1, 1968
*by Jerald and Sandra Tanner*
Deals with Joseph's First Vision, changes in Mormon revelations and documents, the Law of Adoption, the Mormon Battalion, suppression of the records, book-burning, the BYU spy ring, and many other subjects.

### The Case Against Mormonism, Vol. 2, 1968
*by Jerald and Sandra Tanner*
Deals with the *Book of Mormon* witnesses, the gold plates, parallels between the *Book of Mormon* and other documents, the influence of the Bible and the Apocrypha upon the *Book of Mormon*, and proof that the *Book of Abraham* is a spurious work. Almost 70 pages are devoted to the papyri and the *Book of Abraham*.

### The Case Against Mormonism, Vol. 3, 1971
*by Jerald and Sandra Tanner*
Deals with the meaning and changes in the facsimiles in the *Book of Abraham*, books Joseph Smith may have had in writing the *Book of Mormon* and the *Book of Abraham*, the plurality of gods doctrine, the Adam-God doctrine, the Virgin Birth, false prophecies of Joseph Smith and Brigham Young, the Word of Wisdom, the priesthood, cursing enemies, animal sacrifice after Christ, the Mormon missionary system, and many other important subjects.

### Hearts Made Glad: The Charges of Intemperance Against Joseph Smith the Mormon Prophet
*by LaMar Petersen*
This book throws a great deal of light on Joseph Smith's Word of Wisdom and his attitude toward it.

### Mormonism Unveiled
*by E.D. Howe*
A photo-reprint of the 1834 edition.

### History of the Saints
*by John C. Bennett*
A photo-reprint of the 1842 edition.

### Reed Peck Manuscript
This manuscript was written in 1839 by Reed Peck, who had been a Mormon. Contains important firsthand information concerning the Mormon war in Missouri and the Danite band.

### Senate Document 189
A photo-reprint of the "testimony given before the judge of the fifth judicial circuit of the State of Missouri, on the trial of Joseph Smith, Jr., and others, for high treason, and other crimes against that State." Gives very interesting testimony on the Danite band.

### Brigham's Destroying Angel
A photo-reprint of the 1904 edition. The confessions of Bill Hickman, who claimed that he committed murder by the orders of Brigham Young and Apostle Orson Hyde.

### Confessions of John D. Lee
A photo-reprint of 1877 edition. Contains important information on the Mountain Meadows Massacre.

### Under the Prophet in Utah
*by Frank J. Cannon*
A photo-reprint of 1911 edition. Cannon was United States Senator from Utah and the son of George Q. Cannon, a member of the First Presidency. Shows how the Mormon leaders broke their covenants to the nation and continued to live in polygamy after the manifesto. Also shows how the leaders interfered in politics.

### Reminiscences of Early Utah
*by R.N. Baskin*
Photo-reprint of the original 1914 edition. Baskin was a Chief Justice of the Supreme Court of Utah who also served as mayor of Salt Lake City. He explains how the Mormon leaders tried to evade the laws of the United States, discusses marked ballots and the absurd election laws, the Mountain Meadows Massacre, the Endowment House rites, blood atonement, the Danites, and the revelation on polygamy.

### Changes in Joseph Smith's History
*by Jerald and Sandra Tanner*
A study of the changes that have been made in the six volumes of the *History of the Church* since its first printing.

### Falsification of Joseph Smith's History
*by Jerald and Sandra Tanner*
Proves that many serious changes were made in Joseph Smith's *History* after his death. Although the Mormon leaders claim that Joseph Smith wrote this *History*, research reveals that less than 40 percent of it was compiled before his death.

### A Critical Look: A Study of the Overstreet "Confession" and the Cowdery "Defence"
*by Jerald and Sandra Tanner*
This pamphlet shows that these two documents are forgeries.

### Answering Dr. Clandestine: A Response to the Anonymous LDS Historian, enlarged edition
*by Jerald and Sandra Tanner*
This is an answer to the booklet, *Jerald and Sandra Tanner's Distorted View of Mormonism*. Also deals with Joseph Smith's magic talisman and the Nag Hammadi documents.

### On Being a Mormon Historian
*by D. Michael Quinn*
One of the best speeches ever given by a Mormon historian. *Newsweek* called it a "stirring defense of intellectual integrity." In this 1981 speech Dr. Quinn, Associate Professor of History at BYU, attacks the suppressive policies advocated by Apostles Benson and Packer.

### Following the Brethren
*Introduction by Jerald and Sandra Tanner*
Contains Apostle Ezra Taft Benson's speech, "Fourteen Fundamentals in Following the Prophets." Also contains Apostle Bruce R. McConkie's speech, "All Are Alike Unto God."

**John Whitmer's History**
Joseph Smith gave a revelation in 1831 commanding John Whitmer to keep this history of the church. Very revealing.

**Elders' Journal**
A photo-reprint of a LDS paper (1837–1838).

**Messenger and Advocate**
A 3-volume set. Photo-reprint of an early LDS church paper (1834–1837).

**Clayton's Secret Writings Uncovered: Extracts from the Diaries of Joseph Smith's Secretary William Clayton**

**Joseph Smith's History, by His Mother**
A photo-reprint of the original 1853 edition. Contains a 15-page introduction by Jerald and Sandra Tanner.

**Changes in the Key to Theology**
by Jerald and Sandra Tanner
A photo-reprint of the 1855 edition, with changes marked between the first edition and the 1965 edition. Changes were made in the teachings on polygamy and the Holy Spirit.

**Our Relationship with the Lord**
by Mormon Apostle Bruce R. McConkie
An attack on the concept of a personal relationship with Christ.

**The Mormon Purge**
by Jerald and Sandra Tanner
A revealing account of how the LDS church is attempting to silence its historians and other dissidents. This book includes information from secret church documents.

## Cassette Tapes
**Sandra Tanner Tape No. 1**
Two lectures given at Trinity Evangelical Divinity School. A helpful overview for those who want to understand Mormonism.

**Sandra Tanner Tape No. 2**
A one-hour interview on Mormonism with a Milwaukee television station. Includes personal comments about why the Tanners left Mormonism and their faith in Christ. Helpful for both LDS and non-LDS audiences.

**Problems in Winning Mormons**
by Jerald Tanner
Shows how to use a loving approach to win Mormons to the Lord.

**Jerald Tanner's Testimony**
Three cassette tapes concerning Jerald's life and the Utah Lighthouse Ministry.

# Notes

**The Confusion Caused by Mormonism**

1. Those who may disagree with us would hopefully examine such evidence, impartially, in more detail. For those without a computer, we suggest perusing the Bibliography in *Ready with an Answer* and the Resource List at the end of this book, and for those on-line, in addition, Probe Ministries (http://www.probe.org/); LeadershipU (http://www.leaderu.com/index.html), and *Point/Counterpoint: The skeptic and seeker's guide for investigating religions and world views through debate, interview, analysis, and discussion* (http://members.aol.com/pointcpt/wp/pcp.html). This latter web site begins with a sentiment close to our own hearts, one we hope the readers of this book, Mormon and Christian alike, will share, or come to share: "Our orientation is biblical Christianity and we believe that anyone who honestly and earnestly seeks spiritual truth from God (on nothing more than the possibility that God is there and deserves our highest love and commitment) will discover that this position is true. But the truth or falsity of this claim must finally be determined by your own inquiry...."

2. Indeed, God is merciful and understanding even with the stubborn doubter, or the openly hostile skeptic. The apostle Thomas doubted Jesus' resurrection. This was even in the face of considerable eyewitness testimony of his friends, who had soberly declared they had seen Him alive: "Unless I see the nail marks in his hands and put my finger where the nails were, and put my hand into his side, I will not believe it." Later, Jesus appeared to the disciples again when Thomas was present. "Then he said to Thomas, 'Put your finger here; see my hands. Reach out your hand and put it into my side. Stop doubting and believe.' Thomas said to him, 'My Lord and my God!'" (John 20:27-28 NIV). Jesus even said to the hostile Jewish leaders, "Do not believe me unless I do what my Father does. But if I do it, even though you do not believe me, believe the miracles, that you may know and understand that the Father is in me, and I in the Father" (John 10:37 NIV).

**Chapter 1—The Mormon Church Today**

1. *The Salt Lake Tribune*, January 23, 1990.
2. Ankerberg, *Mormonism Revisited*, 22.
3. Hannah Wolfson, Associated Press article, October 9, 2000 (Internet article).
4. Jeffery L. Sheler, *U.S. News and World Report*, November 13, 2000 (Internet article).
5. Ibid.
6. *Time* magazine, July 29, 1991; *The Denver Post*, November 21-28, 1982; *Wall Street Journal*, November 9, 1983; *The Arizona Republic*, June 30–July 3, 1991.
7. Ankerberg, *Mormon Officials*, 21. See *Living a Christlike Life: Discussion 5*, 14-15.
8. Martin, *Maze of Mormonism*, 21.
9. Ankerberg, *Mormon Officials*, 21-22.
10. Ankerberg, *Mormonism Revisited*, 31; *Mormon Officials*, 21-22.
11. *The Utah Evangel* (Salt Lake City, UT), November 1981.
12. Martin, *Maze of Mormonism*, 20; Einar Anderson, *Inside Story*, ix; Jerald and Sandra Tanner, *Mormon Spies, Hughes and the CIA* (Salt Lake City, UT: Utah Lighthouse Ministry, l976), 56.
13. Martin, *Maze of Mormonism*, 16-21.
14. *Christianity Today*, October 2, 1981, 70.
15. Benson, *Teachings*, 240.
16. Ibid., 238.
17. Ibid., 237.
18. *This People* (Mormon periodical), Spring 1990, 21.
19. Ibid.
20. *Los Angeles Times*, January 6, 1990.

**Chapter 2—The Beginning of Mormonism**

1. Joseph Smith, *History of the Church*, 13. (The *Pearl of Great Price* excerpts are originally taken from this text.)

2. Ibid., 4-6.
3. Ibid.
4. Ibid.
5. Ibid.
6. Ibid.
7. Ibid.
8. Ibid.
9. Ibid.
10. Ibid., 8.
11. Ibid., 9.
12. Ibid., 11-12.
13. Ibid., 12-14.
14. Ibid., 15.
15. Most of these are recorded in the most important doctrinal scripture of Mormonism, *Doctrine and Covenants;* see note 16.
16. Cf. *Doctrine and Covenants,* vi-viii for a chronological listing.
17. Cf. Joseph Smith, *History,* 1:39-48, 80.
18. Jerald and Sandra Tanner, *The Changing World of Mormonism,* 10.
19. *Dialogue: A Journal of Mormon Thought,* Autumn 1966, 29; David O. McKay, *Gospel Ideals,* 85; John A. Widtsoe, *Joseph Smith, Seeker After Truth,* 19; Paul R. Cheesman, "An Analysis of the Accounts Relating Joseph Smith's Early Visions," Brigham Young University Master's thesis, May 1975, 75, cited in Jerald and Sandra Tanner, *Changing World,* 151; Jerald and Sandra Tanner, *Joseph Smith's Strange Account of the First Vision,* 1; Jerald and Sandra Tanner, *Mormonism—Shadow or Reality?* 143; Martin, *Maze,* 26-30; Jerald and Sandra Tanner, *Changing World,* chapter 6.
20. Jerald and Sandra Tanner, *Changing World,* 152.
21. Ankerberg, *Mormonism Revisited,* 13-14.
22. Jerald and Sandra Tanner, *Changing World,* 155.
23. Ibid., 156.
24. Church of Jesus Christ of Latter-day Saints, *Sure Foundation,* 169-170.
25. John Ankerberg and John Weldon, *Do the Resurrection Accounts Conflict? And What Proof Is There Jesus Rose from the Dead?* (Chattanooga, TN: Ankerberg Theological Research Institute, 1989).
26. Ankerberg, *Mormonism Revisited,* 13.
27. Gordon Fraser, in the foreword to Jerald and Sandra Tanner, *Changing World,* 10.
28. John Weldon, chapters on "New Age Intuition," "Visualization," and "New Age Inner Work," in John Ankerberg and John Weldon, *An Encyclopedia of New Age Beliefs* (Eugene, OR: Harvest House Publishers, 1996).
29. Elias Smith, *The Life, Conversion, Preaching, Travels and Sufferings, 1816,* 58-59; *The Christian Baptist,* March 1, 1824, 1:148-149; *The Wayne Sentinel,* October 22, 1823, cited in Jerald and Sandra Tanner, *Changing World,* 159-160.
30. Jerald and Sandra Tanner, *Changing World,* 160.
31. John Ankerberg and John Weldon, *Cult Watch: What You Need to Know About Spiritual Deception* (Eugene, OR: Harvest House, 1991), parts 5, 7.
32. Raphael Gasson, *The Challenging Counterfeit* (Plainfield, NJ: Logos, 1969), 125.

**Chapter 3—Mormon Teachings on God and the Trinity**
1. Church of Jesus Christ of Latter-day Saints, *Doctrines of the Gospel,* 6.
2. Joseph Smith, *Teachings,* 343.
3. Talmage, *Articles of Faith,* 47.
4. Church of Jesus Christ of Latter-day Saints, *Sure Foundation,* 93.
5. McConkie, *Mormon Doctrine,* 579.
6. Robinson, *Are Mormons Christians?* 65.
7. Ibid., 69.
8. Ibid.
9. *The Oxford American Dictionary,* s.v. "polytheism."
10. McConkie, *Mormon Doctrine,* 576-577.
11. Ankerberg, *Mormon Officials,* 1.

12. Church of Jesus Christ of Latter-day Saints, *Doctrines of the Gospel*, 8.
13. Ibid.
14. Ibid.
15. Ibid., emphasis added.
16. Ibid., 10.
17. Ibid., 16.
18. *Pearl of Great Price, Book of Abraham* 4:1,5-11,14-17,25-29; 5:7-8,11,14.
19. McConkie, *Mormon Doctrine*, 317.
20. Church of Jesus Christ of Latter-day Saints, *Doctrines of the Gospel*, 6.
21. Ibid., 9.
22. McConkie, *Mormon Doctrine*, 576-577.
23. *Journal of Discourses*, 7:333.
24. Duane S. Crowther, *Life Everlasting*, 361.
25. Robinson, *Are Mormons Christians?* 88, emphasis added.
26. Ibid., 79, emphasis added.
27. Ibid., 71, emphasis added.
28. Richard L. Evans, interviewed in Leo Rosten's, *Religions of America* (NY: Simon & Schuster, 1975), 189.
29. Joseph Smith, *Teachings*, 372; cf. Joseph Fielding Smith, *Answers to Gospel Questions*, 1:3.
30. Joseph Smith, *Teachings*, 370.
31. Church of Jesus Christ of Latter-day Saints, *Sure Foundation*, 96.
32. McConkie, *Doctrinal New Testament Commentary*, 2:77,113,158.
33. E. Calvin Beisner, *God in Three Persons* (Wheaton, IL: Tyndale, 1984); Edward Henry Bickersteth, *The Trinity* (Grand Rapids, MI: Kregel, 1969).
34. Joseph Smith, *Teachings*, 347-348.
35. Church of Jesus Christ of Latter-day Saints, *Gospel Principles*, 293.
36. Joseph Smith, *History*, 6:305.
37. Church of Jesus Christ of Latter-day Saints, *Gospel Principles*, 6.
38. Ankerberg, *Mormon Officials*, 9.
39. Joseph Smith, *Teachings*, 373; cf. McConkie, *Doctrinal New Testament Commentary*, 3:434-437.
40. Joseph Smith, *Teachings*, 345-346.
41. Ibid., 348-349.
42. Joseph Smith, *History*, 6:476, cited in Crowther, *Life Everlasting*, 364.
43. McConkie, *Doctrinal New Testament Commentary*, 2:78.
44. Ibid., 3:225.
45. Ankerberg, *Mormonism Revisited*, 5.
46. Church of Jesus Christ of Latter-day Saints, *Doctrines of the Gospel*, 17.
47. Robinson, *Are Mormons Christians?* 60.
48. See *Journal of Discourses*, 1:93,123; 6:120.
49. *Journal of Discourses*, 6:120.
50. Ibid., 1:93.
51. McConkie, *Mormon Doctrine*, 544-545.
52. *Journal of Discourses*, 11:286.
53. Musser, *Michael Our Father*, 25, citing *Deseret Weekly News*, 22:309.
54. Pratt, *Seer*, September 1853, 132.
55. McMurrin, *Theological Foundations*, 29.
56. Ibid., 36.
57. Ibid., 35.
58. Joseph Smith, *Teachings*, 181.
59. Benson, *Teachings*, 3-4.
60. Church of Jesus Christ of Latter-day Saints, *Sure Foundation*, 97,99.
61. McConkie, *Mormon Doctrine*, 250.
62. Church of Jesus Christ of Latter-day Saints, *Doctrines of the Gospel*, 6.
63. McConkie, *Mormon Doctrine*, 117-118; cf. Einar Anderson, *Inside Story*, 89.
64. McConkie, *Mormon Doctrine*, 239.
65. Benson, *Teachings*, 537.

66. McConkie, *Mormon Doctrine*, 117-118.
67. Ankerberg, *Mormon Officials*, 21.
68. Church of Jesus Christ of Latter-day Saints, *Gospel Principles*, 9.
69. Ibid., 11.
70. Benson, *Teachings*, 540, citing *Discourses of Brigham Young*, 197.
71. Benson, *Teachings*, 542-543.
72. Ankerberg, *Mormon Officials*, 24.
73. Jerald and Sandra Tanner, *Changing World*, 233-234.
74. Ibid., 231-236 for documentation.
75. McConkie, *Doctrinal New Testament Commentary*, 2:160.
76. McConkie, *Mormon Doctrine*, 516-517; cf. Talmage, *Articles of Faith*, 443.
77. Joseph Fielding Smith, *Answers to Gospel Questions*, 3:142; cf. 143-144.
78. Ibid., 144. See *Achieving a Celestial Marriage*, 132, where it teaches women also become gods.
79. *Journal of Discourses*, 13:309.
80. Pratt, *Seer*, November 1853, 172.
81. Ibid., October 1853.
82. *Journal of Discourses*, 3:93.
83. Jerald and Sandra Tanner, *Changing World*, 177, citing Milton Hunter (a member of the First Council of Seventy), *The Gospel Through the Ages* (1958), 104, 114-115.
84. Pratt, *Seer*, February 1853, 23, emphasis added.
85. Jerald and Sandra Tanner, *Changing World*, 188, citing Marion Romney, member of the First Presidency, *Salt Lake City Tribune*, October 6, 1974, 1, emphasis added. See *Achieving a Celestial Marriage*, 129.
86. Robinson, *Are Mormons Christians?* 88.
87. Ibid., 79.
88. Benson, *Teachings*, 4.
89. Jerald and Sandra Tanner, *Changing World*, 191.
90. McConkie, *Mormon Doctrine*, 90.
91. Joseph Fielding Smith, *Doctrines of Salvation*, 3:286.

**Chapter 4—Mormon Beliefs About the Holy Spirit**
1. Talmage, *Articles of Faith*, 160,163,167.
2. Ibid., 166.
3. Jerald and Sandra Tanner, *Changing World*, 188.
4. *Journal of Discourses*, 2:338.
5. Joseph F. Smith, *Gospel Doctrine*, 60-61.
6. Ibid., 60.
7. Ibid.
8. Ibid., 61.
9. *Doctrine and Covenants*, 1835 ed., 52-58.
10. Ibid.
11. Joseph Fielding Smith, *Doctrines of Salvation*, 1:39; *Journal of Discourses*, 5:179.
12. Joseph Fielding Smith, *Doctrines of Salvation*, 1:39.
13. Ibid., with Jerald and Sandra Tanner, *Changing World*, 190.
14. *Journal of Discourses*, 2:338.
15. Joseph F. Smith, *Gospel Doctrine*, 60-61.
16. McConkie, *Doctrinal New Testament Commentary*, 3:338.
17. Ibid., 341.
18. McConkie, *Mormon Doctrine*, 359, 752.

**Chapter 5—The Mormon View of Jesus Christ**
1. Church of Jesus Christ of Latter-day Saints, *What the Mormons Think of Christ*, 1982 (pamphlet), 16.
2. Ibid., 4.
3. Robinson, *Are Mormons Christians?* 111, emphasis added.
4. Ibid., 112, 114.
5. McConkie, *Doctrinal New Testament Commentary*, 2:79.

6. McConkie, *Mormon Doctrine*, 587.
7. Ibid., 590.
8. Talmage, *Articles of Faith*, 471.
9. McConkie, *Mormon Doctrine*, 169; cf. Joseph Fielding Smith, *Doctrines of Salvation*, 1:75.
10. Jerald and Sandra Tanner, *Changing World*, 519, citing Milton Hunter, *Gospel Through the Ages*, 21.
11. Talmage, *Articles of Faith*, 472.
12. Church of Jesus Christ of Latter-day Saints, *Sure Foundation*, 224.
13. J.H. Evans, *An American Prophet*, 1933, 241, cited in Hoekema, *Four Major Cults*, 54.
14. McConkie, *Mormon Doctrine*, 129.
15. *Journal of Discourses*, 10:223.
16. Ibid., 1:50-51, emphasis added.
17. Jerald and Sandra Tanner, *Changing World*, 180, citing *Dialogue: A Journal of Mormon Thought*, Autumn 1967, 100-101.
18. Joseph Fielding Smith, *Doctrines of Salvation*, 1:18, emphasis added.
19. McConkie, *Mormon Doctrine*, 547.
20. Benson, *Teachings*, 6-7.
21. Jerald and Sandra Tanner, *Changing World*, 180, citing *Deseret News*, October 10, 1866.
22. Pratt, *Seer*, October 1853, 158.
23. *Journal of Discourses*, 4:218.
24. Hoekema, *Four Major Cults*, 56.
25. Joseph Fielding Smith, *Way to Perfection*, 37.
26. McConkie, *Mormon Doctrine*, 257.
27. Church of Jesus Christ of Latter-day Saints, *Doctrines of the Gospel*, 15.
28. Ibid., 9-10.
29. Benson, *Teachings*, 6.
30. McConkie, *Doctrinal New Testament Commentary*, 2:215.
31. Ibid., 3:238.
32. McConkie, *Mormon Doctrine*, 129.
33. Church of Jesus Christ of Latter-day Saints, *What the Mormons Think of Christ*, 1982 (pamphlet), 22; cf. McConkie, *Doctrinal New Testament Commentary*, 3:140.
34. McConkie, *Mormon Doctrine*, 76, citing Joseph Smith for the last clause.
35. Ibid., 77.
36. *Journal of Discourses*, 1:346.
37. Ibid., 345.
38. Ibid., 2:210.
39. Pratt, *Seer*, November 1853, 172.
40. See the citations in Jerald and Sandra Tanner, *Changing World*, 254; cf. their *Mormonism—Shadow or Reality?* 128.
41. Ankerberg, *Mormonism Revisited*, 28. See Resource List.

**Chapter 6—What Mormons Say About Jesus' Work on the Cross**
1. McConkie, *Mormon Doctrine*, 61.
2. Talmage, *Articles of Faith*, 76.
3. Church of Jesus Christ of Latter-day Saints, *Doctrines of the Gospel*, 22.
4. Benson, *Teachings*, 14.
5. Talmage, *Articles of Faith*, 481; Joseph F. Smith, *Gospel Doctrine*, 214-215.
6. Ankerberg, *Mormonism Revisited*, 7, 25, 37.
7. McConkie, *Doctrinal New Testament Commentary*, 2:242; cf. McMurrin, *Theological Foundations*, 71.
8. McMurrin, *Theological Foundations*, 71.
9. Crowther, *Life Everlasting*, 233.
10. Ankerberg, *Mormonism Revisited*, 7; Church of Jesus Christ of Latter-day Saints, "The Gospel of Jesus Christ" (pamphlet).
11. McMurrin, *Theological Foundations*, 83.
12. *Journal of Discourses*, 4:220.
13. Ibid., 4:54.
14. Ankerberg, *Mormonism Revisited*, 37.

15. Kimball, *Miracle*, 14.
16. *Doctrine and Covenants*, 76:50,52; cf. Joseph Fielding Smith, *Way to Perfection*, 206.
17. Hal Hougey, *Mormon Missionary Handbook*, 62.
18. Ibid., 73.
19. Ibid., 83-84.
20. Kimball, *Miracle*, 208-209, emphasis added.
21. Benson, *Teachings*, 14, emphasis added.
22. Ibid., 23.
23. Church of Jesus Christ of Latter-day Saints, *Sure Foundation*, 156, emphasis added.
24. Talmage, *Articles of Faith*, 87, emphasis added.
25. McMurrin, *Theological Foundations*, 90.
26. Ankerberg, *Mormonism Revisited*, 25.
27. McConkie, *Doctrinal New Testament Commentary*, 2:242-243.
28. Ankerberg, *Mormon Officials*, 8.
29. Church of Jesus Christ of Latter-day Saints, *Gospel Principles*, 66,68-69.
30. Ibid., 118.
31. Ibid.
32. Ibid., 120-121.
33. Ibid., 121-122.
34. Ibid., 122.
35. Ibid.
36. Joseph Fielding Smith, *Doctrines of Salvation*, 2:131.
37. Joseph Smith, *Teachings*, 347-348.
38. *Journal of Discourses*, 21:80-81,84.
39. Church of Jesus Christ of Latter-day Saints, *Doctrines of the Gospel*, 22.
40. Robinson, *Are Mormons Christians?* 104.

**Chapter 7—What the Mormon Church Teaches About Salvation**
1. McConkie, *Mormon Doctrine*, 670.
2. Ibid., 671.
3. Ibid., 234.
4. Ibid., 671.
5. Ibid.
6. Ibid., 669.
7. Ibid.
8. Crowther, *Life Everlasting*, 329.
9. Joseph Fielding Smith, *Doctrines of Salvation*, 2:133-134, emphasis added.
10. Church of Jesus Christ of Latter-day Saints, *Doctrines of the Gospel*, 91-92.
11. James Talmage, *Jesus the Christ*, 31.
12. McConkie, *Mormon Doctrine*, 671.
13. Ibid., 29.
14. Ibid., 176-177, 234.
15. Ibid., 670.
16. Crowther, *Life Everlasting*, 327, emphasis added.
17. Ibid., 332.
18. McConkie, *Doctrinal New Testament Commentary*, 3:284-285.
19. Church of Jesus Christ of Latter-day Saints, *Doctrines of the Gospel*, 29.
20. Ibid., 77.

**Chapter 8—Mormonism, God's Grace, and Man's Works**
1. Church of Jesus Christ of Latter-day Saints, *What the Mormons Think of Christ*, n.d., 27.
2. Robinson, *Are Mormons Christians?* 104-105, emphasis added.
3. Ibid., 109, emphasis added.
4. McConkie, *Mormon Doctrine*, 434-436.
5. Ibid., 3:259.
6. Ibid., 2:257-258, emphasis added.
7. McConkie, *Mormon Doctrine*, 434-436.

8. Ibid., 108, emphasis added.
9. Cf. Anderson, *Inside Story*, 13, 19.
10. Talmage, *Articles of Faith*, 107.
11. Ibid., 479-480.
12. McConkie, *Mormon Doctrine*, 671.
13. Joseph Fielding Smith, *Doctrines of Salvation*, 2:139.
14. Richards, *Marvelous Work*, 25.
15. Pratt, *Seer*, January 1854, 199-200.
16. McConkie, *Mormon Doctrine*, 339.
17. McConkie, *Doctrinal New Testament Commentary*, 2:215; see also LeGrand Richards, *A Marvelous Work*, 275.
18. McConkie, ibid., 229.
19. Marvin W. Cowan, *Mormon Claims Answered*, 88, citing John A. Widtsoe, *Evidences and Reconciliations*, 190.
20. McMurrin, *Theological Foundations*, 70.
21. McConkie, *Doctrinal New Testament Commentary*, 2:238.
22. Ibid., 230.
23. Church of Jesus Christ of Latter-day Saints, *Doctrines of the Gospel*, 49-50.
24. Joseph Fielding Smith, *The Way to Perfection*, 189.
25. McConkie, *Doctrinal New Testament Commentary*, 3:402.
26. Kimball, *Miracle*, 207-208.
27. Richards, *Marvelous Work*, 275.
28. McConkie, *Doctrinal New Testament Commentary*, 2:248.
29. Ibid., 231, emphasis added.
30. Kimball, *Miracle*, 203.
31. Ibid., 203-204.
32. Church of Jesus Christ of Latter-day Saints, *Doctrines of the Gospel*, 49-50, emphasis added.
33. Church of Jesus Christ of Latter-day Saints, *Sure Foundation*, 157.
34. Ibid., 158.
35. Talmage, *Articles of Faith*, 1.
36. Joseph Smith, *History*, 6:223; cf. Joseph Smith, *Teachings*, 253, 357.
37. Joseph Smith, *History*, 5:65.
38. Brigham Young, *Discourses of Brigham Young*, 220.
39. *Discourses of Brigham Young*, 390.
40. *Journal of Discourses*, 13:213.
41. Ibid., 11:138.
42. Ibid., 4:189.
43. Ibid., 192-193.
44. Joseph Fielding Smith, *Way to Perfection*, 186.
45. Joseph Fielding Smith, *Answers*, 3:26-27.
46. Kimball, *Miracle*, 6.
47. Ibid., 16.
48. Ibid., 206.
49. Ibid., 207.
50. Benson, *Teachings*, 20.
51. Ibid., 26.
52. Ibid., 343.
53. Talmage, *Jesus the Christ*, 5.
54. McConkie, *Doctrinal New Testament Commentary*, 2:279,294.
55. Ibid., 298.
56. Ibid., 3:251.
57. Ibid., 265, emphasis added.
58. Ibid., 377.
59. Church of Jesus Christ of Latter-day Saints, *Doctrines of the Gospel*, 47.
60. Ibid., 48.
61. Ibid.

62. Ibid., 52, citing *The Teachings of Spencer W. Kimball*, 28.
63. Church of Jesus Christ of Latter-day Saints, *Sure Foundation*, 205.
64. Ibid., 206, citing Joseph Smith, *Teachings*, 348.
65. Ibid., citing Joseph Fielding Smith, *Doctrines of Salvation*, 2:18.
66. Ibid., 206-207.
67. McConkie, *Doctrinal New Testament Commentary*, 3:285-286.
68. McConkie, *Mormon Doctrine*, 318.
69. McConkie, *Doctrinal New Testament Commentary*, 3:67.
70. Ibid., 2:296, emphasis added.
71. Ibid., 3:248.
72. McConkie, *Mormon Doctrine*, 45.
73. Church of Jesus Christ of Latter-day Saints, *Master's Church Course A*, 21-22.
74. *Doctrine and Covenants*, 130:18-19.
75. Joseph Smith, *Teachings*, 354-355.
76. Ibid., 357.
77. Ibid., 297.
78. *Doctrine and Covenants*, 131:6.
79. Joseph Fielding Smith, *Way to Perfection*, 208.
80. Pratt, *Seer*, January 1854, 206, emphasis added; cf. McConkie, *Doctrinal New Testament Commentary*, 3:191.
81. McConkie, *Mormon Doctrine*, 581.
82. Pratt, *Seer*, April 1854, 255.
83. Joseph Fielding Smith, *Way to Perfection*, 190-191.
84. Joseph F. Smith, *Gospel Doctrine*, 272.
85. Joseph Fielding Smith, *Doctrines of Salvation*, 2:87-89, emphasis added.
86. Cowan, *Mormon Claims*, 83, citing apostle Mark E. Petersen, *Deseret News*, Church Section, April 14, 1973, 14, emphasis added.
87. Ibid., 85, citing Brigham Young, *Deseret News*, Church Section, July 20, 1968, 14, emphasis added.
88. Cf. Ibid., 91-99.
89. McConkie, *Mormon Doctrine*, 779.
90. Church of Jesus Christ of Latter-day Saints, *Gospel Principles*, 247, emphasis added.
91. Joseph Heinerman, *Spirit World Manifestations*, 7.
92. *Improvement Era*, 39 (April 1936): 200.
93. *Times and Seasons*, 2:546.
94. Heinerman, *Spirit World*, 29.
95. Einar Anderson, *Inside Story*, 84, reporting on a Dr. Ironside's quoting of a Mormon elder. Mormons frequently teach that they are the "saviors" of men.
96. Joseph Smith, *Teachings*, 192.
97. Joseph Fielding Smith, *Way to Perfection*, 153.
98. Joseph Fielding Smith, *Doctrines of Salvation*, 2:141-145, emphasis added.
99. Ibid., 145.
100. Ibid., 146-148.
101. Church of Jesus Christ of Latter-day Saints, *Doctrines of the Gospel*, 85.
102. Ibid.
103. Ibid.
104. Ibid.
105. Ibid., 86.
106. Ibid., citing Joseph Smith, *History of the Church*, 6:365.
107. Ibid., citing Joseph Fielding Smith, *Doctrines of Salvation*, 2:148-149.
108. Ibid., citing Spencer W. Kimball, "Things of Eternity," 5.
109. Joseph Fielding Smith, *Doctrines of Salvation*, 2:131.
110. Jerald and Sandra Tanner, *Changing World*, 516-517.
111. For an excellent popular study, see James I. Packer, *God's Words: Studies of Key Bible Themes* (Downers Grove, IL: InterVarsity, 1981).
112. Sinclair Ferguson, *Know Your Christian Life: A Theological Introduction* (Downers Grove, IL: InterVarsity, 1981), 71.

113. Ibid., 73.
114. James Packer, in Everett F. Harrison et al., eds., *Baker's Dictionary of Theology* (Grand Rapids, MI: Baker, 1972), 305.
115. Bruce Milne, *Know the Truth: A Handbook of Christian Belief* (Downers Grove, IL: Inter-Varsity, 1982), 155.
116. J.I. Packer, *God's Words*, 139-140.
117. J.I. Packer, in *Baker's Dictionary of Theology*, 306.
118. J.I. Packer, *God's Words*, 141-142.
119. J.I. Packer, in *Baker's Dictionary of Theology*, 306.

## Chapter 9—Mormons and the *Book of Mormon*

1. Cited in Jerald and Sandra Tanner, *Changing World*, 368; see *Journal of Discourses*, 7:23 for a similar statement.
2. *Journal of Discourses*, 7:22.
3. Ibid., 35.
4. Hugh Nibley, *An Approach to the* Book of Mormon, 13, cited in Jerald and Sandra Tanner, *The Case Against Mormonism*, 2:63.
5. Joseph Fielding Smith, *Answers*, 2:199.
6. Church of Jesus Christ of Latter-day Saints, *Sure Foundation*, 61-62.
7. Benson, *Teachings*, 48.
8. David Whitmer, *An Address to All Believers in Christ by a Witness to the Divine Authenticity of the* Book of Mormon (1887, reprint, Concord, CA: Pacific Publishing Co., 1972), 12.
9. *The Saints Herald*, November 15, 1962, 16, citing the Chicago *Inter-Ocean*, October 17, 1886, from Jerald and Sandra Tanner, *Joseph Smith and Money Digging*, 9.
10. *The Saints Herald*, May 19, 1888, 310.
11. See Jerald and Sandra Tanner, *Joseph Smith and Money Digging*, passim.
12. Joseph Fielding Smith, *Doctrines of Salvation*, 3:225-226.
13. Jerald and Sandra Tanner, *Changing World*, 84.
14. Einar Anderson, *Inside Story*, 61.
15. Fawn M. Brodie, *No Man Knows My History*, 2d ed. (NY: Alfred A. Knopf, 1976), 69-70, 72-73.
16. Hal Hougey, *A Parallel*, 4; Ropp, *Mormon Papers*, 36.
17. Originally cited in *The Rocky Mountain Mason*, Billings, MT, January 1956, 17-31; also in Jerald and Sandra Tanner, *Did Spaulding Write the* Book of Mormon? 17.
18. Hougey, *A Parallel*, 21.
19. Hoekema, *Four Major Cults*, 85.
20. Cf. Martin, *Maze*, 68.
21. B.H. Roberts, *Defense of the Faith and the Saints*, Salt Lake City, UT: *Deseret News* 1907, 1:329.
22. See Resource List.
23. Jerald and Sandra Tanner, *Changing World*, 115-116, 118-119, 122-124.
24. Jerald and Sandra Tanner, *Mormonism—Shadow or Reality?* 72, 84-85; *Changing World*, 112-113; *Case Against Mormonism*, 2:63-112.
25. Martin, *Maze*, 59-69; cf. Crowdery et al., dedication section.
26. James Bjornstad, *Contemporary Christianity*, Winter 1977–1978, 4.
27. Jerald and Sandra Tanner, *Did Spaulding Write the* Book of Mormon? 5.
28. Taken from the *Book of Mormon* and in part from McConkie, *Mormon Doctrine*, 528-529; Martin, *Maze*, 47-49; McElveen, *Will the Saints?* 59-61; Fraser, *Is Mormonism Christian?* chapter 16; and Arthur Wallace, *Can Mormonism Be Proved Experimentally?* chapter 9.
29. Personal conversation with Sandra Tanner, 1990.
30. McConkie, *Mormon Doctrine*, 528-529; cf. *Book of Mormon*, Mormon 1:7; Helaman 3:1-11; Jarom 5-8; 1 Nephi 5:5-6,13-21,28.
31. Martin, *Maze*, 328.
32. Ankerberg, *Mormon Officials*, 13. Mormon critics of Crane should see his response at www.lightplanet.com/response/crane2.htm.
33. Fraser, *Is Mormonism Christian?* 135.
34. Ankerberg, *Mormon Revisited*, 17.
35. Fraser, *Is Mormonism Christian?* 143, 145.

36. Ankerberg, *Mormonism Revisited*, 18.
37. Hal Hougey, *Archaeology and the* Book of Mormon, rev. ed., 3-4.
38. Jerald and Sandra Tanner, *Archaeology and the* Book of Mormon, 4-6.
39. Fraser, *Is Mormonism Christian?* chapters 16–17.
40. Ibid., 143-145.
41. See John Sorenson, *Progress and Archaeology—An Anthology* (Provo, UT: Brigham Young University Press, 1963), 103-116 for a critical review.
42. See *Dialogue: A Journal of Mormon Thought*, 4:2 (Spring 1966): 74, 145-146.
43. Ropp, *Mormon Papers*, 50-51.
44. Jerald and Sandra Tanner, *Archaeology and the* Book of Mormon, 1-6.
45. Jerald and Sandra Tanner, *Changing World*, 136, citing *Dialogue: A Journal of Mormon Thought*, Spring 1966, 149.
46. See Resource List.
47. See the forthcoming text by the Tanners.
48. Cowan, *Mormon Claims Answered*, 50.
49. Jerald and Sandra Tanner, *Mormonism—Shadow or Reality?* 108-116; cf. Ropp, *Mormon Papers*, 49-50.
50. *Dialogue: A Journal of Mormon Thought*, Summer 1973, 46, from Jerald and Sandra Tanner, *Changing World*, 134; see Resource List.
51. Walter Martin, *The Kingdom of the Cults*, 162.
52. McElveen, *Will the Saints?* 62-64.
53. Letter on file; also cited in Jerry and Marian Bodine, *Whom Can You Trust?* (pamphlet), 16.
54. Letter of Frank Roberts, Jr., Director to Marvin Cowan, January 24, 1963, cited in Bodine, *Whom Can You Trust?*, 3.
55. Letter of May 29, 1978 to G.R. Shannon from A.T. Hermansen of the Research Correspondence Department, cited in Bodine, *Whom Can You Trust?*, 13.
56. *Dialogue: A Journal of Mormon Thought*, Summer 1969, 76-78, cited in Jerald and Sandra Tanner, *Changing World*, 139.
57. Jerald and Sandra Tanner, *Changing World*, 140-141.
58. Sir William M. Ramsay, *The Bearing of Recent Discovery on the Trustworthiness of the New Testament* (1915, reprint, Grand Rapids, MI: Baker, 1979), 79, emphasis added.
59. Ibid., v, emphasis added.
60. Jerald and Sandra Tanner, *Archaeology and the* Book of Mormon; *Changing World*, 133-148; Ropp, *Mormon Papers*, 47-54.
61. Norman L. Geisler, William E. Nix, *An Introduction to the Bible*, revised and expanded ed. (Chicago, IL: Moody Press, 1986); F.F. Bruce, *The New Testament Documents: Are They Reliable?* (Downers Grove, IL: InterVarsity Press, 1971).
62. Ibid.
63. Cf. Jerald and Sandra Tanner, *Changing World*, 370-373.
64. Ibid., 369-370.
65. Wesley Walters, "Whatever Happened to the *Book of Mormon?*" *Eternity* magazine, May 1980, 32.
66. From Bob Witte, comp., *Where Does It Say That?*, 4.
67. Jerald and Sandra Tanner, *Changing World*, 560, citing *Improvement Era*, 16:344-345.
68. Church of Jesus Christ of Latter-day Saints, *Sure Foundation*, 14-15.
69. Benson, *Teachings*, 41.
70. Letter to Marvin Cowan March 23, 1966; cited in Jerald and Sandra Tanner, *Changing World*, 144.
71. Brodie, *No Man Knows My History*, 63.
72. Ibid., 73-74.
73. Ibid., 77-78.
74. Ibid., 79.
75. Ibid., 79-80.
76. Cf. Nandor Fodor, s.v. "Apports" and "Mediumism" in his *Encyclopedia of Psychical Science*.
77. See Resource List.

78. Jerald and Sandra Tanner, *Changing World*, 95-96.
79. Ibid., 96, 102, 105.
80. *Journal of Discourses*, 7:164.
81. Jerald and Sandra Tanner, *Changing World*, 95-105; cf. *Journal of Discourses*, 7:114-115,164; Smith, *History of the Church*, 1:109-110; 3:228-232; *Doctrine and Covenants*, 3:12-13; 10:7; 28:11; *Elders Journal* (edited by Joseph Smith), August 1838, 59; David A. Whitmer, *An Address to All Believers in Christ*, 27-28.
82. McConkie, *Mormon Doctrine*, 842-843.
83. Jerald and Sandra Tanner, *Changing World*, 103, citing LaMar Petersen, *The Historical Background for the* Doctrine and Covenants, unpublished manuscript, 58.
84. Jerald and Sandra Tanner, *Changing World*, 103-104.
85. Ibid., 103.
86. Joseph Smith, *History*, 1:109-110.
87. Ibid., 104; cf. David Whitmer, *An Address*, i-ii.
88. *Times and Seasons*, 2 (1841): 42.
89. Whitmer, *An Address*, 27.
90. Ibid., 38.
91. Benson, *Teachings*, 89.
92. Gordon Fraser in foreword, Jerald and Sandra Tanner, *Changing World*, 10.
93. Jerald and Sandra Tanner, *Changing World*, 102, 105, 107.
94. Bernard De Voto, "The Centennial of Mormonism," *American Mercury*, 19 (1930): 5.
95. Ankerberg, *Mormonism Revisited*, 18-19.
96. Letter from President Joseph Fielding Smith to Marvin Cowan, March 18, 1966, cited in Bodine, *Whom Can You Trust?* 5.
97. Ellis T. Rasmussen, in Church of Jesus Christ of Latter-day Saints, *Sure Foundation*, 27.
98. Ibid.
99. John W. Welch, in ibid., 61.
100. Steve Gilliland, in ibid., 153.
101. Martin, *Maze*, 68-69.
102. Benson, *Teachings*, 53.

## Chapter 10—Documented Changes in the Mormon Scriptures

1. Martin, *Maze*, 318.
2. Smith, *History*, 1:54-55; cf. 52-56.
3. Ibid., 53.
4. Ibid., 4:461.
5. See W.C. Woodruff, *Joseph Smith Begins His Work*; John Gilbert memorandum, 1-2; Jerald and Sandra Tanner, *Mormonism—Shadow or Reality?* 1-2. They cite B.H. Roberts, *Defense of the Faith*, 280-281, 295; and the Gilbert interview in George Reynolds, *The Myth of the "Manuscript Found,"* 59.
6. George Reynolds, *Myth of the "Manuscript Found,"* Salt Lake City Juvenile Instructor, 1883, 91, cited in Jerald and Sandra Tanner, *Mormonism—Shadow or Reality?* 89.
7. Reynolds, *Myth*, 71.
8. Oliver B. Huntington, *Journal of Oliver B. Huntington*, from typed copy at Utah State Historical Society, 168, cited in Jerald and Sandra Tanner, *Changing World*, 132.
9. Hoekema, *Four Major Cults*, 84.
10. Church of Jesus Christ of Latter-day Saints, California Mission, 1591 East Temple Way, Los Angeles, CA 90024.
11. *Saints Herald*, November 15, 1962, 16, from Jerald and Sandra Tanner, *3913 Changes in the Book of Mormon*, 15.
12. Jack Free, *Mormonism and Inspiration*, 111, cited in Arthur Budvarson, "Changes in Mormonism," 5 (pamphlet).
13. Jerald and Sandra Tanner, *3913 Changes*, 16.
14. Jerald and Sandra Tanner, *Changing World*, 132.
15. Wilford C. Woodruff, *Joseph Smith Begins His Work* (verse citations not given).
16. Ibid., 353.
17. Ibid., 127.
18. Ibid., 64.

19. Ibid., 173.
20. Ibid., 284.
21. Ibid., 309.
22. Ibid., 560.
23. Ibid., 142.
24. Jerald and Sandra Tanner, *3913 Changes*, 6-9.
25. Woodruff, *Joseph Smith Begins His Work*, 52.
26. Ibid., 303.
27. Hoekema, *Four Major Cults*, 85.
28. Woodruff, *Joseph Smith Begins His Work*, 200.
29. Ibid., 546.
30. Ibid., 25.
31. Ibid.
32. Joseph Fielding Smith, *Answers*, 2:200.
33. Mark Petersen, *As Translated Correctly*, 3-5; cf. Jerald and Sandra Tanner, *Changes in the* Pearl of Great Price: *A Photo Reprint*, Introduction, 7, citing Joseph Fielding Smith, Jr., *Religious Truths Defined*, 175, 337.
34. Joseph Fielding Smith, *Doctrines of Salvation*, 3:198-199.
35. *Lectures on Faith* (deleted) is approximately 25,000 words. For other changes see Jerald and Sandra Tanner, *Flaws in the* Pearl of Great Price: *A Study of Changes and Plagiarism in Joseph Smith's* Pearl of Great Price, 89-155.
36. Jerald and Sandra Tanner, *Changing World*, 64.
37. Ibid., 43.
38. John Widtsoe, *Joseph Smith: Seeker After Truth* (Salt Lake City, UT: Deseret News, 1951), 119; Joseph Fielding Smith, *Doctrines of Salvation*, 1:170, cited by Jerald and Sandra Tanner, *Changing World*, 39.
39. Smith, *History*, 1:173 n.
40. Jerald and Sandra Tanner, *Changing World*, 64-65.
41. Ibid., 62.
42. Ibid., 185-186.
43. *Lectures on Faith* (originally delivered before a class of the elders, Kirtland, OH, and printed in the 1835 edition of *Doctrine and Covenants*), 53, from Jerald and Sandra Tanner, *Changing World*, 185.
44. Ibid., 12, 26.
45. Ankerberg, *Mormon Officials*, 14.
46. See Resource List.
47. *Doctrine and Covenants*, "Explanatory Introduction," 1982, 1989 eds.
48. Jerald and Sandra Tanner, *Changes in the* Pearl of Great Price: *A Photo Reprint*; see Resource List.
49. *The Pearl of Great Price*, "Introductory Note," 1982, 1989 eds., 1.
50. Jerald and Sandra Tanner, *Changes in the* Pearl of Great Price: *A Photo Reprint*, 14-15; the entire preface is also deleted from modern editions.
51. Jerald and Sandra Tanner, *Changing World*, 344-345.
52. Ankerberg, *Mormonism Revisited*, 18.
53. Personal conversation with Dr. Gleason Archer, October 19, 1991.
54. Gleason Archer, "Anachronisms and Historical Inaccuracies in the Mormon Scriptures," appendix in *A Survey of Old Testament Introduction*, rev. ed. (Chicago, IL: Moody Press, 1974), 504.
55. Jerald and Sandra Tanner, *Changing World*, 362, citing the *New York Times*, May 3, 1970.
56. Ibid., citing *Salt Lake Tribune*, May 4, 1970.
57. Ibid., 362-363.
58. See Resource List; cf. Martin, *Maze*, chapter 6.
59. F.S. Spaulding and A.B. Samuel Mercer, *Why Egyptologists Reject the* Book of Abraham (see Resource List).
60. Martin, *Maze*, 155.
61. Ibid.
62. Photocopy of letter in Ropp, *Mormon Papers*, 105.

63. *The Utah Evangel*, November 1981, 1, 5; cf. *Salt Lake Tribune*, September 30, 1981; Idaho Falls, *Post Register*, September 30, 1981.
64. Church of Jesus Christ of Latter-day Saints, *Gospel Principles*, 51.

**Chapter 11—Mormons and New Revelations from God**
1. James Talmage, *The Study of the Articles of Faith*, 296.
2. Ibid., 311.
3. *Journal of Discourses*, 3:155-157; cf. 2:338.
4. Benson, *Teachings*, 102.
5. Talmage, *Articles of Faith*, 311.
6. McConkie, *Mormon Doctrine*, 645.
7. McConkie, *Mormon Doctrine*, 644-45; see *Journal of Discourses*, 1:13-15; 2:44-46.
8. Ibid., 645.
9. McConkie, *Mormon Doctrine*, 650.
10. See, e.g., *Journal of Discourses*, 16:46.
11. In Joseph W. Musser, *Michael Our Father and Our God*, 20, citing *Deseret Weekly News*, 26:274.
12. *Journal of Discourses*, 13:264.
13. Ibid., 13:95.
14. Musser, *Michael Our Father*, 13-29; see Jerald and Sandra Tanner, *Changing World*, 202-203.
15. *Journal of Discourses*, 16:375. Mormons are to receive the words of Joseph Smith and Brigham Young "as from the mouth of God."
16. *Journal of Discourses*, 16:46.
17. Ibid.
18. *Journal of Discourses*, 1:50.
19. *Journal of Discourses*, 5:331; see *Deseret News*, June 18, 1873.
20. *Millennial Star*, 16:543, from Einar Anderson, *Inside Story,* 105-106.
21. *Millennial Star*, 15:801.
22. Ibid., 16:530.
23. Gerald and Sandra Tanner, *Changing World*, 199, citing *Women of Mormonism*, 196.
24. *On the Mormon Frontier*, 2:435, in Jerald and Sandra Tanner, *Changing World*, 200.
25. *Journal of Discourses*, 4:1.
26. *Sacred Hymns and Spiritual Songs for the Church of Jesus Christ of Latter-day Saints* (1856), n.p., 375.
27. Abraham Cannon's diary of June 23, 1889, 2:39, from Jerald and Sandra Tanner, *Changing World*, 201.
28. Musser, *Michael Our Father,* 1-136; for example, 1-6, 13-19, 31-38, 133, etc.; Martin, *Maze*, 84-90; Jerald and Sandra Tanner, *Changing World*, chapter 8; Jerald and Sandra Tanner, *Mormonism—Shadow or Reality?* chapter 10.
29. McConkie, *Mormon Doctrine*, 18.
30. Joseph Fielding Smith, *Doctrines of Salvation*, 1:96; cf. his discussion through 106.
31. Ankerberg, *Mormon Officials*, 16.
32. Stenhouse, *Tell It All*, 299-300.
33. Joseph Fielding Smith, *Doctrines of Salvation*, 1:96; this is Smith's description of Brigham Young's alleged teaching, something Smith agrees with.
34. Mark E. Petersen, *Adam: Who Is He?* 16-17.
35. Ibid., 14.
36. Robinson, *Are Mormons Christians?* 19.
37. Ibid.
38. Ibid., 20.
39. Ankerberg, *Mormon Officials*, 17, in the words of Walter Martin.
40. Benson, *Teachings*, vi-vii, second emphasis added.
41. Ankerberg, *Mormon Officials*, 11, 14.
42. The *Utah Christian Tract Society Newsletter*, 12, 8, (March/April 1980): 2; see Resource List for transcript of Benson's original lecture.
43. Ibid.
44. McConkie, *Mormon Doctrine*, 649.
45. See Point/Counterpoint Web site at http://members.aol.com/pointcpt/wp/pcp.html.

**Chapter 12—Contradictory Teachings in Mormonism**
1. Church of Jesus Christ of Latter-day Saints, *Sure Foundation*, 48.
2. Benson, *Teachings*, 116.
3. Hugh Nibley, *No Ma'am, That's Not History*, 46, from Jerald and Sandra Tanner, *Mormonism—Shadow or Reality?* 5.
4. Ankerberg, *Mormon Officials*, 28.
5. Ankerberg, *Mormonism Revisited*, 17.
6. Jerald and Sandra Tanner, *The Case Against Mormonism*, 1:86-87.
7. Ibid., 84-86.
8. See Resource List and Jerald and Sandra Tanner, *The Case Against Mormonism*, 4; Martin, *Maze*, 38 and chapter 7.
9. Jerald and Sandra Tanner, *The Case Against Mormonism*, 1:35, citing *Dialogue: A Journal of Mormon Thought*, Spring 1966, 49-52.
10. Jerald and Sandra Tanner, *Changing World*, 37.
11. D. Michael Quinn, *On Being a Mormon Historian*, 5.
12. Ibid., 23.
13. Ibid.
14. Ibid., 20-21, emphasis added.
15. Ibid., 16.
16. Ibid., 8.
17. *Journal of Discourses*, 11:269.
18. Ibid., 30:31.
19. McConkie, *Mormon Doctrine*, 522, 523; 1966 edition, 578-579 is somewhat softened.
20. McConkie, *Mormon Doctrine*, 765.
21. See "doctrine" in ibid., 204-205.

**Chapter 13—The Track Record of Mormon Prophets**
1. Talmage, *Articles of Faith*, 7-8.
2. McConkie, *Doctrinal New Testament Commentary*, 1:252-253.
3. *The Evening and Morning Star*, July 1833, 1, emphasis added.
4. From an analogy by Bob Witte, "And It Came to Pass" (tract), Safety Harbor, FL: from Ex-Mormons for Jesus, Box 946, 33572, n.d.
5. Whitmer, *An Address*, 30-31.
6. Pratt, *Seer*, February 1854, 213. Yet Pratt also stated in the same article (p. 212) concerning the *Book of Mormon* and the Bible, "Both books being of Divine origin, they will of course agree; for God never disagrees with himself; and his words spoken in ancient America are just as true as his words spoken in ancient Palestine."
7. Pratt, "The Bible Alone an Insufficient Guide," in *Orson Pratt's Works* (Liverpool, England, 1851), 46; cf. 44-47.
8. Ankerberg, *Mormon Officials*, 7.
9. Smith, *History*, 1:400.
10. Ibid., 394, 400, 402; Martin, *Maze*, 353-354.
11. *Journal of Discourses*, 10:344, cited by Jerald and Sandra Tanner, *Changing World*, 421.
12. *Journal of Discourses*, 13:362, cited in ibid.
13. *Doctrine and Covenants*, 1890 edition, Section 84, 289.
14. *Dialogue: A Journal of Mormon Thought*, Autumn 1966, 74, cited in Jerald and Sandra Tanner, *Changing World*, 422.
15. Joseph Fielding Smith, *Way to Perfection*, 268-270.
16. Joseph Fielding Smith, *Answers*, 4:112.
17. Ibid., 111-115.
18. See, e.g., Ankerberg, *Mormonism Revisited*, 19.
19. Talmage, *Articles of Faith*, 25.
20. *Doctrine and Covenants*, 87:1-8.
21. Joseph Smith, *History*, 5:324, in Jerald and Sandra Tanner, *Changing World*, 428, emphasis added.
22. See "Rebellion in South Carolina" in *The Evening and Morning Star*, January 1833 (this magazine was available to Smith in December); Joseph Smith, *History*, 1:301; Larry S.

Jonas, *Mormon Claims Examined*, 1961, 52, in Jerald and Sandra Tanner, *Changing World*, 424-425.
23. A civil war was considered a possibility even before 1832. This fact was discussed on *American Adventure*, a two-part program on Jacksonian America on WTCI-TV 45, Saturday, November 2, 1991, 7:00 to 8:00 A.M., produced by the Dallas Community College. See also Jerald and Sandra Tanner, *Changing World*, 425; Martin, *Maze*, 357.
24. Ropp, *Mormon Papers*, 64.
25. Jerald and Sandra Tanner, *Changing World*, 430.
26. Ibid., 428-430.
27. *Journal of Discourses*, 9:142-143, cited in Jerald and Sandra Tanner, *Changing World*, 426.
28. *Journal of Discourses*, 10:250; see *The Millennial Star*, 25:787.
29. Jerald and Sandra Tanner, *Changing World*, 430.
30. Ibid., 404-408.
31. Joseph Smith, *History*, 5:336.
32. Cited in Jerald and Sandra Tanner, *Changing World*, 419.
33. Ibid., 420.
34. This was copied from the microfilm original at the Mormon Church Historian's Library; cf. Jerald and Sandra Tanner, *Changing World*, 420.
35. Smith, *History*, 6:58, emphasis added.
36. Brodie, *No Man Knows*, 392.
37. Ibid., 393-394.
38. Smith, *History*, 3:170-171.
39. Ibid., 171.
40. Joseph Smith, *Teachings*, 302; cf. Smith, *History*, 5:394.
41. Joseph Smith, *Millenial Star*, 22:455, cited in Bob Witte, "And It Came to Pass" (tract).
42. *Journal of Discourses*, 5:219.
43. Smith, *History*, 1:323.
44. Colleen Ralson, *Dissecting the* Doctrine and Covenants, 4-7.
45. Martin, *Maze*, Appendix G on unfulfilled prophecies.
46. Jerald and Sandra Tanner, *Mormonism—Shadow or Reality?* 195.
47. Bob Witte, *Witnessing to Mormons*, 17.
48. Church of Jesus Christ of Latter-day Saints, *The Doctrine and Covenants Student Manual*, 181.
49. Ibid.
50. Ibid., 194.

## Chapter 14—The Mormon View of Christianity
1. *Journal of Discourses*, 6:198.
2. Brigham Henry Roberts, Introduction to Joseph Smith's *History*, lxxxvi.
3. Ibid.
4. *Elders Journal*, 1, 4:59-60; this journal was edited by Joseph Smith. From Jerald and Sandra Tanner, *Mormonism—Shadow or Reality?* 3.
5. See *Book of Mormon* index references under "Babylon," "Church of the Devil," "Church, Great and Abominable," and "Churches, False."
6. Joseph Smith, *Teachings*, 270.
7. Ibid., 322.
8. Ibid., 345.
9. Ibid., 15.
10. Church of Jesus Christ of Latter-day Saints, *Sure Foundation*, 200-201.
11. *Journal of Discourses*, 8:199.
12. Ibid., 8:171; cf. 7:333.
13. Ibid., 5:73.
14. Ibid., 5:229.
15. Ibid., 6:167.
16. Ibid., 5:240.
17. Ibid., 13:225.
18. Ibid., 6:25.

19. *Pamphlets by Orson Pratt*, 183, cited in Jerald and Sandra Tanner, *Case Against Mormonism*, 1:6.
20. B.H. Roberts, *The Mormon Doctrine of Deity*, 233.
21. Pratt, *Seer*, May 1854, 259-260.
22. Pratt, *Seer*, March 1854, 237, 239, 240.
23. Joseph Fielding Smith, *Doctrines of Salvation*, 3:267, 287.
24. McConkie, *Mormon Doctrine*, 132.
25. Ibid., 137-138.
26. McConkie, *Doctrinal New Testament Commentary*, 2:240, 274; cf. 3:265.
27. Ibid., 2:280.
28. Ibid., 3:85.
29. Ibid., 247, 550-551.
30. This makes its pretended friendship with Christianity all the more inexcusable. See Andersen, "Love Thy Minister, Neighbor Worship Outline," photocopy and his *Soft Answers*.

## Chapter 15—What Mormons Really Mean When They Use Christian Terms

1. John Ankerberg, John Weldon, and Walter Kaiser, *The Case for Jesus the Messiah: Incredible Prophecies That Prove That God Exists* (Chattanooga, TN: Ankerberg Theological Research Institute, 1989).
2. *The Oxford American Dictionary*, s.v. "Christian."
3. Deseret Sunday School Union, *Master's Church Course A*, 229.
4. Talmage, *Articles of Faith*, 28.
5. Benson, *Teachings*, 10.
6. Church of Jesus Christ of Latter-day Saints, *Sure Foundation*, 155.
7. Ankerberg, *Mormonism Revisited*, 13.
8. Darl Andersen, *Soft Answers*, 58, 86.
9. Stephen E. Robinson, *Are Mormons Christians?* vii.
10. Ibid., 2.
11. Ibid., 7.
12. Ibid., 34.
13. Ibid., 72, 77.
14. Ibid., 60, 88.
15. Harry L. Ropp, *The Mormon Papers*, 119.
16. Ibid., 13.
17. Ibid., 11.
18. *The Utah Evangel*, November 1981, 3.
19. Ibid., May 1981.
20. *Journal of Discourses*, 16:46.
21. The Church of Jesus Christ of Latter-day Saints, *Apostasy and Restoration* (pamphlet), 14.
22. Personal conversation with Sterling M. McMurrin.
23. Sterling M. McMurrin, *The Theological Foundations of the Mormon Religion*, x.
24. Ibid., ix, 26.
25. Gordon Fraser, *Is Mormonism Christian?* 10.
26. Martin, *Maze of Mormonism*, 45.
27. Jerald and Sandra Tanner, *Changing World*, 559.
28. Hoekema, *Four Major Cults*, 30.
29. Irving Hexham, in Walter A. Elwell, ed., *Evangelical Dictionary of Theology* (Grand Rapids, MI: Baker Book House, 1984), 736.
30. *Encyclopedia Britannica*, 15th ed., Macropaedia, s.v. "Mormonism."
31. *The New Schaff-Herzog Encyclopedia of Religious Knowledge*, s.v. "Mormonism."
32. Anthony A. Hoekema, in J.D. Douglas, ed., *The New International Dictionary of the Christian Church*, rev. ed. (Grand Rapids, MI: Zondervan, 1979), 678.

# Index